P. Adkins

WAVES

OF

POWER

DYNAMICS OF
GLOBAL TECHNOLOGY LEADERSHIP
1964–2010

David C. Moschella

American Management Association

New York • Atlanta • Boston • Chicago • Kansas City • San Francisco • Washington, D.C.
Brussels • Mexico City • Tokyo • Toronto

This publication is designed to provide accurate and authoritative information in regard to the subject matter covered. It is sold with the understanding that the publisher is not engaged in rendering legal, accounting, or other professional service. If legal advice or other expert assistance is required, the services of a competent professional person should be sought.

Library of Congress Cataloging-in-Publication Data

Moschella, David C.
    Waves of power : dynamics of global technology leadership, 1964–2010 / David C. Moschella.
        p. cm.
    Includes index.
    ISBN 0-8144-0379-4
    1. Computer industry—United States. 2. Computer software industry—United States. 3. Computer industry. 4. Computer software industry. 5. Information technology. 6. Market surveys. I. Title.
HD9696.C63U52628   1997
338.4'7004'09045—dc21   96-49652
                                             CIP

Printing number

10 9 8 7 6 5 4 3 2 1

CONTENTS

Introduction and Overview

The computer industry has proved to be remarkable in many ways. Its rate of technological advance is unprecedented in business history. Consider that computer hardware price/performance has improved more than 100,000-fold over the past twenty years, with a similar pace of innovation expected for at least another decade. The rate of market growth has been nearly as dramatic. An industry that didn't exist in 1950 grew to $50 billion in 1980 and exceeded $500 billion in 1995, again with no end in sight.

From a more abstract perspective, the general purpose nature of digital technology seems applicable to an almost infinite array of uses. Not since the development of electricity itself have so many different tasks been able to take advantage of a single technological capability. Each generation of improved product price/performance merely widens the range of cost-effective potential uses, often in unexpected ways.

Within the computer industry, these unique and truly marvelous attributes have developed so predictably for so long that they are now taken for granted. Constant technology improvement, nearly constant market growth, and ever widening usage levels are merely the backdrop against which competition and value creation occur.

When the computer community tries to understand itself two issues often stand out—a series of dramatic waves of technology change and a consistently high concentration of supplier market power.

In addition to the obvious list of industry executives, economists, consultants, competitive strategists, and antitrust lawyers, even the general public tends to be fascinated by the computer business's unusual pattern of strong, almost monopoly, vendor leadership. From its beginnings in the early 1950s and through the present period, this industry has granted special power, mystique, and profitability first to IBM, then to Microsoft and Intel. In addition, since it was IBM itself that unwittingly passed its mantle on to today's leaders, this seemingly fast-changing business has, at least arguably, been characterized by a single, and as yet unbroken, chain of command now more than forty years old.

Even more curiously, since the sources of IBM's mainframe computer market dominance actually go all the way back to its more than 80 percent share of the mechanical accounting equipment business of the 1920s, 1930s, and 1940s, industry historians can rightly argue that the power that Microsoft and Intel wield today actually stems directly from events and developments of some seventy-five years ago, well before the first electronic computer was invented. Clearly, the sources of computer industry power can reveal much about the industry itself.

Perhaps most surprising of all is that this monopoly power has passed so smoothly through an industry characterized by constant technology and supplier turmoil. The industry's history clearly shows that once in a generation, the market's orientation and its underlying technology and business structure have unexpectedly shifted, with even the strongest competitors soon finding their worlds turned upside down. IBM, once the most admired of all corporations, suddenly begins to lose billions. Giant Japanese electronics firms, previously viewed with awe, become slow, lumbering, and out of touch. Whenever the existing leaders have stumbled, a whole new set of vendors has rushed in to fill the void.

Put simply, the story of computer industry competition has been one of new waves of technology, led by new waves of vendors, rapidly overpowering much of the existing order. As has often been noted, there have been few, if any, better business examples of what the great Austrian economist Joseph Schumpeter labeled in 1939 "creative destruction." Most important, this pattern of wavelike evolution continues. As Internet and Worldwide Web user populations swell into the tens of millions, it is becoming clear that once again a new computer industry is being born.

Just as the information technology (IT) industry of the 1980s shifted away from mainframes and toward personal computers, so is the personal computer (PC) era now giving way to an industry that increasingly revolves around a global network infrastructure. As this "network-centric" era begins, the prospects for new vendors, current market leaders, and future sources of IT industry market power are once again topics of intense competitive and investment industry speculation.

This book will explain why the network-centric era will result in market and supplier restructuring every bit as great as those of the PC revolution. As the computer, telecommunications, consumer electronics, and publishing/media industries converge, the IT industry will once again witness the emergence of new vendors, new business models, and new patterns of global market leadership. Even if they continue to exist, the product monopolies of today will shrink in significance as network services and applications become the driving force in IT business expansion.

In addition to explaining and exploring these overall developments, this book will attempt to answer a number of specific industry questions. How will the IT industry of the twenty-first century be organized? Who, if anyone, will control the Internet? Which market sectors will emerge as the new centers of leverage and power? How will the competitive landscape change over the next decade and beyond? Can U.S. vendors maintain their currently enviable global market leadership position?

In sum, the work that follows is primarily intended to help the reader understand the nature and direction of IT market competition in the network-centric era. In addition, all of the analysis is presented within an overall framework of long-term IT industry evolution. Just as IBM's mainframe power became the source of the great monopolies of the PC era, so does the PC market provide the necessary starting point for analyzing the forces behind the network-centric wave. From a more futuristic perspective, the network-centric era itself should be seen as just another step along the path toward a true information society.

A Fifty-Year View of IT Industry Evolution

Figure 1 provides a pictorial representation of long-term IT industry development. As the graphic shows, the computer business has already lived through two major waves of change, with the network-centric third wave really just beginning in 1993–1994. Each of these waves has managed to redefine existing computing paradigms.

Although today the word *paradigm* is often used loosely, in this book, the phrase "paradigm shift" is reserved for those rare times when a wide range of essential IT industry dimensions begin to change

Figure 1. Stages of industry growth.

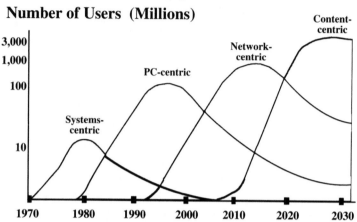

Number of Users (Millions)

fundamentally, simultaneously, and systematically in reaction to a common force or set of forces. A partial list of these key dimensions includes the target customer audience and applications, the primary technology focus, the underlying market economics, the nature of supplier product and service offerings, the dominant distribution channel, and the overall IT industry structure and value chain composition. Taken together, these factors define the required supplier business model for each period.

Figure 2 provides a summary of these dimensions across the four great waves covered by this book. In addition to defining some of the key differences between each of the major industry periods, figure 2 shows why, in this book, the minicomputer industry is seen as an important branch of the systems business but not as a paradigm shift in and of itself. Many of the dimensions shown in figure 2 remained the same for mainframes and minicomputers, hence the broad "systems-centric" label used throughout this text.

More than any specific technology change, it is the sheer breadth and scope of a major paradigm shift that has made it so difficult for industry leaders to maintain their position from one era to the next. When virtually everything that a large and successful organization is doing suddenly needs to be radically overhauled, it's not surprising that a new company starting from scratch might have some compelling advantages.

Figure 2. IT industry evolution, 1964–2015.

	Systems-centric 1964–1981	PC-centric 1981–1994	Network-centric 1994–2005	Content-centric 2005–2015
Key Audience	Corporate	Professional	Consumer	Individual
Key Technology	Transistor	Microprocessor	Communications bandwidth	Software
Governing Principle	Grosch's Law	Moore's Law	Metcalfe's Law	Law of transformation
Vendor Offerings	Proprietary systems	Standard products	Value-added services	Custom services
Channel	Direct	Indirect	Online	Customer pull
Network Focus	Data center	Internal LANs	Public networks	Transparency
User Focus	Efficiency	Productivity	Customer service	Virtualization
Supplier Structure	Vertical integration	Horizontal computer value chain	Unified computers & communications chain	Embedded
Supplier Leadership	U.S. systems	U.S. components	National carriers	Content providers
Number of Users at End of Period	10 million	100 million	1 billion	Universal
End of Period Market Size	$20 billion	$460 billion	$3 trillion	Too embedded to be measurable

Although all of the dimensions cited in figure 2 are important components of competitive success, one of the major themes of this book is that changes in industry structure have been and will continue to be the most difficult for current leaders to accommodate. In addition, as the following review of the systems and PC eras will show, changes in industry structure have led directly to shifts in both supplier market power and global IT industry leadership. Given the great structural transformation forecasted, much of this history will likely be repeated through the coming network-centric era.

Looking Back at the Systems and PC Eras

By general consensus, the modern computer era began in 1964 when IBM, with its S/360 series, introduced the industry's first broad family of compatible systems that could be steadily upgraded over time. It was the huge, and largely unexpected, success of this series that assured that the monopoly position IBM had built up in the mechanical age would be successfully passed on to the emerging electronic era.

There is also general agreement that the key event in launching the second wave was IBM's introduction of its personal computer in 1981. Although PCs had existed since the mid-1970s, it was not until the arrival of the open architecture, 16-bit system from IBM that market expansion accelerated and customer computing began to be transformed. IBM provided both product standardization and its unique stamp of approval.

In retrospect, the subsequent evolution of the PC industry now seems obvious and inevitable. To improve information sharing, stand-alone PCs were soon tied together into local area networks (LANs). Each LAN needed to be managed by at least one shared LAN server. These ever more powerful servers became capable of running increasingly complex multiuser databases and applications, empowering departments and making obsolete many existing minicomputer systems. Over time, these isolated, individual LANs were linked together via various internetworking technologies, forming robust enterprise environments. In short, within a decade, this new bottom-up PC-centric approach had matched the core functionality of all but the largest mainframe systems. The revolution was complete.

All of the existing mainframe and minicomputer vendors struggled to cope with these powerful changes, usually without success. The PC era's emphasis on new customers, new technologies, new distribution channels, new sales and marketing skills, and greatly increased time-to-market and pricing pressure radically redefined supplier priorities. Even more important, it soon became clear that a new, horizontal supplier structure would prove the most effective business model for exploiting the changed market reality.

From the industry's earliest beginnings, the market leaders, be they American, European, or Japanese, were all vertically integrated suppliers, each responsible for all key aspects of design, manufacturing, software, sales, service, and support, all tied together through each vendor's proprietary system architecture. IBM's S/360 series and subsequent mainframe offerings were merely the signature examples of what was the overwhelming global mainframe and minicomputer supplier model.

In contrast, the PC industry from its earliest beginnings adopted a purely horizontal supplier structure. Companies such as Intel, Microsoft, Novell, Lotus, Compaq, Seagate, Oracle, 3Com, Electronic Data Systems, and many others all thrived by being specialists in particular layers of a newly emerging IT industry value chain. By focusing on just one technology area, the horizontal companies moved with a speed, deftness, and openness that the older systems companies simply couldn't match.

This new industry chain was held together by a curious, and largely unforeseen, mix of de facto and de jure standards. Controllers of de facto standards such as Microsoft, Intel, and Novell grew and profited greatly. In contrast, vendors competing in de jure segments such as PCs, disk drives, and monitors experienced similar growth but also a brutal, increasingly commodity-like competition unlike anything the IT industry had ever seen.

From a global perspective, this change in vendor business models led to an even more dominant U.S. competitive position. Most of the companies that mastered the horizontal model turned out to be American, usually from the western half of the country. Neither Europe nor Japan developed the start-up, venture-capital-driven culture of the United States. Instead, they relied primarily on their traditional systems companies: Fujitsu, Hitachi, and NEC in Japan and Siemens (Germany), Bull (France), ICL (United Kingdom), and Olivetti (Italy) in the major European markets.

The European and Japanese companies faced all of the same problems as the American systems companies, often from an even weaker computer business base. By the early 1990s, U.S.-based horizontal firms were clear leaders in, among other areas, microprocessors and other specialized semiconductors, PCs, disk drives, printers, networking hardware, and virtually all manner of software. Only in commodity markets such as DRAMs (Dynamic Random Access Memory), displays, and CD-ROMs were Japanese vendors still globally successful, while the major European vendors had been almost completely marginalized except in their respective home country markets. In short, to the surprise of many, U.S. national competitiveness benefited greatly from the PC era.

Understanding the Network-Centric Era

Just as the systems era succumbed to the power of the PC wave, so is the PC era now giving way to a network-centric paradigm. Over the next decade, much of the industry's energy and effort will be aimed at empowering the network as opposed to the desktop. The goal of the period will be to make computer connections as simple and as ubiquitous as telephone connections are today. The long talked about merger of computers and communications is finally happening.

As in the PC era, the current paradigm shift will be characterized by fundamental changes across a wide range of customer, technology, distribution, sales, marketing, and supplier business model dimensions. A number of these key changes are described briefly below. Each will be explained in detail in subsequent chapters.

From microprocessor to communications bandwidth. To understand the industry's changing technological priorities, consider that today a doubling of modem speeds would almost certainly do more to move the industry forward than a doubling of microprocessor speeds. Technologies such as cable modems, ISDN (Integrated Services Digital Network), and ADSL (Asymmetric Digital Subscriber Line) are now more strategic to the industry than faster PCs. As will be shown, the implications of this are multifaceted and profound.

From graphical interfaces to network browsers. Products such as Netscape's Navigator should be seen as the "windows" into the Internet and as such constitute a major challenge to the Windows-centric PC industry. However, Microsoft has shown a remarkable ability to respond to this challenge, and its competition with Netscape will prove to be one of the defining aspects of the network-centric era.

From Moore's to Metcalfe's law. The doubling of semiconductor performance every twenty-four months predicted by Moore's law has driven the hardware industry for three decades and will continue to do so. However, Metcalfe's law, which states that the value of a network increases exponentially as the number of users increases, while networking costs only increase linearly, will be the real driver of the upcoming network-centric industry. Tapping into the power of network economics is the key to next-generation financial success.

From internal to external networks. Just as most companies rely on telephone carriers for most voice services, so will most wide area computer communications be managed by public providers offering virtual "intranets." Proprietary, in-house networks are now too costly and inflexible and, once security concerns are resolved, will provide little additional value. The opportunities for traditional telephone service suppliers are immense if they can move quickly enough to take advantage of them.

Product subordination. Commodity-like PC hardware and software products have driven the industry for the last decade. Over the next decade, it will be diverse network services that will push the industry forward. Vendors of standard PC products will be moved farther down the industry value chain, requiring real changes in marketing, positioning, and price points. Symbolic of this overall subordination, hardware and software products will increasingly be bundled or even given away as part of higher value service offerings. The very image of PCs and related software will change as they come to be seen as intelligent peripherals subservient to the larger network capability.

From indirect to on-line distribution. Most PC products are currently sold and serviced through indirect, retail channels. The IT industry will likely be a leader in moving business directly on-line. This is especially so in the software market, where network-centric software "freeware" strategies from Netscape, Adobe, Sun, and, more recently, Microsoft are revolutionizing marketing, sales, delivery, and service and greatly accelerating software technology adoption. The network's ability to rapidly and efficiently distribute software is now ending the historical pattern of new hardware's being adopted much more quickly than new software. Increasingly, the opposite will be the case.

From a horizontal computer industry to a converged computer and communications structure. Like the PC wave, the network wave will bring about radical changes in global supplier industry structure. The key change will be the long predicted merger of the computer and telecommunications industries. This will then be followed by the integration of first the cable TV industry and then, eventually, consumer electronics. In the end, today's overlapping computer, telecom, and consumer electronics worlds will rationally recombine to create a new converged, but still horizontal, structure for devices, software, and transmission services. Supplier adjustments to this new environment will define long-term global competition. These changes will likely prove particularly difficult for today's pure play PC companies.

From U.S. to national supplier leadership. Although U.S. vendors are extremely well positioned for many opportunities in the network-centric era, the fundamental shift toward an industry led by network services delivered as part of a telephone-like grid favors the owners of communications infrastructures. Today, these are almost always national telephone, cable, and other service providers. Given the importance of communications infrastructures, few countries are likely to tolerate significant levels of foreign ownership or control. Thus, the power and influence of national communications carriers will increase dramatically, leading to a much less homogenous global technology market.

From single vendor to distributed power. Industry power itself will continue to evolve. Thus far it has, like a baton, been passed smoothly throughout the history of the industry. However, with the arrival of the Internet, the IBM/Intel/Microsoft chain of command has been suddenly disrupted. The most powerful force in today's market is controlled by no single vendor. Indeed, the most important competitive battles over the next few years will involve vendor attempts to gain dominance over various aspects of the Internet. No one vendor will dominate the communications content industries.

Taken together, the scope of change is likely to match or exceed that of the PC era. The industry's center of gravity has shifted to the network; the leaders of the current period are under direct challenge from the new order; and, perhaps most important, a new industry structure promises to reshape both the mission of the IT supplier as well as the current global balance of power. Standard products such as PCs, microprocessors, and software will remain global in nature, but network services, now the highest organized level of value-add, will maintain diverse country characteristics. Over time, nation-specific network services and their suppliers will accumulate the majority of IT market power.

The bulk of this book will attempt to take the reader through these massive decade-long transformations from a product, customer, supplier, and global perspective. Despite the tremendous excitement and publicity associated with the Internet, these fundamental developments have really only just begun. Indeed, for at least the next five years, today's PC-centric industry will continue to fund most of the industry. However, given the extraordinary power of network, software, and content economics, great new fortunes will surely be made and lost. From a more futuristic and humanistic perspective, the developments of the upcoming era will prove essential to this industry's long-term mission of building a true information society.

A Network Infrastructure Is Not an End in Itself

Although the process of wiring the developed world with high bandwidth connections should be largely completed by the year 2005 or so, it is important to keep in mind that IT industry evolution will clearly not cease at this stage. Once the global information infrastructure is in place, the industry's focus will shift to making maximum use of that infrastructure. This newly dominant emphasis upon content and applications will mark the beginning of real progress toward a true information society.

The defining aspect of this fourth wave will be that an increasing share of key societal output, whether for businesses, entertainment, lifestyle, or education will have been designed first and foremost around the newly available cyberspace. Equally important, information technology will extend beyond today's world of bits and encoded information to become embedded in the great majority of business and consumer products, eventually bringing most of the physical, and especially the analog, world into the information technology domain. Smart cameras, sensors, and other embedded technologies will make information technology so pervasive as to become essentially unmeasurable.

In these future waves, notions of being connected, or wired, will be taken as a given, as common and as transparent as today's telephone services. Indeed, an easy way to judge the success of the third wave will be to assess the extent to which a high bandwidth, ubiquitous network infrastructure can be made largely invisible. Such an infrastructure is the platform on which a powerful fourth wave can be built. Speculation regarding what this content-centric world might look like comprises the final chapter of this book.

A Guide for the Reader

This book is about the dynamics within the global IT industry. As such it is not intended to forecast all the important new ways in which technology will be used, only those necessary and likely to drive the industry forward. It also spends very little time discussing the pros and cons of the ever-increasing role of technology in our overall society. These important topics have been covered at length by others. This book's mission is simply to explain how this most dynamic of all industries works today and how it will likely behave over the coming tumultuous decade.

The organization is largely chronological, covering the period of roughly 1900–2010. About one-third of the text is devoted to the developments of the mainframe and PC eras. Although this portion of the book is much more of an interpretive analysis than a formal presentation of IT industry history, the author believes that an understanding of the computer market's past is critical to appreciating the full power and multifaceted implications of any major paradigm shift.

Just as one could not truly comprehend what happened to the mainframe and minicomputer companies during the PC era without some knowledge of their vertically integrated past, an understanding of the defining forces of the global PC industry is needed to accurately assess the challenges faced by today's PC-centric industry leaders. Each wave of industry expansion not only builds on but in many cases is defined by the weaknesses of the previous generation. With this as background, the key contents of each of the chapters are described briefly.

Chapter 1 summarizes some of the key lessons of the mainframe era with particular emphasis on the origins of IBM's power and the rise of the vertically integrated systems model. It ends with IBM's momentous and costly decision to use Intel microprocessors and Microsoft operating system software for its first personal computer. IBM clearly facilitated, and at least arguably caused, the loss of its dominant market position.

Chapters 2 to 4 examine various aspects of the PC era. Knowledgeable readers will be familiar with some of this material, which is designed to set the stage for network-centric era competition. Chapter 2 provides an overview of the growth, power, and implications of the PC wave, including the roots of the horizontal model, the unique status of Intel and Microsoft, and the increasing commoditization of much of the IT business.

Chapter 3 assesses the global implications of the PC era, with particular emphasis on why Japan has thus far fared so poorly in the worldwide PC business. This segment also reviews the current weaknesses of the major Western European nations as well as the important contributions of Korea, Taiwan, and India. This background will be critical to an understanding of global competition in the network-centric era.

Chapter 4 describes the late stages of the PC era, particularly Microsoft's and Intel's increased focus on the enterprise market, the adjustments of the systems companies, and the ongoing reconciliation of the horizontal and vertical supplier models. With its emphasis on current market data, chapter 5 concludes the analysis of the past and present by providing a statistical look at the composition of today's global IT business.

Chapters 6 to 8 focus on various aspects of the network-centric era. Chapter 6 reviews the key dimensions implied by this particular paradigm shift. It expands on the generational changes described in this overview and discusses the issue of why Internet usage exploded with such force and suddenness. Chapter 7 introduces the key concept of a converged computer/communications/consumer electronics value chain. As these three industries steadily come together, a new integrated and greatly extended IT business will emerge. Chapter 8 outlines the relationship between changing applications, technology requirements, and resulting structures.

Chapters 9 to 11 discuss the implications of this converged value chain for global hardware, software, and transmission services competition, respectively. The hardware discussion in chapter 9 focuses on the impact of both hardware product subordination and an expanded product set of PCs, PDAs (personal digital assistants), cable set top boxes, WebTV, and Internet terminals on today's supplier business model. The chapter forecasts increased end user device competitiveness from Japan, Korea, and Taiwan, real microprocessor challenges to Intel, and major changes in the long-term hardware vendor business model, especially for pure play PC companies.

Chapter 10 presents a similar analysis of the global software market. The two main themes are the revolutionary impact of networking on software marketing, distribution, and economics and the effects of software subordination on the overall market power of the major U.S. software suppliers. The key thesis is that as software ceases to be the industry's highest level of organized value-add, software companies' ability to dictate market standards is likely to significantly diminish, particularly if the emergence of Netscape results in real multivendor software competition.

Chapter 11 examines the U.S. network services market. Perhaps the single biggest force in restructuring the IT industry will be the rise of telecommunications. As mission-critical voice and data services become increasingly intermingled, today's supplier structure, which includes many small Internet access providers, will prove unsustainable. Over time, the owners of telecom facilities are also likely to be the primary service providers. Consequently, it is the integration, cooperation, and competition between these infrastructure owners that will set the pace of overall bandwidth improvements. These owners will differ greatly on a country-by-country basis. As the computer and communications industries merge, IT industry power will increasingly be shared.

Chapter 12 moves away from product and service attributes to discuss global competition between the national network infrastructures themselves. Given different starting points, different suppliers, and different regulatory and cultural dictates, individual country infrastructures are likely to vary widely. Since advanced network infrastructures are rapidly becoming a cornerstone of a modern economy, countries with superior infrastructures are likely to gain significant economic and social benefits. The comparative positions of the United States, Japan, and the major nations of Western Europe are assessed using a global competitiveness model developed by Michael Porter of the Harvard Business School. Overall, the outlook for the U.S. national infrastructure looks extremely positive.

Chapter 13 and 14 look at the network era from a customer perspective. Chapter 13 focuses specifically on the implications of the network era for enterprise computing. The main emphasis is placed on understanding the transition to a network-centric era from an information systems user perspective. The chapter suggests that certain "bit-based" industries will likely be transformed far more radically than other "atom-based" sectors, to use the terminology popularized by Nicholas Negroponte, founder and current head of the Media Lab at the Massachusetts Institute of Technology. It also describes how new network-centric applications compare with other important information systems (IS) priorities.

Chapter 14 addresses these changes from a consumer perspective. This section assesses efforts to use cheaper PCs, network computers, and cable set top boxes to expand the consumer computing user base beyond today's limited PC demographics of those who have high incomes and high education and are less than forty-five years of age. A second important concept is that as consumers increasingly use networks to reach banks, schools, insurance companies, governments, and other large organizations, the boundaries between business and consumer applications will steadily shrink in importance.

Chapter 15 steps back to take a broader look at the critical role of government both over time and during the network-centric period. Whether as an advanced user, R&D sponsor, standards arbitrator, price regulator, competitive reformer, consumer protector, or antitrust overseer, government has made important, but often largely unrecognized, contributions throughout much of the IT industry's history. As the unregulated world of computing merges with the heavily regulated world of telecommunications, public sector involvement can only increase. Supportive government actions will be essential for a successful third wave rollout. The February 1996 U.S. telecom reform legislation provides an excellent and important example.

Chapter 16 looks beyond the third wave to speculate what will happen early in the next century when all of this advanced infrastructure is in place. The main purpose will be to forecast the underlying dynamics of the next paradigm shift, which will increasingly revolve around network content and services. Beginning early in the next century, the content-centric era will likely define a new paradigm, again with profound multidimensional implications. It will mark the true arrival of a multimedia IT industry, as many businesses and social activities are redesigned to take advantage of the now ubiquitous cyberspace.

The book concludes with a retrospective look at the nature and evolution of computer industry power. In the end, issues of technology, structure, and the individual decisions of competitors have emerged as the deciding attributes. If the PC era is any example, fifteen years from now, the industry will look back and see the changes of today as inevitable and highly predictable. It is the goal of this book to try to forecast what those broad patterns of change will be.

Acknowledgments

I would like to thank all of my friends and colleagues at the International Data Group, particularly IDG President Kelly Conlin and

Computerworld President Gary Beach for giving me the time, support, and encouragement necessary to complete this work. I am also indebted to my longtime employer, International Data Corporation, for providing the environment in which many of this book's ideas were created, tested, and refined. I would also like to thank IDC for permission to use its valuable research data.

Special gratitude is due to Dr. Robert Metcalfe, who originally suggested that all the work I had done over many years should be pulled together into this single volume. Similar thanks are due to Matt Wagner at Waterside Productions and Tony Vlamis at Amacom for their belief in and enthusiasm for this project. I would also like to recognize the work of Dorothy Anderson in editing my original manuscript, as well as Cindi Sparrow for producing virtually all of this book's many graphics.

REASSESSING IBM'S LEGACY

Although this book is by no means de-signed to be a historical reference, the early history of the computer business re-mains remarkably relevant to many as-pects of today's information technology industry. This chapter provides a brief his-tory of the commercial mainframe com-puter industry, the first great wave of computer growth and expansion. Particu-lar attention is paid to three lasting lega-cies: computer industry supplier struc-ture, vendor market share concentration, and the sources of IBM's power.

Although the origins of computing machines go back to the 1930s, the years up until the early 1960s are often viewed as essentially a premodern phase, characterized by experimental and usually short-lived machines trying to make do with highly immature, electrome-chanical technologies.

Although from a technology perspective this is largely correct, from the perspective of the structure of the computer industry and the sources of supplier market power, nothing really could be further from the truth. In fact, to understand why the computer industry has evolved the way it has, one has to go all the way back to the late nineteenth century, to the very idea of using machines to process in-formation. One question can serve as a simple starting point: Exactly why did IBM become so dominant?

Surprisingly, given all that has been written about IBM's ups and downs, there is still not an accurate and widely shared view of exactly how IBM became the industry colossus it did. Why did this huge new industry take on a competitive balance consisting essentially of IBM and then everyone else?

Industry jargon of the time reflected this two-tier reality. For a long time, the mainframe industry competition was referred to as "IBM and the seven dwarfs," and then after RCA and General Electric dropped out it became IBM and the BUNCH (Burroughs, Univac, NCR, Control Data, and Honeywell). IBM grabbed a steady 70 per-cent mainframe market share for itself and seemed to let the others divide up the rest.

In an age when Microsoft is often seen as having IBM-like power, the question is hardly academic. In fact, IBM's power in its day dwarfed that of Microsoft today. As recently as 1984, IBM had roughly one-third of all computer industry revenues and more than half of all industry profits. Microsoft today has less than 2 percent of worldwide IT revenues and less than 10 percent of overall industry profits. Moreover, since much of Microsoft's initial power was effec-tively bestowed upon it by IBM, the source of IBM's power is directly relevant to Microsoft as well.

Certainly, IBM's hugely dominant share was not typical of other global hardware manufacturing business at that time. In sectors such as automobiles, consumer electronics, consumer durables, telephone exchanges and other comparable areas, no one firm could grab and hold the majority of the worldwide market. Today's PC industry would be another good example of a more typical competitive structure.

The airplane manufacturing business is perhaps the closest parallel to IBM's mainframe success, but Boeing's long dominant position has always been greatly helped by that industry's extraordinarily high barriers to entry, barriers largely not existent in a start-up driven computer industry. Even in the mainframe era of the 1960s and 1970s, there were usually more than a dozen worldwide system suppliers, with a steady stream of companies entering and exiting the market.

So why didn't the computer industry of the 1960s come to look like today's PC business, with a strong leader or two being closely pursued by a number of comparably sized rivals?

Industry legend often has it that IBM's S/360 family was a huge and highly innovative gamble that left the rest of the industry in the dust. Among the many problems with this view is the inconvenient fact that IBM's computer market share was already dominant years before the S/360 was announced.

A conventional business explanation that perhaps IBM's products were either technically superior or materially less expensive also fails to convince. Even at the time, many observers believed that IBM's systems were often inferior to those of Remington (eventually Sperry), Control Data, Honeywell, or Burroughs. They manifestly were not cheaper. This admission has left two main lines of general explanation.

The positive story, closely associated with the Watson family legend, is that IBM simply outmarketed everyone else by focusing on the commercial market, understanding customers' data-processing needs, and providing excellent service. The second, more jaundiced, view comes from some of IBM's trampled opponents who claim that through a mix of predatory pricing and strategic vaporware IBM often cheated its way to success. There is certainly considerable truth to the former and some legally recognized evidence of the latter, but neither can adequately explain IBM's overwhelming competitive position.

In fact, the roots of IBM's computer industry dominance go back to the late nineteenth century and Herman Hollerith's original "statistical piano" built for the U.S. Government's census efforts. This initial tabulating product led to the various but only moderately successful accounting machines of the Computing, Tabulating, and Recording Company (CTR), which an aggressive forty-year-old named Thomas Watson, Sr., joined as general manager in 1914.

Although certainly no secret, an often neglected aspect of the Tom Watson story is that he spent his formative years at National Cash Register Corporation (NCR). Today, NCR is a company of modest position with a culture of being, if anything, almost too nice. However, in the early years of this century, NCR, under the leadership of John Patterson, was one of the most feared companies in the nation, with a near monopoly on the huge market for mechanical cash registers.

Through aggressive, often predatory pricing, with ruthless control over channels and the used market, and with powerful financial advantages over its competitors, NCR dominated what was a pure hardware and services market. Obviously, there was no software component.

Tom Watson brought the lessons and practices he learned at NCR to CTR, which in 1924 he renamed International Business Machines (IBM). Over the course of the next three decades, in a period where antitrust regulations were just beginning to be enforced, a highly aggressive IBM came to totally dominate the huge punch-card-based accounting machine market, reaching a market share of roughly 90 percent.

In his important, but often overlooked, 1986 book, *Big Blue,* former U.S. Government antitrust economist Richard Delamarter describes how, in the 1920s, 1930s, and 1940s, IBM lived on the edge of antitrust law using highly aggressive tactics to drive rivals out of the punch-card business.* In fact, the first antitrust suit against IBM goes back to 1932, with a second suit filed in 1952.

Legal history aside, IBM's dominant position with corporate data managers was clearly established well before the computer was even invented. IBM's great accomplishment was maintaining this position through the transition to the electronic age. However, since the early computers were in fact a mix of electronic tabulators and electromechanical punch-card equipment, IBM had a natural base from which to move into and dominate the computer business.

---

*Richard Delamarter, *Big Blue: IBM's Use and Abuse of Power* (New York: Dodd, Meade, 1986).

Indeed, IBM's punch-card position was so strong that even IBM's computer competitors needed to buy and provide punch-card equipment and the paper cards themselves from IBM, an enormous advantage. The IBM 80-column card format became the industry standard, perhaps the first example of the many software lock-ins to come. However, as the example of NCR suggests, given sufficient aggressiveness and a lax antitrust environment, near monopoly positions can, in fact, be established in hardware even without a software dimension.

IBM deserves great credit for making the transition to the computer era, but it did have some important advantages. Its huge profits from both card machines and the paper cards themselves allowed it to invest heavily in the new data-processing technologies and, perhaps more important, to respond aggressively to any competitive threat. From a customer perspective, IBM's dominance of the accounting machine market gave it ready access to and deep knowledge of virtually all major corporate accounts.

In retrospect, the controversial but ultimately highly successful 1964 launch of the S/360 family served to make it clear to everyone that IBM's monopoly had been successfully moved from the mechanical to the electronic age. (Interestingly, the controversy stemmed from the fact that many observers believed that the S/360 family was deliberately announced early to stop competitive losses; many machines would not be delivered for well over a year.)

The lesson of all of this is often forgotten. If IBM had not had such a huge share of the accounting machine business, it is highly unlikely that it would have so dominated the early years of the computer industry. More than anything else, the aggressive strategies of Thomas Watson, Sr., in the 1920s and 1930s went on to define the computer industry of the 1960s, 1970s, and beyond.

Structural Legacy

In addition to this dominant vendor legacy, the very structure of the computer industry also goes back to the pre-electronic age. During the 1950s, in order to build workable systems, IBM, Remington Rand, RCA, Burroughs, and others designed and built proprietary systems, relying largely on in-house resources for systems, peripherals, software, sales, service, and support. At the time, they really didn't have much choice. As will be discussed in chapter 2, vertical integration has historically been an early phase for most new emerging technology-driven businesses.

This initial U.S. computer industry structure was eventually emulated in Europe by companies such as ICL, Bull, and Siemens and also in Japan by Fujitsu, Hitachi, NEC, and others. In an otherwise rapidly changing market, the vertically integrated approach remained the dominant IT supplier model until the early 1980s. In fact, this means of organization became so well entrenched that many participants had trouble imagining a functional IT industry organized any other way. IBM's S/360 family was emblematic of the staying power of this approach.

The Real Impact of IBM's S/360 Family

From a commercial computing perspective, it is now standard practice to view the modern computer era as beginning in 1964. In April of that year, IBM introduced its System/360 family of computers. Looking back, we see that these systems were significant in two main regards:

From a technological standpoint, the S/360 systems introduced the concept of a family of compatible machines spanning, for that time, a very wide performance range, using common software and peripherals. The entire S/360 family was based on a single architecture that could be evolved steadily over time. Indeed, even today, the designs of IBM's most advanced mainframes still have their roots in this original family of machines now more than thirty years old.

From a market perspective, the S/360 series of products sold in record, and unexpectedly high, numbers, cementing IBM's place as the overwhelming industry leader, a position it would indisputably hold for the next twenty years. IBM is still, in terms of revenues, by far the world's largest computer company.

More than any other single product line, the S/360 family entrenched the vertically oriented industry structure depicted in figure

1-1. As in the 1950s, IBM built, sold, and serviced all of its key main-frame system parts. But, unlike the 1950s, the overall S/360 business proved big enough and stable enough that various third-party companies could, often after much legal squabbling, build businesses in S/360 services, peripherals, software, and financing. Some of the leaders in establishing these third-party markets were Applied Data Research in software, Telex in storage, Electronic Data Systems in services, and Greyhound in equipment leasing.

Many of these businesses were, at least initially, simply too small for IBM to pay attention to; others brought important innovations. However, nearly all of these new third-party companies were initially targeted at the large S/360 base, further strengthening that family's competitive position, ironically, despite IBM's often vehement opposition. This early example of the strong getting stronger has since become a familiar industry pattern; some call it increasing returns, others, such as Bill Gates, label it more simply as a positive feedback cycle.

This model of specialty companies providing products and services that revolved around a central systems company soon extended beyond just IBM to become the dominant computer industry pattern up until the early 1980s. It was a stable and profitable business structure that was largely adopted by the minicomputer industry as well. It created a long list of consistently profitable, billion-dollar-plus systems companies and an even longer, but much less stable, list of smaller, specialty companies. According to International Data Corporation (IDC), global spending on mainframe and minicomputer hardware rose from $2 billion in 1964 to more than $25 billion in 1984, a compound annual growth rate of 14 percent per year.

From a computer customer's point of view, this model was a com-

Figure 1-1. Systems company business model, 1964–1981.

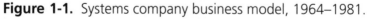

fortable, if expensive, compromise. On the positive side, supplier and architectural stability simplified user technology decision making and facilitated long-term customer/supplier partnerships. Customers became very closely tied to their particular set of vendors.

On the other hand, the proprietary vendor approach tended to lock customers into a particular mainframe or minicomputer vendor for long periods of time. Switching vendors generally meant obsoleting costly and increasingly mission-critical applications software, a decision not to be made lightly or often.

In the end, vendors had a quasi-monopoly position within their own customer base, and thus the bulk of vendor competition focused on getting new customers. Once a vendor was selected, customers had a simpler, more predictable environment, but they paid dearly for it.

This mainframe industry structure of the 1960s was largely repeated with minicomputers with a few important and revealing variants. Unlike the mainframe suppliers, most of the minicomputer companies of the 1960s and 1970s were start-ups, especially the successful ones. With a shortage of funds and a growing computer industry around them, early minicomputer vendors such as Digital Equipment and Data General had a strong incentive to use outside components and peripherals, and most in fact did so. However, as these companies grew, they invariably became more vertically integrated; Digital eventually started making most of its own semiconductors, disk drives, printers, and terminals.

This suggests that, at least in terms of the computer industry, the vertical model began as a necessity, but it also grew because it was seen as desirable. It was this preference for internally developed hardware and software that defined the engineering-driven system-centric industry culture. This attitude eventually took on its own pejorative label: "the not invented here syndrome."

The IBM 360 and eventually 370 software environment went on to become the de facto standard for mainframes. Fifteen years later, Digital's VAX VMS enjoyed a similar, operating system driven dominance as it distanced itself from its supermini rivals. Microsoft's success with MS-DOS has much in common with what IBM and Digital did in their day. Strong de facto system software leadership has deep roots in the history of the information technology business. Indeed, there has never been any other way. This is a theme that will recur numerous times throughout this book.

Unlike Microsoft, of course, IBM could leverage its software dominance across its hardware and services offerings. It was this combination of software control married to a vertically integrated business structure that led to IBM's still unmatched size and long-standing industry leadership. As the next section will show, the only company capable of loosening IBM's grip on the industry turned out to be IBM itself.

IBM Divests Its Power and Is Cheered for It

As the seminal event in the development for the PC industry, IBM's 1981 decision to outsource its critical PC components to Microsoft and Intel is now widely recognized as one of the most damaging corporate decisions in business history. The monopoly power that IBM had so carefully built up over some sixty years was inadvertently and suddenly bestowed upon two companies that were then just a tiny fraction of its size.

Obviously, IBM failed to appreciate the strategic importance of both personal computers and microprocessor technology. But then again, so did just about everyone else in the IT industry. IBM's decision to use existing technologies to quickly get to market was almost universally applauded, especially as IBM went on to dominate the PC industry of the early 1980s. After all, none of the major PC pioneers—Apple, Commodore, Tandy—made their own microprocessors. In 1983, IBM's worldwide PC share reached a stunning 70 percent, with numerous other suppliers scrambling to divide up the rest. Although a true IBM-compatible market was already developing, it looked anything but threatening.

William F. Zachmann, then head of research for International Data Corporation (IDC), was one of the few to clearly and strongly voice the view that personal computers were not just another IBM plug-compatible market such as mainframes, disk and tape drives, printers, and terminals. Without control of the critical component technologies, IBM's high cost structure, slow time-to-market, and paralyzing bureaucratic in-fighting would soon make it extremely vulnerable to direct and open competition. This view, in retrospect now considered obvious, was generally ignored and often ridiculed until the second half of the 1980s when the evidence became indisputable.

Even after the potential danger of its decisions had become clear, IBM and much of the rest of the industry continued to believe that it was only a matter of time before IBM would take back what it had given away. It is to the great and lasting credit of vendors such as Intel, Compaq, and especially Microsoft that almost all of these efforts— the PC XT/370, the Topview user interface, the Microchannel bus architecture, OS/2, Workplace OS, and most recently the Power PC— have either disappointed or have proved to be outright failures.

Given that most of the rest of the industry saw many of IBM's moves in the same positive way that IBM did, there is no real need to cast blame on the particular IBM executives involved. Perhaps all that needs to be said is that at a time when companies are constantly pushed to reassess their business models and challenge their basic market assumptions, IBM has been savagely punished for doing just that. Its decision to use Microsoft and Intel was precisely the type of nontraditional or "outside the envelope" move often considered necessary today. As Bill Gates mulls solicited and unsolicited advice concerning Microsoft's approach to various Internet-based competition such as Netscape's Navigator and Sun's Java, he is no doubt reminded of the source of his own great success.

Could It Have Been Otherwise?

Business historians will debate for years to come what would have happened if IBM had built its own PC, with its own components, in the same vertically integrated manner that had served it so well in the past. Obviously, there is no definitive answer about what would have or could have happened. However, there is good reason to think that things might have developed very differently, at least for a considerable period of time.

Two real-world examples stand out. In Japan, until the last couple of years, unlike the rest of the global IT market, there was no single PC standard. Each Japanese PC vendor developed its own PC operating system. Although all of these operating systems were based on Microsoft's DOS software, they were all sufficiently incompatible to make interoperability of PC applications impossible.

The result was that, as with mainframes and minicomputers, each vendor had a monopoly-like control over its portion of the PC customer base. The interesting result was that Nippon Electric Corporation (NEC) consistently held an IBM-like 50 percent share of the Japanese PC market, and overall supplier competition was greatly restrained. However, the price for this vendor protection was much slower PC market growth. High system prices and limited software portability were among the key reasons why the Japanese PC market lagged far behind those of comparably developed nations. The unusual and important history of the Japanese PC industry will be covered at length in chapter 3.

Closer to home, the U.S. workstation market continues to operate according to a proprietary systems model. Although virtually all of today's high-performance workstations are based on the Unix operating system, each vendor produces its own Unix software that is incompatible with the other vendors' offerings. In this case, a handful of vendors—Sun, Hewlett-Packard, IBM, Silicon Graphics, and Digital—divide the great bulk of the market relatively equally among themselves, with few new entrants.

Obviously, IBM would gladly swap the current PC market reality for either of the above outcomes. Taken together, the two examples do seem to suggest that today's PC industry structure was not inevitable. During a time when many are concerned with limiting Microsoft's power, the industry should not forget that if it weren't for IBM's unwitting and accidental assistance, it would have taken a long time for IBM's power to be so completely broken.

As chapters 2 to 4 will show, the consequences of IBM's power divestiture have proved to be staggering. The problems that beset IBM simultaneously spread to all of the existing systems companies, eventually toppling the vertically integrated market model itself. However, these problems were more than offset by the unprecedented growth of the global PC business. This accelerated process of creative destruction eventually resulted in substantial overall industry gains.

CHAPTER 2

UNDERSTANDING THE SECOND WAVE: THE POWER OF A PARADIGM SHIFT

Although much of the PC industry story is now familiar, a review of its principal forces and results will provide the starting point for understanding the current network-centric era. This chapter defines the nature of the PC paradigm shift and explains why existing mainframe and minicomputer companies found it so hard to cope with. It then describes the emergence of a bifurcated monopoly/commodity industry and the surprising global ascendancy of horizontally structured U.S. firms.

The explosion of the personal computer business during the 1980s was one of the great industrial takeoffs of all time. From just $2 billion in 1980, the PC business grew to $83 billion in 1990. This growth has continued virtually unabated through the 1990s, with the 1995 world-wide PC hardware business, according to IDC, reaching $160 billion in sales. This story is well known to all.

But beyond the staggering growth and wealth creation, the arrival of the personal computer, particularly the IBM PC, signaled the beginning of a fundamental and now well-understood IT industry paradigm shift. An industry that had in the past revolved around the mainframe or minicomputer system now had a new center of gravity—the desktop personal computer. This change in orientation went on to revolutionize the industry.

The history of the PC business is, of course, interesting and important in and of itself; however, it will also prove to be essential in understanding the origins of the network-centric era. Not only does the PC era provide an ideal example of the power and scope of a multidimensional paradigm shift, it also defines the industry upon which the network-centric focus will be built. As will be shown throughout this book, many of the supplier characteristics and idiosyncrasies that evolved to meet the needs of the PC market are likely to be ill suited to the demands of a network-driven industry. Figure 2-1 shows some of the defining characteristics of the PC wave, each of which is summarized as follows:

From systems-centric to PC-centric. Over the course of the 1980s, most of the industry's energy went into empowering the personal computer. During the second half of that decade, there were few major

Figure 2-1. Understanding the PC paradigm shift.

1964–1981	1981–1994
Systems-centric	PC-centric
Corporate computing	Individual computing
Grosch's law	Moore's law
Data center	Client/server
Proprietary	Commodity
Direct sales	Indirect channels
Vertical integration	Horizontal value chain

innovations in mainframe or minicomputer systems, with the word "downsizing" capturing user interest in substituting microprocessor-based systems for traditional proprietary designs wherever possible.

From corporate to individual computing. In the 1960s and 1970s, customer IT emphasis was on corporate efficiencies, mostly through administrative systems. In the PC era, the focus shifted to individual and ultimately workgroup productivity. As part of this change, computers moved out of the domain of the trained professional to be increasingly used by the average white collar worker. The number of people owning and using computers increased by an order of magnitude.

From Grosch's law to Moore's law. In the 1940s, Grosch's law, named after computer pioneer Herb Grosch, stated that computer power increases as the square of the cost. In other words, a computer that is twice as expensive as another should have four times the processing power. This was the core argument in favor of large systems, and it largely held true during the 1960s and 1970s.

In contrast, Moore's law (named after Intel cofounder Gordon Moore) stated that semiconductor performance would double every two years for the foreseeable future. Because of their more modern designs and much greater volumes, merchant microprocessor based systems would ride this curve more quickly and easily than proprietary designs. By the mid-1980s, Grosch's law had been inverted (except in the eyes of some diehard cost-to-use defenders), and the best price/performance was now clearly with PCs and other microprocessor-based systems.

From the data center to the client/server. Data center management was at the heart of the systems era's information processing efforts. During the 1980s, much of this energy shifted to end user management, support, and training. The complex integration of PCs, LANs, servers, and, when necessary, existing legacy systems came to be called client/server computing.

From proprietary to commodity systems. The 1960s and 1970s were characterized by proprietary systems that presented users with high vendor switching costs. Since all IBM-compatible PCs ran the same software, PC vendor switching costs were close to zero. PC software and peripheral products also took on commodity-like characteristics.

Direct versus indirect selling. Virtually all mainframe sales and a significant portion of the minicomputer business reached customers, especially large customers, through direct sales channels. Because of their low sales prices and commodity features, the great majority of PC business went through indirect channels, mostly stores and dealers. Direct PC sales were conducted mostly via the telephone.

From a vertical to a horizontal supplier model. All of the above combined to change the very nature of what it meant to be a computer vendor. As discussed in chapter 1, the major mainframe and minicomputer players were large vertically integrated manufacturers. The PC era ushered in a new supplier model where smaller companies specialized in a particular layer of the industry value chain. The reasons for and the implications of this crucial change in industry structure will be explained in detail in subsequent sections.

When coupled with the enormous new business opportunities created, changes of this magnitude easily justify the use of the often overused term *paradigm shift.* But exactly why did these radical changes occur the way they did? Understanding the roots and drivers of this paradigm shift can help provide insight into future ones.

Recognizing the Nature of Change

In the late 1980s and early 1990s, the conventional wisdom said that there had been two great drivers of these prodigious upheavals: (1) the invention of the microprocessor and (2) the arrival of so-called open systems that would increasingly standardize hardware and software products.

Clearly, the microprocessor was critical. By riding down the path predicted by Moore's law, microprocessors enabled the industry to provide ever more powerful personal computers at largely constant costs. These unprecedented price/performance improvements clearly enabled the revolution. Analogous increases in communications bandwidth will be the critical driver of the network-centric era.

At a more theoretical level, the microprocessor fundamentally altered existing computer principles. Before the microprocessor, the computer's CPU (central processing unit) was a scarce resource that computer architectures were designed to optimize, hence the emphasis on so-called timesharing. Microprocessors offered computing power so cheaply that computing cycles could be regularly sacrificed for end user productivity, convenience, and ease of use. There is no doubt that the arrival of powerful and inexpensive microprocessors radically reshaped computer designs and architectures.

But what about open systems? The examples of the Japanese PC market and the U.S. workstation market cited in chapter 1 show that there was nothing inherent in microprocessors themselves that would necessarily lead to standardized software markets. It is certainly imaginable that PCs, LANs, and their interconnection could have proceeded along vendor-specific lines for a considerable period, perhaps forever. It was only IBM's endorsement of Intel and Microsoft that so quickly broke down the proprietary model.

Thus, although the microprocessor revolution was inevitable, open systems were considerably less so. Indeed, the idealized form of open systems has never really happened. The so-called open systems era was characterized by three great de facto monopolies—Microsoft, Intel, and Novell—all three of which were rapidly assuming IBM's recently divested market power.

Indeed, the real change was not one of moving from so-called proprietary systems to so-called open ones. The real change was the move away from a world where standards were set by vertically integrated systems vendors toward one where they were set by vendors who concentrated on particular parts of the industry value chain. This remains a crucial point and, as will be shown later, one that is still highly relevant as the battle for Internet and Worldwide Web standards heats up. There is still no clear evidence that long-term processor and operating system standards can be set through anything other than strong, de facto, usually single vendor leadership.

For a brief period in the late 1980s, the industry fooled itself into believing that it had truly entered an open systems era where key industry standards would be set by various committees, alliances, and consortia. High-profile efforts such as the Advanced Computer Environment (ACE), the Open Software Foundation, X/Open, Unix International, and others were founded essentially to try to set a number of core hardware and software design standards. In this mission they have had only minor successes and a number of embarrassing failures. Virtually all have been disbanded or significantly scaled back. As discussed throughout the second half of this book, these lessons loom large as one considers the future effectiveness of the Internet Engineering Task Force and other standards bodies.

By the early 1990s, the industry had fully realized that rather than create an open systems revolution, they had more accurately exchanged one master, IBM, for three—Microsoft, Intel, and Novell. More abstractly, they had shifted from a vertically integrated industry structure to an increasingly horizontal one. Even more than the microprocessor, it was this structural shift that proved so difficult for the existing order to cope with.

Lessons From Other Industries

Perhaps a movement toward some sort of horizontal structure was inevitable. Certainly business history suggests that over time many major industrial sectors have become characterized by a separation of products (particularly any kind of hardware equipment) from related software and services.

During the 1940s, in the early days of television, companies such as RCA, Zenith, and Dumont were all heavily involved in television manufacturing, broadcasting services, and program content. All three needed program content to drive the sales of their various hardware offerings. For example, many of the original color TV programs came from NBC, whose parent RCA just happened to be the leading supplier of color TV sets. Similar device/content synergy was part of the early years of radio in the 1920s and 1930s.

But by the mid-1950s, the success of independent television and record companies made it clear that a separation of hardware and software activity would be the dominant model within the consumer electronics and related entertainment businesses. Today, companies such as Matsushita, Toshiba, and Sony build a wide variety of hardware devices, but historically they have not been involved in providing the required programming and broadcast services. Equally, no major music or television programming company has chosen to get into the hardware manufacturing business.

The largely unsuccessful early 1990s attempts by both Sony and Matsushita to buy into the content side of the entertainment business actually support the overall separation thesis. In both cases, the companies managed their hardware and content businesses largely independently. Any synergies are achieved largely at the branding level. It's not as if Sony tells its customers that in order to see its latest music video, one needs to have a Sony VCR, television, or CD player. This sort of linkage has been tried but has almost always failed in consumer electronics, but through the 1980s it was still considered normal in much of the IT business.

Similarly, before the deregulation of the U.S. telecommunications industry in the 1980s, the telephony market was dominated by a vertically integrated AT&T, which made its telephones and switches while controlling virtually all the available network services. AT&T was an almost totally vertically integrated organization, as were the telephone companies in many other major nations.

Since the United States and other governments began to force global communications deregulation, an increasingly horizontal industry structure has emerged. Sony, Panasonic, AT&T, and General Electric have moved into the telephone business; Alcatel, NEC, Northern Telecom, Ericsson, and AT&T dominate the voice switching equipment market, while relative newcomers such as MCI and Sprint have focused exclusively on services.

Although AT&T continued to compete in all three segments, each product group was increasingly asked to stand on its own. In 1995, the company confirmed the overall trend by announcing that it would split its equipment and services divisions into legally separate companies, with the equipment company taking on the name Lucent. (In 1991, the author labeled the process by which vertically integrated computer companies break themselves up into horizontal units "IT industry dis-integration.")

Similar patterns can be seen with airplanes, automobiles, and many other major industry sectors. Boeing may be the world's biggest airplane manufacturer, but today people would think it quite strange if Boeing suddenly decided that if people wanted to fly on a Boeing plane, they would have to fly on Boeing Airlines. (Historians might note, however, that this was exactly the case up until 1934 when Congress, through the Black-McKeller bill, legally separated the airline services business from the airplane manufacturing business, thereby forcing the break-up of the then dominant United Aircraft and Air Transport Corporation, chaired by William E. Boeing. The resulting break led to the creation of today's Boeing, as well as United Airlines.)

The clear lesson to be learned from examining these mature sectors of the world economy is that, over time, products and services tend to become unbundled and that companies often find it counterproductive to try to translate an edge on one side into leverage on the other. However, as the airplane, telecommunications, computer, and other industries show, often the initial push toward this dis-integration has come from the government. Market forces alone have not always been sufficient to break the strong vertically integrated market structure that often dominates the early stages of a new industry.

The government's main reason for requiring such product and services unbundling has been to diminish or eliminate monopoly power that has clearly constrained market evolution in certain industries, especially telecommunications. Once unbundling begins, market momentum tends to make it irreversible due to the differing product and services business models described in the next section.

The Economics of Hardware, Software, and Services

By examining some simple economic realities, this section will explain why the hardware, software, and services businesses will tend to stay separate over time. These same underlying economics, especially when combined with the powerful economics of networks, will continue to shape the IT industry through the network-centric era and beyond.

Figure 2-2 provides a conceptual view of the underlying economics of the three sectors. The figure shows that the average cost curves for all three businesses are quite different, resulting in diverse supplier dynamics.

Hardware. Although many hardware markets follow the pattern shown, the PC market is perhaps most illustrative. Clearly, from a PC vendor's point of view there are considerable volume manufacturing/ marketing and distribution economies. It is generally believed that unless a manufacturer can sell at least several million PCs per year, it will be at a considerable cost disadvantage versus its larger competitors.

However, these scale economies are not infinite. After a certain point (which no doubt changes over time), the cost curve flattens. Indeed, at some point it may even start to rise. Imagine if Compaq had to make all of the some 60 million PCs built in 1995. Would this really lead to increased efficiency? Almost certainly it would not.

Figure 2-2. Underlying economics—hardware, software, professional services.

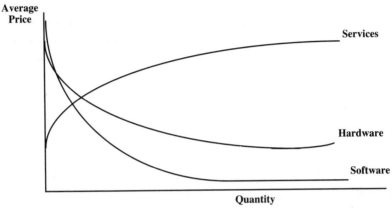

The result of this underlying economic reality is that a mature PC hardware market should be characterized by a limited number of major suppliers. Without sufficient volumes, smaller players will not be competitive beyond certain niche markets. However, since manufacturing scale economies are ultimately limited, no one vendor is capable of taking over such a commodity market.

This is generally the way the PC hardware business has been evolving over the first half of the 1990s. It is a typical consumer electronic structure found with both televisions and VCRs. The biggest difference is the continued existence of large numbers of very small players that continue to hold a significant share of the desktop (although not the laptop) market. These companies can compete because of the availability of all key PC parts from the component industries. Nevertheless, as technology sophistication rises and the major vendors continually cut costs, the outlook for these firms is not bright.

Software. In contrast to hardware, the cost curve for software continues to move downward, eventually approaching zero. This is due to software's unique economics. Once developed, the marginal cost of a second copy is effectively the price of a diskette or tape or, in the case of electronic distribution, virtually nothing at all, as the ample amount of freeware on the Internet is now making quite clear. Thus there are tremendous scale economies in the software business, a characteristic that tends to lead to highly concentrated markets. Vendors who can operate far down the cost curve have a huge advantage over those who produce at significantly lower volumes.

Therefore, it is no accident that many sectors of the software business tend to become highly concentrated over time. In this sense, Microsoft's strong position in both operating systems and certain applications is more the norm than the exception, following in a long tradition of strong leaders: IBM's MVS, Novell's Netware, Lotus 1-2-3 (in the DOS era), Autodesk's Autocad, Adobe's Postscript, Netscape's Navigator, and others.

Professional services. This often overlooked sector shows yet a third distinct pattern. Unlike hardware and software, services may in fact have no net scale economies at all. Clearly, there are some volume efficiencies on the marketing and company branding side, but these are largely offset by the inherent inefficiencies in scaling a people-based business. If a project can be done by one person in the time required, that's often the cheapest way to do it.

Thus professional service firms of all types tend to follow the same pattern—the bigger the firm, the higher the prices. This holds true for major accounting firms such as Price Waterhouse, management consulting firms such as McKinsey, legal firms such as Baker and Mckensie, or computer service firms such as Electronic Data Systems (EDS) and Andersen Consulting. One doesn't generally hire these firms unless there is a big job to be done.

These economics have led to a bipolar services industry structure. At the low end, there are more than 100,000 computer services firms worldwide. Most of these firms are quite small, often less than five people. In addition, there is a much smaller group of branded, increasingly global, large professional services firms that meet the needs of comparably sized customers. Interestingly, there are relatively few companies in between, especially at an individual country level. Various firms have tried to target or franchise efforts in this middle space, usually without success. US Web is the latest, trying to build a network of Internet services companies.

These sharply different economics make it difficult to effectively pursue all three businesses through any sort of integrated model. Should Compaq want to develop software only for its machines, it would miss out on the more than 80 percent of the potential market that doesn't use Compaq PCs. Microsoft would have the opposite problem should it try to move into the PC hardware business. Any effort by a services firm to take a strong product orientation faces the obvious problem of serving customers either having or desiring a different product environment.

In short, the natural economics of hardware, software, and services argue strongly for the long-term adoption of the horizontal model. Whereas with the airlines and telecommunications industries it was government intervention that provided the force necessary to break the entrenched vertically integrated structure, in the case of the IT industry it was IBM's PC outsourcing decisions.

Underlying Business Model Conflicts

These underlying economics are implicit in the business models of the major IT suppliers. In order to be successful, most companies must choose one path or the other. Companies wishing to compete as both, such as IBM and Digital, can try to create similar autonomy through both holding company and company-within-a-company strategies, but this can be difficult. Figure 2-3 provides a simplified view of these business model differences broken out by key product and customer issues.

Two real-world examples from IBM in the early 1990s can serve to clarify the appeal of the horizontal model. (IBM under Louis Gerstner has actually reversed some of these changes, a subject that will be

Figure 2-3. Key business model differences, technology manufacturers and providers.

	Product Issues	Customer Issues
Technology Manufacturers	**Build best products Sell to almost anyone**	**Focus on time-to-market Low end-user contact Inherently global**
Technology Providers	**Provide best products Buy from almost anyone**	**Focus on time-to-adoption High end-user contact Inherently local**

explored in chapter 4.) The first historical example looks at the issue of building versus buying the best products. Consider IBM's laptop computer business circa 1991.

For years, many IBM customers required significant numbers of laptop computers. In general, the IBM sales force would bid the IBM-manufactured product even though it was often not the most competitive laptop in the market. (Remember, this was before the highly successful IBM ThinkPad.) Not surprisingly, the customer often chose a Toshiba or the then popular Zenith portable machine. Thus, not only did IBM usually lose the laptop business but its overall relationship with the customer was diminished as well.

In the early 1990s, as IBM moved toward a more independent business unit approach, the IBM service division gained the freedom to choose the products it wanted to offer. If it didn't believe that the IBM-manufactured product was the best solution for a customer, it had the authority, at least theoretically, to offer whatever it believed best for its markets.

In other words, a true service company needs to provide the best products available. It is highly unlikely that all of these will come from a single supplier. Consequently, to remain competitive, the service company must be free to choose from the entire supplier marketplace. For a pure play services company such as EDS or Andersen, this is easy. For companies that also make computer hardware or software products, it can only be done if there is a sufficient degree of independence between the product and service operations.

A second example from that period, IBM's Power microprocessors, illustrated the need for a manufacturer to sell to almost anyone. IBM as a manufacturing organization had invested considerable resources in developing an advanced new Reduced Instruction Set Computer (RISC) computing platform. Since there are significant scale economies in microprocessor production, in order to maximize this investment IBM needed to try to reach as wide a market as possible.

Under the old vertically integrated IBM this was basically impossible. IBM technology was generally only available through the traditional IBM sales and marketing organization. This end user driven channel simply could not reach many potential component buyers. The solution was to give the Power PC division the freedom to form a joint venture with Motorola and sell the product to virtually anyone, most prominently to competitors such as Apple and Groupe Bull, something that never would have happened at the IBM of the 1960s and 1970s.

In addition to these make versus buy and market access decisions, there are three other important business model differences that tend to lead to separate product and service providers.

Time to market versus time to implement. Manufacturers are concerned with getting new products to market as quickly as possible. Service providers are much more concerned with the optimal path for long-term end user implementation; a good example would be the current competition between Netware, Windows NT, Unix, and OS/2. At various times each has probably been the best solution for many users, but this leadership position has clearly changed over time.

Levels of end user contact. Service providers generally organize themselves along customer lines. Witness the success of the industry-specific groups within EDS. In contrast, many manufacturing organizations have found that the product organization tends to remain predominant, often obstructing effective service delivery. Virtually all of the reorganizations within the systems companies over the 1985–1994 period were attempts to balance product and service division needs, an inevitably difficult process.

Local versus global products. The product side of the business is inherently easier to globalize, with many IT products now sold successfully all around the world. In contrast, there are very few, if any, true global service providers. Local languages, business practices, and customization have traditionally allowed local suppliers to remain strong. However, given the ever increasing importance of multinational corporations in so many economic sectors, true global service capabilities are a real market requirement. The race to build such capabilities is proving to be one of the most important and lucrative competitions of the 1990s.

In summary, it is important to understand that neither the product manufacturing nor the service provision business is inherently better than the other. The key point is that strategies that work for one will, as a rule, not be effective for the other. Companies that try to do both, such as IBM and Digital, face enormous management challenges. They must keep these organizations separate enough to pursue their own interests. As will be shown in chapter 4, it took the systems companies nearly a decade to figure out how to do this.

Computer Industry Implementation

Although this analysis suggests that some breakup of the old vertical industry model was perhaps inevitable, the computer industry version of this was more extreme than in any of the other industries discussed. The rapid pace of technology change, the relatively low barriers to entry, and especially in the United States an active venture capital market led quickly to a highly horizontal supplier structure (see figure 2-4).

Virtually every slice of the PC market—including keyboards, monitors, disk and diskette drives, CD-ROMs, DRAMs, microprocessors, graphic chips, communications boards, sound cards, most applications, and various delivery and service channels—is led by a different set of vendors. The level of supplier specialization has been truly extraordinary.

This highly horizontal structure could not exist without reliable and well-defined standards between each layer of the industry chain. Standards such as the PC AT-bus, SCSI disk drives, EGA and VGA monitors, the Windows Application Programming Interface, and many others were required to allow vendors to focus fully on their particular area of value added with the confidence that their product

Figure 2-4. IT industry structure, 1964–1994.

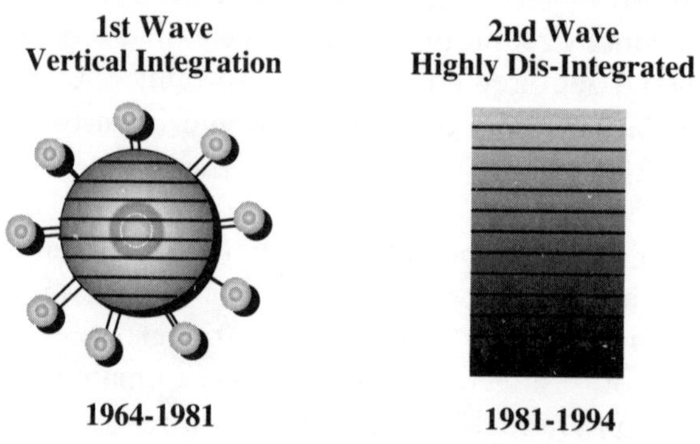

1st Wave Vertical Integration	2nd Wave Highly Dis-Integrated

1964-1981	**1981-1994**

would actually function once bundled into a full system offering. Indeed, for the horizontal system to work, a reliable standards process must be in place between each layer of the chain.

Although the path has not always been smooth, the establishment and evolution of these layered interfaces was one of the great accomplishments of the PC era. In fact, if during the 1980s there was any real meaning to the term "open systems," it lay in the industry's ability to generate a highly horizontal model that could still function even during periods of rapid product innovation. As we will see shortly, the leadership of IBM, Microsoft, and Intel was critical to this remarkably reliable performance. In areas without strong supplier leadership, the establishment of important new standards can prove difficult, as the PC and storage industry's current inability to evolve past the 1.4MB diskette format attests.

This standards-setting process became the new source of overall industry power. In areas where de jure, nonvendor-controlled standards existed, open, direct, and increasingly fierce competition became the norm. In areas, where de facto control existed, monopoly supplier patterns resulted. It was certainly not a historical accident that the two key de facto areas—microprocessors and operating systems—were the two outsourced by IBM.

The Inability to Adjust

The new horizontal industry structure first blossomed during the 1981–1986 period. By the late 1980s, its vendors had largely equaled the existing vertical order in size, and by the early 1990s, they had clearly surpassed it. The vertically integrated structure that had existed since the industry's inception was superseded in less than a decade. Such is the power of a true paradigm shift.

Why did the new order seem to have such an easy time replacing the existing one? Certainly, it was not a matter of either resources or expertise. The mainframe and minicomputer systems companies had far greater financial and technical resources. They also had research and development labs that were still far and away the industry's most advanced. Consider the following:

Digital with its DECNET offerings had a much stronger sense of all issues related to networking than Novell did. Unfortunately, Digital saw its networking software as primarily a means to sell more Digital computers. To use DECNET you needed to use Digital's VAX computer systems. Novell took a broader, more open approach to linking diverse, primarily PC-based systems. This was what the market wanted.

IBM largely invented relational database software, and its in-house database input systems research was the clear industry leader. However, IBM database software ran only on IBM computers, usually quite expensive ones. Companies such as Oracle, Ingres, Informix, and later on Sybase tried to make their software as hardware independent as possible, focusing especially on volume minicomputer platforms. This allowed them to sell their software on substantially cheaper, microprocessor-based systems, filling a large unmet market need.

Unisys had a strong field service organization and real industry-specific expertise, but their services were almost always packaged with the use of Unisys hardware and software that by the mid-1980s had fallen out of favor with many customers. Electronic Data Systems could claim rightfully that it was largely a product-independent company, greatly simplifying sales to many customers.

These are but some of the most obvious examples of a prevailing trend where proprietary vendors, often despite clearly superior technology, consistently lost share to more specialized, more open rivals that were more in touch with customer requirements.

Perhaps the most remarkable aspect of the period is how long it took the systems companies to realize that their old models were no longer working. These vendors spent a good part of the mid-1980s in various stages of denial. Although there was often some truth to their views, repeated statements that PCs were an immature technology, that proprietary systems were more robust and reliable, and that the horizontal approach was confusing, wasteful, and probably unsustainable clearly put the system vendors on the wrong side of history until it was nearly too late.

In their defense, the systems companies found themselves in a very awkward position. The changes demanded by the horizontal model threatened the very core of what they were. The process of repositioning, reorganizing, and rationalization took the better part of a decade to complete. The lack of clear identity, the inability to be best of breed in either products or services, and the resulting strategic dilemmas are shown in figure 2-5, which shows the mainframe and minicomputer companies as they existed as recently as 1992.

Some vendors, such as Sun and Hewlett-Packard (HP) increasingly saw themselves as primarily technology product manufacturers. Those without as strong a technology base, such as Unisys and Bull, increased their emphasis on services. IBM and Digital had such large presences in products and services that they understandably were determined to find a way to pursue both businesses. AT&T's Global Information Solutions (the former and now once again NCR) had a modest presence in both. While this painful and seemingly endless self-examination occurred, the PC business continued to surge mightily.

Missing the huge PC market opportunity was bad enough. But it was also clear from at least the middle of the 1980s that the horizontal model would inevitably spread beyond the desktop into traditional systems and server markets. The rapid rise of relational database management software companies and the increasing acceptance of Unix showed that a layered approach could succeed even in more complex IT environments, this despite frequent and vociferous statements to the contrary from many of the leading systems vendors.

Figure 2-5. Evolving supplier business models, 1992.

Technology Manufacturers	Technology Manufacturers & Providers	Technology Providers
Intel	◄——IBM ——►	EDS
Microsoft	◄— DEC—►	Andersen
Apple	AT&T/NCR	VADs
Novell		VARs
Borland	◄——HP—► Europeans	MIS
Start-ups	◄—Sun Wang	
Japanese/Asia	Unisys	
	Prime	

A New Set of Industry Leaders

While the system vendors underwent their individual identity crises, companies aligned with the ascendant horizontal model steadily took over the industry. Even in retrospect, the long list of new billion-dollar-plus, horizontally focused companies is staggering—Intel, Microsoft, Novell, Apple, Compaq, Dell, Seagate, Cisco, Oracle, EMC, EDS, Computer Associates, and so on. Taken together, they comprise one of business history's most rapid creations of new wealth.

Figure 2-6 shows the core segments of the IT industry value chain as of 1992. It also shows the market leader at that time as well as the primary competitors. The two most notable aspects of this are the absence of the traditional systems companies and the total dominance of U.S. vendors, most of whom were from the western part of the country, often from Silicon Valley itself.

(Technically, because its proprietary businesses were still so huge, IBM, in terms of revenues, was often still number one or two in virtually all of the categories, but in terms of industry leadership as measured by almost any definition besides revenues, IBM was no longer the market driver in any specific horizontal sector other than mainframes.)

The geographic aspects of this shift are not to be minimized. Within the United States, the vertically integrated companies had their roots in the eastern half of the country. IBM in New York; Digital, Wang, Prime, Data General, and most of the other minicomputer companies in Massachusetts; Unisys (via the former Sperry) outside

Figure 2-6. An industry led by specialists.

	Leader	Others
Services	EDS	Andersen, CSC
DBMS	Oracle	Informix, Sybase
Systems SW	Microsoft	Novell
Datacomm	Cisco	3Com, Bay Networks
PCs	Compaq	Apple, Dell
Printers	HP	Epson, Canon
Disks	Seagate	Quantum, Conner
Microprocessors	Intel	Motorola

of Philadelphia; and NCR in Dayton, Ohio. Only Hewlett-Packard, Tandem, and Amdahl represented California.

In contrast, while a few of the leading horizontal companies were on the East Coast, particularly in software and networking, the great majority were in the West—Intel, Microsoft, Novell, Seagate, Oracle, Compaq, Apple, Dell, EDS. By the end of the 1980s, the industry power structure had moved decisively from the Northeast to primarily the Northwest, with a second power center emerging in Texas.

It is almost certainly not an accident that the one systems supplier that actually benefited from this transition, Hewlett-Packard, is also located in Silicon Valley. With its valley culture and deep roots in the horizontally structured calculator and measurement equipment businesses, HP found the new industry order much easier to understand and internalize, although even it took a long time to become fully competitive in the PC hardware business. (Additional analysis of the HP business model is provided in chapter 4.)

Global Competitive Shift

The global competitive changes were even more significant. Within the United States, the principal vendor impact of the PC era's shift to a horizontal structure was a transfer of wealth and power from one set of older U.S. vendors to another group of newer U.S. companies. This enabled a truly radical supplier restructuring to occur without unmanageable public controversy or significant government intervention. Despite the huge financial losses at many of the major mainframe and minicomputer companies and even the bankruptcy of a few, there was never any serious talk of Chrysler-like system company bailouts.

However, from the perspective of London, Paris, Munich, or, most important, Tokyo, the changes were much more terrifying. From the IT industry's inception, U.S. vendors had been the clear global market leaders, but in their own domestic markets, European and Japanese vendors had been able to hold their own. Japanese vendors had even started to make significant progress in the then critical IBM-compatible mainframe hardware markets through their close cooperative efforts with U.S. entities such as Amdahl, partly owned by Fujitsu, and National Advanced Systems, now Hitachi Data Systems.

The shift toward a layered industry structure set these efforts back by at least a decade, perhaps longer. Without the venture capital and start-up culture of the United States, few if any significant new firms began in either Europe and Japan. Meanwhile, the existing major players, ICL, Bull, Siemens, Olivetti, Fujitsu, Hitachi, and NEC, faced all of the problems of the U.S. systems vendors but, at least in the case of the European entities, from an even weaker business base.

By the end of the 1980s, not only had the horizontal model triumphed over the vertical one but U.S. companies had so dominated the horizontal model that, overall, U.S. IT leadership became one of the rallying points of an overall improvement in U.S. economic competitiveness. This critical development, which went largely unnoticed by most of the political and media establishment for several years, will be examined in much more detail in the global PC-era competitive analysis provided by chapter 3.

Sources of Power Within a Horizontal Structure

As the horizontal model took hold, new ways of analyzing the industry were needed—many of these focused on what is now commonly called value chain analysis—the flow of economic activity from basic components through completed systems and related services.

There are several ways of looking at the IT industry value chain. Figure 2-7 provides the most common way, showing the horizontal structure in terms of the traditional measures of value added. (The

Figure 2-7. IT industry by value chain contribution, 1992.

- Vendor Support and Professional Services --   36%
- Distribution channels --   11%
- Packaged software --   16%
- Peripherals --   12%
- Processors --   14%
- Semiconductors --   11%
- Total   100%

Source: International Data Corporation.

simple economic definition of value-add is to take the total revenues of a company and then subtract the total amount paid by that company to all other companies. What's left is then the value added by any particular firm.)

According to that view, as the chart shows, IT industry value contribution is a fairly egalitarian proposition. When we look at the industry as a whole, we often forget that roughly one-third of the value added comes from specific services, either performed by an IT vendor or by users themselves with their own IT staff. The remaining two-thirds is divided remarkably evenly between software, peripherals, processors, and semiconductors, areas that get most of the media and financial market attention.

Although precise measurements of this type are difficult, the data are clearly indicative of the overall process of value creation within today's industry. Yet the data seem to contradict the prevailing sense both within and outside of the computer business that the combination of Intel and Microsoft, often referred to as the "Wintel" standard (named by combining the names of Intel and Windows), controls so much of the industry.

Part of the explanation lies in the fact that the Wintel influence is in fact limited to a relatively narrow but pervasive slice of the industry and therefore does tend to be in a public spotlight. But, more important, the fact is that not all layers of the value chain are created equally; some have considerably more leverage and profitability than others.

The degree of leverage within a given value chain is derived by one simple attribute: the relative ease or difficulty of producing a compatible, competitive product. In most hardware sectors—disk drives, printers, monitors, and so on—products adhere to sufficiently rigorous specifications as to be largely interchangeable; therefore, fierce competition usually results. Services firms also compete head-on, with relatively low supplier switching costs over time.

For reasons that will be explored more deeply later, despite many attempts over many years there has never been a successful cloning of a computer operating system. This accounts for much of Microsoft's and Novell's success. The history of compatible processor manufacturing cloning is slightly more positive but still full of many more failures than successes, thus accounting for Intel's dominant position.

Virtual Vertical Integration

From a business history perspective, the IT industry in the 1980s will be remembered for many things; the extraordinary growth of the PC business, the rise of the horizontal model, and the transition to a new generation of vendor leaders will certainly be high among them.

But future students of supplier competition might well be equally fascinated by the period's unique competitive dynamic—the mutually self-reinforcing monopolies among three different vendors, Intel, Microsoft, and Novell. The relationship between these vendors up until early in 1994 is shown in figure 2-8.

For more than a decade, each vendor had a monopoly or in the case of Novell a near monopoly in its targeted segment. Microsoft had nearly 90 percent of the PC operating systems market. Intel had nearly 90 percent of the PC microprocessor market, and Novell had roughly two-thirds of the PC LAN operating system (OS) software market.

Having three critical industry sectors so dominated by three vendors was odd enough, but perhaps even stranger was that because each occupied essentially neighboring layers on the IT value chain, during this period what was good for one was almost inevitably good for the other. Faster Intel chips could run more powerful applications that often required networking, which then needed faster chips, and so on and on.

Figure 2-8. Mutually reinforcing monopolies—Microsoft, Intel, Novell.

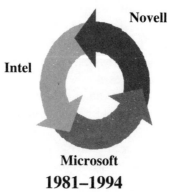

1981–1994

It was indeed a rare and powerful virtuous circle, and since each was a monopoly, each could extract very high profits. In the end, their core interests were in such alignment that in terms of actual behavior the three may have well have been one company. In this sense, they could be seen as virtually vertically integrated, comprising in many ways the accumulated legacy passed on from IBM.

(For simplicity's sake, this analysis deliberately leaves out Microsoft's repeated but largely unsuccessful 1980s efforts to move into the LAN OS business as well as Novell's quixotic dabbling in the DOS-compatible operating systems market and, more recently, its disastrous forays into the word processing and spreadsheet businesses.)

More specifically, the Intel 86 architecture, the Microsoft DOS/Windows operating system, and Novell's Netware became the modern equivalent of IBM's 370 processor family, the MVS operating system, and the Systems Network Architecture (SNA) networking software. In both examples, the vendor who controlled the de facto standards enjoyed a monopoly-like position. Almost everyone else competed at a lower level.

In this sense, from an industry power perspective, not much had really changed other than the names of the companies making all the money. Remarkably, despite all that the PC revolution accomplished, a monopoly legacy established by Tom Watson, Sr., and now some sixty years old was in many ways still the guiding force in the industry. As Microsoft and Intel moved up into more complex systems realms, it would soon become more so.

Additional Sources of Microsoft's Power

IBM is not the only vendor whose decisions have unwittingly contributed to Microsoft's power. At times it has seemed that the whole industry has been deliberately trying to help things go Microsoft's way. Consider the following three examples:

Apple's decision not to license its Macintosh operating system gave Microsoft years to develop a comparable graphical user interface. By the time Apple realized the value of its software assets, it was largely too late to make a difference. If it had acted earlier, the PC market might well have been much more evenly split.

The potential merger of Lotus and Novell in the early 1990s would have been a powerful competitor to Microsoft in the enterprise. The merger collapsed largely because of the egos of Lotus's Jim Manzi and Novell's Ray Noorda, who couldn't agree on who would run the combined company. Novell went on to lose its focus on its core networking business and make an extremely unwise acquisition of Word-Perfect. Lotus was eventually acquired by IBM.

A decade of countless failed attempts to build a standard version of Unix has given Microsoft years to build and position Windows NT as the server operating system standard. Just five years ago, Microsoft control over the enterprise server environment was viewed by many as laughable. Now the only question is how powerful its position will be. The Unix vendor community has largely given up on complete standardization.

As the overwhelming provider of Microsoft-compatible processing power, these events, which have so greatly benefited Microsoft, have directly helped Intel as well.

This is in no way meant to imply that Microsoft, Intel, and Novell have not done many smart things on their own. Microsoft has managed to extend its operating system position into applications, languages, tools, and other areas; owning the operating system guaranteed none of this. Novell carved out its LAN dominance without any help from IBM or anyone else. Intel has refused to rest on its laurels. The company continues to invest heavily in both development and manufacturing capacity, keeping chip costs low and making life extremely difficult for both potential Intel-compatible vendors and alternative microprocessor architectures.

In short, IBM gave Microsoft and Intel a great initial opportunity, and both have taken maximum advantage of it. Novell created its own opportunity but during the early 1990s squandered much of its power by not recognizing its true interests and trying to challenge Microsoft's key desktop positions. Under new management, the company is trying to go back to its networking software roots, having divested itself of its Unix and applications businesses at steeply discounted prices.

Commodity Markets for Almost Everyone Else

While these three companies enjoyed IBM-like power, the rest of the PC industry was becoming increasingly commoditized. There was no better example of this than the PC hardware industry.

Figure 2-9 provides a simplified view of the PC hardware value chain as it existed around 1990. There are two key points: (1) Other than the microprocessor, virtually all of the hardware in a PC was a commodity product, and (2) nearly all of these components were provided by vendors other than the PC hardware vendor itself. In other words, the PC hardware vendor was responsible for only a small share of the value added in the actual PC. Even this portion generally comprised soft features such as the shape, packaging, feature mix, service policies, and, of course, the price.

Future business students will also study the PC hardware business as another unusual situation, one where the major IBM PC-compatible suppliers—Compaq, Dell, Packard Bell, and so on—were totally dependent on the overall PC supplier chain. IBM and Apple are modest exceptions. IBM does make a number of its key components, especially for its laptop products, while Apple, of course, controls its own hardware and systems software designs, but even IBM and Apple are very far from the old vertically integrated model.

It is true that many other industries rely heavily on extended supplier chains; automobile companies have come to outsource most of

Figure 2-9. Decomposing the PC industry value chain.

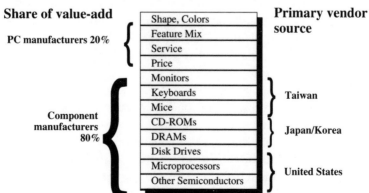

their transmission, steering, braking, cooling, exhaust, and electrical systems, and even engines may well eventually go this way. However, in other industries the development of fully capable supplier chains has often taken decades to emerge. In the computer industry, it exploded in just the few years between 1981 and 1984.

The inevitable result, of course, was that this new industry structure made it virtually impossible for PC suppliers to differentiate their products, since everyone was basically using the same component sources. Product competition shifted toward one of channel management, time-to-market, the service, price, and feature mix, and most important, product and company branding. Compaq Computer has emerged as the current master of this particular type of competition. As will be shown in subsequent sections, the network-centric era will likely redefine the role of the consumer device manufacturer, necessitating significant and difficult changes in today's PC hardware business model.

From a broader perspective, as the physical differences between products diminished, the importance of psychological competition rose dramatically. Advertising, image, and reputation became critical components of PC hardware competition. Once the domain of engineers, the PC business became increasingly managed by marketing people, particularly those adept at building positive brand image and awareness. All of this was the direct result of this extreme implementation of the horizontal model and the concentration of power in the hands of Intel and Microsoft.

As will be discussed in chapter 3, globalization was another important legacy of the PC hardware industry structure. Since, other than microprocessors, virtually all components were essentially commodities, they could easily be sourced from anywhere in the world. This allowed for significant global specialization. U.S. firms dominated the microprocessor, disk drive, printer (thanks to HP), custom semiconductor, software, networking, and system assembly sectors. Japanese firms were strong in DRAMs, CD-ROMs, floppy disks, and displays, while Taiwanese firms had a strong presence in motherboards, keyboards, mice, and low-cost PC clones.

This specialization was greatly accelerated by the movement to the horizontal model. In the earlier, vertically integrated days, IBM and Digital made most of these products themselves. Often they would use offshore manufacturing facilities, if only for the tax and political benefits of contributing to their local markets. However, in terms of speed and effectiveness, a vendor-owned, offshore site can rarely match a dedicated company trying to serve the broader global market. More than any country other than the United States, it was Taiwan that benefited by the particular way that the PC industry evolved.

Summary of the Second Wave

We have seen how the arrival of the microprocessor and IBM's decisions to outsource critical PC components set in motion a total restructuring of the worldwide IT industry. A horizontal model characterized by specialized companies focusing on each and every part of the industry value chain made obsolete most of the existing vertical industry structure within a decade.

But as powerful as the paradigm shift was, links to the past were not severed. The monopoly power that IBM had enjoyed since the 1930s was largely passed on to Intel and Microsoft, and less directly to Novell, where it lived on throughout the 1980s and beyond. These three companies became the privileged beneficiaries of the PC revolution.

The rest of the PC industry had to learn to cope with fiercely competitive commodity markets. Time-to-market, quality, price, and increasing brand awareness became critical success factors as the industry became characterized by ever faster product cycles and ever more severe pricing pressure. The resulting supplier turmoil proved a challenge to all, with few vendors consistently profitable through the period and many dropping by the wayside. However, the result of this heightened competition was a rate of innovation and improved price/performance sufficient to drive a decade's worth of strong growth, transforming the personal computer business into a giant global industry.

By the mid-1980s, it had become clear that the horizontal model would spread into higher priced products and services as well. The great success of the relational database companies, especially Oracle, and the improved prospects for professional services firms such as Electronic Data Systems and Andersen Consulting assured that the horizontal structure could handle even the industry's most demanding requirements. Although proprietary mainframe solutions still domi-nate the high end of the enterprise systems market, outsourcing ser-vices had broken the traditional hardware vendor control of even this lucrative and strategic segment.

By and large, it was new vendors who understood and exploited this business model in a way that existing vendors either would not or could not. The result was not just a reshuffling of the U.S. supplier structure but a global shift where U.S. companies gained powerful po-sitions in most key IT industry sectors, forcing Japanese and other Asian vendors to focus on certain commodity markets while margin-alizing most of the European IT players. As chapter 3 makes clear, it was the horizontal model's simultaneous ability to bring out the strengths of U.S. companies while diminishing those of its major rivals that led to the dramatic competitive changes of the PC era.

GLOBAL COMPETITION IN THE PC ERA: WHAT HAPPENED TO JAPAN?

From a competitive perspective, perhaps the biggest surprise of the PC industry was the almost total failure of Japanese firms to gain a presence in the worldwide desktop computer marketplace. Despite the great opportunities of the PC era, for most of the period, Japanese vendors had little success outside of commodity markets such as CD-ROMs, displays, floppy disks, and DRAMs. This chapter explains why Japan consistently lost its share to U.S. rivals while introducing a frame of analysis for evaluating global competition in the network-centric era. In the final sections, the current positions of Taiwan, Korea, the major nations of Western Europe, and other emerging countries are also reviewed.

One of the less recognized impacts of the PC-centric era was the creation of a much more homogenous, global IT industry. Intel microprocessors, Seagate disk drives, HP printers, Microsoft operating system and application software, Novell LAN software, and many other hardware and software products eventually became successful in virtually all major world markets. Only the PC hardware market itself showed high levels of national variation, due to the largely commodity and assembly nature of that business.

In contrast, in the earlier mainframe and minicomputer systems era, the computer industry exhibited strong national differences. Although U.S. firms, especially IBM, competed successfully in most world markets, in each individual major country market the local competition was strong, for example, ICL in the United Kingdom, Bull in France, Siemens in Germany, Olivetti in Italy, and Fujitsu, Hitachi, and NEC in Japan.

During the 1980s, it was the combination of this increasingly homogenous global technology market and U.S. leadership within most major PC technology sectors that led to the dominant U.S. position that exists today. Given the steadily rising importance of information technology in the overall world economy, this leadership has been a source of celebration in the United States but a significant source of frustration and concern elsewhere.

Looking back, it's worth remembering that this competitive outcome was not generally forecasted and indeed was not even widely recognized for some time. During the second half of the 1980s, the conventional IT industry wisdom in the United States and around the world was that Japan and emerging powerhouses such as Korea and Taiwan would soon dominate the global computer market, at least on the hardware side. Observers at that time witnessed the following, seemingly inevitable, trends:

The personal computer was turning computer hardware into a consumer electronics commodity. Japanese companies were long dominant in this area.

Semiconductor memory was believed to be the core chip design and manufacturing competency. Japanese dominance of the DRAM market was widely seen as a precursor to dominance of the broader semiconductor industry.

The Japanese domestic IT market and the overall Japanese economy continued to surge. In contrast, both the U.S. economy and U.S. IT market of the late 1980s were sluggish. Doomsayers rashly extrapolated that the Japanese IT market would soon equal that of the United States despite a population just 50 percent as large.

The strong Japanese yen and soaring Japanese stock and real estate values enabled an aggressive investment and acquisition strategy. Japanese firms began to invest heavily in both new and troubled U.S. technology companies, triggering fears of an imminent industry takeover.

The deepening problems at IBM and the breakup of AT&T were steadily reducing these two giants' R&D capability. Horizontally focused U.S. suppliers appeared to be too small to fill the void. Meanwhile, Japanese technology R&D spending was soaring.

Giant diversified Japanese technology companies could use cross-subsidization and predatory pricing as well as formal and informal trade barriers to crush smaller U.S. rivals in a sector-by-sector strategy.

Although much of this pessimism had been grossly overstated for several years, these industry attitudes persisted until roughly 1992 when the Japanese bubble economy finally burst and the signs that IT competitiveness had decisively shifted toward the United States had become obvious to all. Perhaps the most symbolic moment was Intel's 1992 emergence as the world's largest semiconductor company. But even more telling, by the early 1990s a wide variety of U.S. IT companies were eagerly developing ambitious plans for the Japanese domestic market, once considered to be an impregnable fortress.

Media recognition took even longer to set in. As late as the 1992 U.S. presidential campaign a common phrase used by former Massachusetts senator Paul Tsongas, considered to be a knowledgeable realist regarding economic and technology matters, was: "The cold war is over: Germany and Japan have won." Even today, the extent of the turnaround is not always fully appreciated. Although stories about the rise of Japan were commonplace in the late 1980s, analyses of the stunning U.S. competitive victories are still relatively rare.

To help assess how long the current U.S. good fortune will last, it is important to understand exactly why these dramatic changes have occurred and what sort of forces have been set in motion. Much has been written about the speed and effectiveness of highly focused U.S. PC hardware, semiconductor, software, peripheral, and networking companies and the powerful synergy that now exists between these companies' U.S. design operations. What has received far less industry and media attention is the role played by the strategies and structures within the Japanese IT industry itself.

In the following section, we will examine the issue of global IT competitiveness from a Japanese market perspective. The discussion will show that many of the Japanese vendor problems stemmed from unusual rigidities within the Japanese domestic market itself. Understanding the likely evolution of market forces within Japan provides the key to developing a realistic assessment of the prospects for the wounded, but still formidable, Japanese suppliers, particularly as the network-centric era emerges.

An Academic Perspective on Global Competition

In his influential 1990 book *The Competitive Advantage of Nations,* Harvard Business School professor Michael Porter undertakes a systematic effort to understand why some countries are competitive in some industries but not in others.* Not surprisingly, his work shows that a country's global competitive strengths and weaknesses inevitably stem from particular and identifiable country attributes. Defining and gauging the relative importance of these attributes accounts for much of this book's work.

In an important conceptual breakthrough, Porter developed an analytical model that identifies a set of mutually reinforcing traits that characterize global leaders across a wide variety of industries. (Computers were not one of his main areas of focus.) As shown in figure 3-1, this model is generally referred to as "the diamond." In this chapter, we will borrow Porter's general industry model and terminology

---

* Michael Porter, *The Competitive Advantage of Nations* (New York: Free Press, 1990), p. 72.

Figure 3-1. Application of Porter competitive model to global PC competition, 1992.

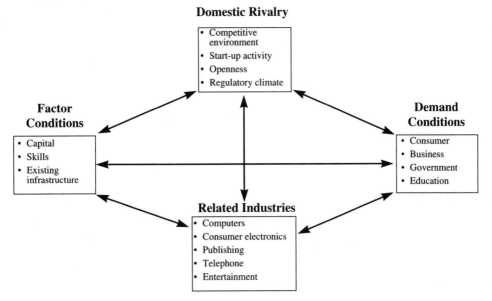

and apply it to the specific issues of global IT competition in first the PC and then the network-centric era.

Porter focuses on four main competitive issues, which are listed in order of increasing importance and briefly defined below:

1. *Factor conditions.* Basic factors of production: skilled labor, available capital, relevant services, and so on. This is a necessary but insufficient condition for success in any industry

2. *Related and supporting industries.* The presence of an internationally competitive supplier structure in key related industries is often a precursor to success. In other words, success does not often spring out of nowhere. Rather, competencies that drive a new industry usually have their roots in an existing area. Strengths in these industries are important but, again, not decisive competitive factors.

3. *Demand conditions.* The sophistication of the domestic market demand for the industry's product or service. In other words, countries with the most demanding customers often produce the most able vendors. For example, the fact that Germany has a number of large

cities a few hundred miles apart and has no Autobahn speed limits
has created an environment where high performance car makers can
thrive. This domestic demand sophistication is highly correlated with
global competitive success.

   4. *Firm strategy, structure, and rivalry.* The manner in which companies are created, organized, and managed and the intensity of the
domestic rivalry. In other words, strong competition at home leads
to strong, highly competitive vendors. Nationally protected industry
champions virtually never become global leaders. According to Porter's research across a large number of industries, this intense domestic
competition is the single most important success factor.

   Applying this scheme to the domestic Japanese IT situation, we
see that at least for the major hardware markets Japanese vendors
have always been well-positioned in areas 1 and 2. Clearly, they have
strong engineering and manufacturing skills as well as ample capital
resources and a leadership position in key related industries such as
consumer electronics, power supplies, magnetic media, and robotics.
Indeed, it was their strengths in items 1 and 2 that led many observers
to expect Japanese suppliers to thrive in the PC era. However, Porter's
work warns against putting too much weight on these factors.

   According to Porter, it is items 3 and 4 that are likely to be decisive, and in both of these areas significant problems existed for Japanese suppliers throughout most of the PC era. Issues relating to the
less than state-of-the-art Japanese local demand conditions can be
quantitatively demonstrated. The lack of sufficient domestic rivalry
requires a more complex analysis. Combined, these two factors left
Japanese suppliers ill prepared for global PC era competition in the
first half of the 1990s.

A Five-Year Gap in Domestic Demand

Figures 3-2 and 3-3 highlight some of the major differences between
the U.S. and Japanese domestic markets as they existed in 1992. The
four-year-old data are deliberately chosen to make the historical
point. Some, although certainly not all, of the usage gap between the
United States and Japan has closed in recent years and should continue to do so.

Figure 3-2. 1992 Composition of U.S. and Japan domestic IT markets.

	Percent of U.S. Market	Percent Japanese Market
Mainframes and minis	18%	29%
PCs/workstations	24%	19%
Datacomm equipment	5%	2%
Support and professional services	34%	40%
Packaged software	19%	10%
Total	100%	100%

Source: International Data Corporation.

Figure 3-3. 1992 Enterprise computing customer strategies—United States and Japan.

	U.S.	Japan
Percent pursuing client/server	43%	26%
Percent pursuing open systems	51%	24%
Percent pursuing Unix strategy	34%	17%
Percent of PCs on LANs	37%	23%
Percent of PCs running Windows	39%	5%

Source: International Data Corporation.

Figure 3-2 uses IDC data to look at overall 1992 market composition. The chart clearly shows that, compared to the United States, the Japanese domestic market was much more reliant on minis, mainframes, and custom software. Conversely, there was considerably less emphasis on the major worldwide growth areas of PCs, networking, and packaged software. In fact, the composition of the Japanese market in 1992 looked roughly like that of the U.S. market in 1987, suggesting roughly a five-year market development gap.

Figure 3-3 draws on IDC's 1992 customer survey data. This chart also shows a pattern of bias toward older technologies and modes of computing. Specifically, in 1992 Japanese IT customers were much less interested in client/server architectures, open systems, Unix, downsizing, LANs, and Microsoft Windows. Thus, Japanese vendors did not have to face these issues to anywhere near the same extent as their U.S. rivals.

Why did these gaps emerge? In addition to the competitive reasons described in the following sections, the sophistication of Japanese domestic demand has also been diminished by cultural factors, including *keiretsu*-based customer relations, an educational bias toward hardware, conservative business practices, and the Japanese language itself.

The *keiretsu* system, in which groups of large companies have interlocking financial interests and tend to support each other's products, is often viewed (correctly) as a strength in terms of keeping out U.S. rivals. But often not mentioned is the fact that this same system also tends to limit the intensity of competition between the Japanese vendors themselves. Individual technology companies often have a preferred position within particular *keiretsu* groupings, allowing a high degree of informal customer lock-in.

From a customer perspective, Japan's hierarchical, seniority-driven business culture, lack of packaged software, and the fundamental challenges of computing in *kanji,* the Japanese character-based language, have greatly restricted the overall extent of PC computing. Of these, the language issues are perhaps the most significant.

The difficulty in using a Japanese keyboard is one of the main reasons that many executives don't use PCs. Even today, the need for specialized word processing skills often gives PC computing a strong secretarial connotation. In contrast, in the United States and elsewhere, word processing was the single strongest driver of the early PC business, rivaled only by spreadsheets. It wasn't until the early 1990s when computers became powerful enough to more easily handle *kanji* images that Japanese language PC-based word processing began to be viewed as a mass market, consumer activity, more than a decade later than in the West.

Insufficient Domestic Rivalry

In 1992, the statement that the lack of sufficient domestic rivalry was a problem for Japanese vendors may have come as a surprise to many, including the major Japanese vendors themselves. After all, companies such as Fujitsu, Hitachi, NEC, Toshiba, Oki, and others see themselves as fierce rivals, constantly jockeying for market advantage. Additionally, the intense Japanese domestic competition that led to worldwide leadership in automobiles, consumer electronics, and DRAMs are textbook examples of Porter's diamond at work.

But it is important to keep in mind that the issue is not the extent of perceived rivalry but rather whether the competition in Japan was as intense as it was in competitive countries (i.e., the United States), and here the answer has been a clear no.

Personal computers are the most important example. For years, many participants and observers noting the apparent similarities to the consumer electronics business expected the Japanese to be major players in the worldwide PC business. Obviously, this has not happened, and the lack of sufficient domestic PC competition has been a primary but often unrecognized reason. In general, the industry has greatly underestimated the impact of the decade-long lack of a true DOS standard in Japan, which led to a structurally less efficient and competitive Japanese PC industry.

For those unfamiliar with this issue, the history of the Japanese PC market has been much like the first few years of the U.S. market. Each PC vendor produced its own version of Microsoft's DOS operating system that was incompatible with all the other vendors'. However, while this approach had largely vanished from the U.S. market by 1984, only after 1993 with the movement to a common DOS/V and Windows format did a true Japanese PC standard begin to emerge.

The lack of a single PC standard resulted in the following domestic market conditions:

Higher prices. Since there was little direct competition and significant customer lock-in, Japanese domestic market PC prices were far higher than world levels.

Less innovation. With each vendor creating its own machine, the pace of innovation was slowed due to a not-invented-here supplier attitude, which preferred in-house technologies whenever possible. Technology improvements were also slowed by a general lack of compatibility with new software, peripherals, and semiconductors designed around the worldwide "Wintel" standard.

Weak application base. The need to develop different versions of basic spreadsheet and word processing programs for each type of PC retarded the development and availability of many types of PC software.

More difficult migration. The multitude of incompatible PC architectures greatly complicated the movement toward advanced platforms such as local and wide area networks, slowing the movement away from mainframe-based enterprise systems.

Single-vendor control. Up until 1994, NEC had roughly 50 percent of the market, setting the pace of technology change, providing a price umbrella, and making substantial profits.

In short, the historical structure of the Japanese PC industry resembled nothing so much as the U.S. minicomputer or workstation industries, with multiple incompatible architectures providing vendors with a significant amount of customer control and hence price stability. (As noted earlier, industry historians will debate for a long time whether the U.S. PC industry would have a similar structure had not IBM decided to open its PC architecture. IBM, no doubt, wonders the same.)

The midrange Japanese computer business shows a similar pattern, with the proprietary systems of Japanese vendors holding a tight grip on the vast majority of sales. As with PCs, the *keiretsu* culture and Japanese language issues also account for much of this global difference, but an even bigger reason, and another aspect of the missing rivalry issue, is the overall lack of start-ups or other new entrants.

Consider where the U.S. Unix market would be today were it not for one-time start-ups such as Sun, Pyramid, Convex, Silicon Graphics, and Sequent, let alone long-vanished early pioneers such as Altos, Plexus, Onyx, Synapse, Auragen, and others. Successful or not, the spur of these new companies was necessary to break the hold of the established proprietary vendors and to usher in the Unix systems business of today. However, no such start-up push has ever existed in Japan, and thus the Japanese Unix market of the 1980s was largely restricted to the workstation business, giving major Japanese vendors little direct experience in building, selling, and supporting commercial Unix-based systems.

In sum, the domestic market allowed Japanese vendors to enjoy relatively mild competition in many key hardware markets. This protected home environment coupled with the lack of start-up activity made it easy for them not to make the competitive changes necessary to take advantage of emerging worldwide opportunities. Over the 1988–1992 period, Japanese vendor exports failed to expand beyond established mainframe, DRAM, display, and commodity component areas.

Then beginning in 1992–1993, worldwide market forces began to come to the Japanese domestic market itself, putting the major Japanese suppliers on the defensive for the first time since the IBM/Fujitsu/Hitachi mainframe software lawsuits of the early 1980s. Compaq's aggressive push into the Japanese PC market was perhaps the most symbolic event, but many leading U.S. horizontal suppliers began to sense new opportunity in what is easily the world's second largest IT market. This new U.S. aggression formalized the changed competitive reality. However, it also became an important wake-up call that finally has started the major Japanese vendors along the long path to recovery.

Outlook for Japanese Vendors

As the PC era begins to wind down, the key question is to what extent the Japanese vendors can recover in existing businesses and position themselves for future ones. If competitiveness can be restored at home, Japanese vendor global prospects will improve.

A common industry joke from 1993 expressed much of the prevailing sentiment: From its earliest beginnings, Japanese vendors had admired, even revered, IBM, and often it seemed that the entire strategy of, in particular, Fujitsu and Hitachi was to be just like IBM. As these companies' pain, losses, and self-doubt began to mount, it seemed that, unfortunately for them, they had finally succeeded. Another variant had Japanese suppliers so intent on following IBM that they didn't realize that they were heading over a cliff.

As with many industry jokes, there is both truth and exaggeration in this. Although the 1993–1995 financial performance of the major Japanese vendors was shaky, it was not nearly as wrenching or as life threatening as that of an IBM or Digital. Unlike the U.S. systems companies, the existing Japanese worldwide business model was fundamentally sound. Japanese vendors' problems were due to the effects of their local environment and some significant strategic mistakes, not the business model itself.

This last statement is very important and requires further explanation. Although the major Japanese vendors are often correctly described as vertically integrated, it has always been a very different kind of vertical integration than that used by U.S. and European systems vendors. Japanese vendors have always used a mix of integrated and autonomous business unit structures. Therefore, unlike IBM and Digital no major cultural and business model overhaul was required. (See chapter 4 on system vendor recovery.)

More specifically, unlike IBM and Digital, the semiconductor, disk drive, and other groups in Japanese companies were never set up to serve primarily captive purposes. Consequently, these companies have always understood and participated in global, dis-integrated, horizontal markets. Their long-term emphasis on component OEM hardware markets stands in sharp contrast to both IBM's and Digital's relatively recent acknowledgment of this opportunity.

In short, the Japanese vendors' challenge over the 1993–1995 period was to restore the vitality of their current business model rather than strive to find a new one. Even without the emerging opportunities of the network-centric era, the Japanese have already begun to restore key parts of Porter's diamond. Among some of the notable trends:

A true PC standard has become dominant and is supported by virtually all DOS-based vendors, including market leader NEC.

Unix and LAN usage has begun to resemble worldwide trends.

Japanese prices are now comparable to world prices for PC and related products.

PC market growth has taken off.

As the Japanese market comes to more closely resemble that of the United States or Western Europe, it becomes much easier for Japanese vendors' core competence in low-cost manufacturing, R&D, miniaturization, quality, and consumer brand recognition to be productively engaged and for Japanese vendors to once again become formidable global players at many levels of the value chain. Just three years after Compaq's wake-up call, newly competitive Japanese PC firms such as Toshiba, Sony, and NEC are gearing up for another run at the U.S. PC market.

Clearly, this renewed competitiveness will be largely limited to hardware sectors because the Japanese position in worldwide software and services markets is likely to remain quite weak for the foreseeable future. Consequently, U.S. vendor hardware opportunities in Japan are not nearly as attractive as those in software. Although there will certainly be U.S. hardware successes, overall Japanese PC technology competition will strengthen significantly in the second half of this decade.

Equally important, this expected recovery can be achieved without new Japanese start-ups and without major structural changes. Whereas restructuring was clearly the watchword for IBM and Digital, for the Japanese the issue was more one of retrenchment, reawakening, retooling, and recovery. Japanese companies' ability to adjust and bounce back should never be underestimated.

Global Hardware Specialization

Although the main hardware competition has been and will continue to be between U.S. and Japanese companies, both Taiwan and Korea continue to play increasingly significant roles. In addition, Western Europe is still a major source of information technology production, although the major European hardware firms have clearly lost much of their vitality. In this section, we will examine the current global positioning of the United States, Western Europe, and Southeast Asia for existing PC-centric markets. In chapters 9 through 12 we will examine how these regions' prospects will change during the network-centric era.

As the PC industry evolved into a truly global one, country specialization increased. Within the hardware sector, competition revolved around two main dimensions—strength in technology and overall time-to-market. Figure 3-4 depicts a number of key current hardware sectors along these two dimensions.

As is clearly shown, hardware products tend to move to the four corners of the diagram. Within the high technology sectors, micropro-

Figure 3-4. Competitive attributes, key hardware markets.

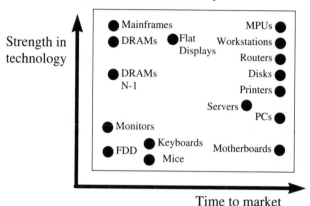

cessors, mainframes, and DRAMs all require large investments in advanced technologies. However, the microprocessor market moves quite quickly, whereas mainframes and DRAMs have long and relatively predictable product cycles.

At the low end of the technology spectrum, rapid delivery of the latest motherboards, graphics cards, and sound boards has become critical to PC vendor efforts to get to market quickly. In contrast, products such as monitors, keyboards, mice, and floppy diskette drives evolve relatively slowly.

Over the last five years or so, these different product attributes have mapped well into particular country competencies, as shown in figure 3-5. Previous sections of this book have covered the dominance of U.S. vendors in fast-moving, high technology sectors as well as Japanese strengths in the slower moving but still high technology markets such as mainframes, high-end disk drives, flat panel displays, DRAMs, and so on.

As one moves down the technology curve, it becomes clear that Korean and Taiwanese firms have each carved out significant and generally different positions. Taiwanese firms have become fully integrated in the global IT production value chain and have dominated many low-cost PC commodities such as keyboards, mice, and motherboards. (However, in the 1995–1996 period, Intel became much more aggressive in the motherboard industry, creating tremendous problems for Taiwanese suppliers.)

Figure 3-5. Country positioning, computer hardware markets.

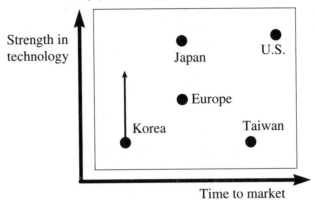

In contrast, Korean firms got off to a slow start during the 1980s, choosing to challenge both U.S. and Taiwanese companies head on, often without success beyond very low end floppy disk and monitor markets. However, during the early 1990s, Korean firms have re-emerged with a powerful overall strategy. Rather than take on the United States and Taiwan, they have instead set their sights on Japan, pursuing a strategy of targeting high technology commodity products.

Over the last two years, Korea has emerged as an important rival to Japan, grabbing a large share of the worldwide DRAM market and becoming increasingly active in flat panel displays. The large, diversified nature of Korean companies such as Samsung, Hyundai, LG Electronics (formerly Lucky Goldstar), and Daewoo makes them well suited to such long-term, capital-intensive markets.

Obviously, many other Asian nations also play important roles by providing subcontracted manufacturing services to mostly U.S. and Japanese multinationals. Singapore has become the world's center for disk drive production; it also produces high volumes of printers, computer subassemblies, and increasingly semiconductors. Malaysia, China, Thailand, and Indonesia play similar offshore manufacturing roles. Whereas in the 1980s and early 1990s, it was mostly U.S. companies that exploited these low-cost manufacturing opportunities, today the Japanese, Koreans, and Taiwanese are also moving much of their manufacturing out of their home country markets.

However, in terms of generating their own competitive companies, only Singapore has made any real impact, with Creative Technologies becoming a major player in sound and video card markets. Additionally, Singapore has emerged as an important regional management center for most U.S. IT firms, largely replacing Hong Kong in this role. The list of U.S. firms with Asian headquarters in Singapore includes Hewlett-Packard, Compaq, Intel, Digital, and Seagate along with many others.

When all of the national efforts described above are combined, they result in an interrelated set of global strategies and positioning that has served both the market and U.S. interests well. Taiwanese firms have provided critical low-cost components that have helped keep prices low. More important from a strategic perspective, the success of Korean firms in the DRAM market has assured fierce competition in a sector where Japan once enjoyed a near monopoly. Korean and possibly new U.S. efforts will challenge Japan's dominance of the flat panel display market as well. CD-ROMs are another Japanese stronghold that is being targeted.

From the Japanese perspective, the challenge from Korea has become a major concern. Unless Japanese hardware vendors can be more successful in the upper right-hand corner of the market, they will increasingly be squeezed by Korea's rising competencies in the upper left.

Taiwanese vendors are also facing pressure on the lower right-hand side of the market from countries such as Singapore, Malaysia, Thailand, Indonesia, and most important China. They also feel the pressure to move up the technology curve as quickly as possible. Whether they should do this on the left side à la Korea or on the right as the United States does is a critical strategic question.

Currently, both approaches are being tested. As the motherboard market shrinks, Taiwanese diversification efforts include laptops, scanners, Macintosh clones, DRAMs, and semiconductor fabrication as well as a variety of custom design, manufacturing, and distribution services. However, most Taiwanese companies remain quite small, with really only Acer being successful in establishing a global brand name. For most other Taiwanese firms, close cooperation with U.S. and Japanese market leaders will still be required; similarly, a direct confrontation with the major Korean conglomerates is quite risky.

What about Europe? Although Western Europe accounts for nearly one-third of global IT market consumption, in terms of global supplier leadership, they have only a minor position. Returning to figure 3-5, it is clear that Europe continues to be generally stuck in the middle. It has significant but not fully competitive capabilities in virtually all technology areas. In an age of international supplier specialization, this is not a good place to be. Although some of the major European firms are learning to cope with these realities, global success in PC-centric markets has almost certainly passed them by.

Elsewhere around the world there are a number of other nations that are important hardware production centers, especially in Latin America, but only one other country has shown the ability to generate world-class hardware vendors. That country is Israel.

However, since many Israeli companies are still quite small and are mostly focusing on networking technologies, their main contribution to the industry will come over the next decade and will be covered in chapter 10 on national competition in the network-centric era.

From a U.S. PC industry perspective, these global developments could hardly have been more favorable. Thanks to the Taiwanese and the Koreans, the United States has been free to enjoy its leadership positions in microprocessors, other specialty chips, networking, PC disk drives, the desktop and laptop machines themselves, and, as always, virtually all manner of software without significant risk of commodity supply interruption. One of the key questions of the second half of this book is, How long can such good fortune last?

Global Software and Services Market Competition

Within both software and services, which together account for roughly half of today's global IT market, the competitive landscape is entirely different. Global positioning can also be shown on a two-axis grid. This time the two dimensions are human skills—principally in design, consulting, implementation, and project management—and organizational reach, that is, the ability to project those skills out into the global market.

Figure 3-6 plots the competitive software and services position of major world regions in terms of these two dimensions. Each is analyzed in turn.

Software. Once again, particular regions tend to gravitate to the corners, with the exception of Europe. U.S. firms continue to have an

Figure 3-6. Country positioning, software and services.

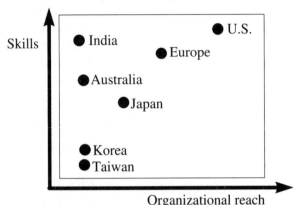

unmatched mix of both specific competencies and global market reach. In contrast, countries such as India, Russia, and Hungary often have highly competitive skills but extremely limited market reach, while most Asian nations have essentially neither.

European firms are again somewhat caught in the middle; the skill base is generally good, occasionally excellent, but market access is often confined to their own domestic markets as well as that of their former colonies. Other English-speaking countries such as Canada, Australia, South Africa, and Israel also have strong skills but generally struggle to reach global market audiences.

The weak Asian position is not due to any inherent lack of software proficiency—quite the contrary. However, there are two formidable barriers that are likely to prevent the emergence of any global Asian software giants for the foreseeable future. The first is the global emphasis on English-language products as the starting point for most new applications and tools. The second major barrier, although serious, is at least more solvable. The lack of intellectual property protection in many Asian countries has made it very difficult for a strong local software industry to emerge.

Overall, from a U.S. competitive perspective, within the existing PC-centric world there are few clouds on the horizon. Cooperative efforts with India and other countries provide ready access to low-cost but highly skilled resources. If interesting products emerge from Europe, Canada, Australia, or elsewhere, marketing partnerships are often simple and attractive. Unlike on the hardware side, the looming threat from Asia simply isn't there. As will be shown in chapter 10, most but not all of this strong U.S. software position will be preserved through the network-centric age.

Services. Figure 3-6 shows the current situation in terms of professional services such as IT consulting, project design, custom programming, systems integration, and outsourcing. Perhaps the most notable observation is that although skill bases are comparable in a number of countries, global market reach varies considerably, and no nation, including the United States, has a truly global IT services industry.

U.S. systems vendors such as IBM and Digital come the closest in terms of global reach, but these same vendors tend, not surprisingly, to have competencies mostly with their own product offerings. Pure play service companies such as EDS, Andersen, and Computer Sciences all have holes in their global operations, sometimes quite large ones. However, building a fully capable unit in one hundred or more significant country markets remains a daunting long-term challenge. Partnerships and occasional acquisitions remain the most frequently chosen path.

Nevertheless, U.S. firms are much closer to having this capability than any of their worldwide rivals. European firms have struggled to even come up with viable pan-European capabilities let alone global ones. Even more tellingly, virtually no Asian firm has made a serious attempt to develop services business outside of its particular home country.

As chapter 4 describes in detail, this global services reach will steadily gain in importance as existing horizontal products from Microsoft and Intel as well as new ones from Netscape begin to take on critical enterprise functions. The combination of leading edge horizontal products with the systems and services companies' global integration capabilities will prove to be the most direct path toward establishing the advanced enterprise information systems of the next decade.

CHAPTER 4

TECHNOLOGY EVOLVES: INTEL AND MICROSOFT HEAD TOWARD THE ENTERPRISE

In the late stages of the PC revolution, Intel and Microsoft technology moves beyond the desktop toward more powerful server environments, essentially trying to take the "/" out of client/server computing. This technological evolution attempts to simplify the hardware and software markets. System vendors finally begin to adapt to a changed industry, eventually leading to a much needed reconciliation of the vertical and horizontal models. However, lest the industry become too complacent, this last phase of PC-era evolution coincides with the first phase of the network-centric era.

The relationship between technology change and evolving industry structures entered an important but clearly evolutionary phase beginning around 1993 and continuing on through the current period. As with the S/360 and IBM PC, this era can also be seen as represented by certain symbolic events, in this case the emergence of Windows NT, the Intel Pentium, and the IBM Power PC. Conceptually, the nature of the change is depicted in figure 4-1.

What does this picture imply? Quite literally, it shows an industry structure that is still layered in nature but with clearly fewer layers. In other words, the horizontal model will continue to hold sway through this current phase. More specifically, the businesses of hardware, software, and services are likely to stay largely separate. As a rule, Compaq is staying out of services, Intel out of software, and Microsoft out of hardware.

But within these broad hardware, software, and services categories, particularly the first two, changing technologies are offering the possibility of a simpler, more homogeneous technology base for core hardware and software platforms. The effect of these changes on both the traditional PC business model and the more complex enterprise environment will likely prove to be profound.

However, the conceptual pattern of fewer layers is by no means suggesting a major industry consolidation of the overall industry. Whatever consolidation might take place in existing domains tends to be more than offset by the creation of entirely new areas such as the Internet and Worldwide Web. Although quite the opposite is often stated, the overall history of the industry continues to be one of more players and steadily fragmenting supplier market shares.

Figure 4-1. Computer industry structure, 1964–2000.

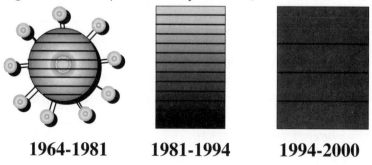

1964-1981   **1981-1994**   **1994-2000**

Simplifying the Hardware Market—Intel Moves Upstream

As has been discussed in previous chapters, the structure of the PC hardware industry is an unusual and perhaps even an unnatural one, with the major name brand PC players having so little say over what is actually inside their machines. To no one other than the existing mainframe and minicomputer manufacturers did this structure look more odd. In many executives' hearts and minds, there has always been a feeling that at some point a more normal world would be restored, and computer makers would be responsible for their own processor designs again. From a computer architecture perspective, the movement to true 32-bit systems seemed like a potential major opportunity to restore the old order, since this was something that all the existing hardware manufacturers knew a great deal about.

Indeed, the arrival of full 32-bit microprocessors promises to once again reshape the hardware industry structure, although not necessarily in the way the systems companies would like. The structure of the PC industry seems more likely to move up into remaining proprietary systems domains.

Consider that before the 32-bit chip was widely available, the boundaries between products, although never beyond debate, were from a market analysis point of view quite discrete. As figure 4-2 shows, there were numerous product categories. Each tended to be defined by its own processor technology, operating systems, perfor-

Figure 4-2. Simplifying the hardware market.

| Supercomputers |
| Mainframes |
| Minicomputers |
| Servers |
| Workstations |
| Personal Computers |

Intel
IBM Power
Digital Alpha
Sun SPARC
HP PA

1994   **2000**

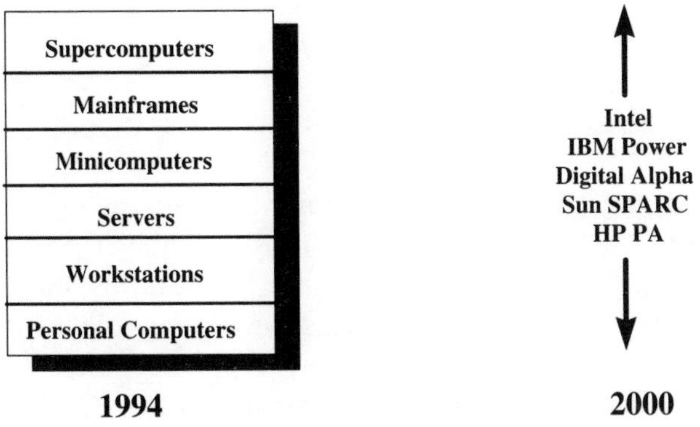

mance specifications, applications, and customer base. Beyond full line suppliers such as IBM and Digital, many of these categories had their own set of vendors as well. Words such as *supercomputer, mainframe, minicomputer, workstation,* and *personal computer,* although never academically pure in definition, did have quite distinct meanings in the marketplace.

Beginning in 1993, the broad-based arrival of full 32-bit microprocessors began to change all of this. As figure 4-2 depicts, microprocessors such as the Intel Pentium, IBM Power PC, Sun Microsystem SPARC, Hewlett-Packard Precision Architecture series, and Digital Alpha family can now define anything from a desktop platform through, when used in parallel, a supercomputer. This new and increasingly seamless scalability presented a direct challenge to the traditional market segmentations. Silicon Graphics' acquisition of supercomputer leader Cray was a good indication of these collapsing product boundaries.

From a technology perspective, all of the non-Intel products were based around so-called Reduced Instruction Set Computer (RISC) architectures. These chips have certain theoretical advantages over the Intel line, which carries not only the legacy of 1975 design principles but also the need to be backward compatible with earlier 8088, 286, 386, and 486 generations.

IBM, Digital, HP, and Sun hoped that their newer designs would eventually provide Intel with strong competition. However, Intel has proved to be highly adept in squeezing the most out of its architecture, incorporating as many RISC-like features as possible. In fact, the technologies have come together to such an extent that Intel and Hewlett-Packard are working together on their next generation of 64-bit systems.

PC/System Vendor Competition

Vendor marketing efforts soon followed the changing technological reality. Traditional PC companies, most notably Compaq, became much more aggressive in server markets by adding multiprocessing features. Although this move carried with it significant implications in terms of expected levels of sales and support, it often seemed to be less of a major strategic decision than it was a natural following of the technology. In contrast, despite much fanfare, all of the systems companies have been rather slow to invade the desktop space, although IBM's Power chip is now successfully used by Apple.

At its core, the reshaped competition comes down to a simple question. Which would have more success: Intel processors moving up into traditional systems markets or RISC chips moving down onto the desktop?

At least some of the answer depends on the time frame. In the short term, products based on Intel microprocessors have clearly been winning big in the market, dominating the low end of the LAN server business and having increasing success with multiprocessor implementations. IBM's long delay in bringing out a true PC version of its Power series is symbolic of the systems vendors' limited efforts to crack the desktop market.

Indeed, so strong is the Intel momentum that even RISC system vendors such as Digital and HP have begun to push Intel-based servers to customers who require them, a clear admission that the PC industry is successfully moving up into the systems realm. For many customers, Intel system costs are considerably lower, the processing power is sufficient, and there is a huge industry familiar with distributing, servicing, and using Intel-based systems. In its own way, IBM makes the same recognition by aggressively selling Intel-based servers running its OS/2 operating system.

All of the RISC system vendors might well agree with this assessment. However, they would also add that Intel is only winning the early rounds of what will be a long competitive struggle for microprocessor business leadership. They point out rightly that Intel still has an enormous advantage in its ability to run MS-Windows-based software. As long as this advantage is in place, alternative architectures have little chance for broad-based acceptance. However, should subsequent software environments become truly portable across different processor designs, then the real chip competition would begin.

In other words, if the tie between PC hardware and PC software, the so-called Wintel standard, could be broken, then Intel might be vulnerable to direct chip-versus-chip competition. After all, despite the popularity of the term "Wintel," Intel and Microsoft are in fact two separate companies. IBM did not just divest its power; it forever divided it. From this perspective, it does seem to be only a matter of time until this is reflected in the marketplace.

In many ways, the long-term strategy for the RISC chip vendors is to survive long enough to see if this severance actually happens. For a decade or more, many vendors hoped that Unix would fulfill this function. Now it is clear that there is really only one viable operating system candidate—Microsoft's own Windows NT. As in the IBM mainframe era, so again it might take a monopoly to break a monopoly. However, thus far the RISC chip vendors have made little headway in the NT market.

Even if their NT hopes don't pan out, vendors of RISC microprocessors have several other viable volume market capabilities. To become a major player in the microprocessor market, a vendor must tap into at least one multimillion unit market. Over the next decade, PCs will cease to be the only market of this size. Some of the most prominent other possibilities include video game machines, cable set top boxes, personal digital assistants, Internet appliances, automobiles, and a widening variety of smart machines, devices, and appliances. The outlook for these future markets is discussed in chapter 9. However, for at least the next few years, the PC industry will continue to be the overwhelmingly dominant segment.

As will be shown in detail in chapter 9, both history and the reasons stated suggest that a permanent hardware monopoly without at least significant program compatible manufacturer (PCM) competition is probably unsustainable. However, in terms of extending its dominance and taking maximum advantage of its opportunity, Intel appears to be doing just about everything possible, making any rapid change in position quite unlikely.

One of the reasons the systems companies are likely to continue to be aggressive in this area is that they realize that in the long run, if they are not a builder of microprocessors, their future in the computer industry will be diminished and can really take only one of two forms: either they will be like today's PC vendors, relying on an outside microprocessor supplier and struggling to differentiate their products or, if portable software does emerge and computer makers begin to once again make both the box and the processor, vendors without their own microprocessor capability could be out of the computer hardware manufacturing business altogether.

In the long run, the stakes are that high. However, the sheer variety of expected future devices argues strongly in favor of the merchant microprocessor model. Vendors who want to use a chip in their own products will need to have a strong merchant OEM business as well. Historically, this has proved difficult. Right now, the microprocessor and computer systems business are still more on the path of separation than unification. This bodes well for Intel but will create room for other microprocessor vendors as well.

Microsoft Simplifies the Software Market

Since so much of the source of Intel's power is drawn from its special relationship with Microsoft, evolution within the software sector is watched closely by hardware and software vendors alike along with, of course, the entire service and end user communities.

As with the hardware industry, over the course of the 1980s the software business went through a process of defining itself according to increasingly distinct layers in its version of a highly horizontal model. Specialized products evolved to meet specific customer needs. A sample of these products is shown in figure 4-3. This structure was optimized for innovation, and overall a tremendous amount of technological progress has been achieved. But the price of this freedom to innovate has been a level of complexity and confusion that has made user software decision making increasingly difficult.

Consider that most of the layered products shown in figure 4-3 come from different and often fiercely competing vendors—desktop applications from Microsoft, server applications from many sources, LAN operating systems from Novell, email systems from a variety of

Figure 4-3. Simplifying the software market.

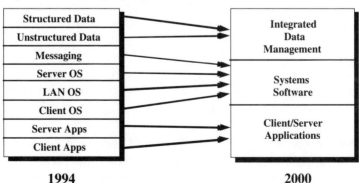

Structured Data	Integrated Data Management
Unstructured Data	
Messaging	
Server OS	Systems Software
LAN OS	
Client OS	Client/Server Applications
Server Apps	
Client Apps	
1994	**2000**

vendors, unstructured data usually via Lotus Notes, and structured data from a relational database management system (RDBMS) company such as Oracle.

Unlike the case with hardware, the interfaces between these products are often fuzzy. Ideally, the LAN, the mail system, the Notes system, and the database system all need similar information concerning system users, their passwords, privileges, and so on. Yet there is no obvious method of having an integrated directory management system. Another example would be the overlapping functions between a LAN OS such as Netware and a server OS such as Unix or Windows NT. Yet a third set of problems comes in coordinating the inevitable overlaps between unstructured data such as Lotus Notes with more structured DBMS information.

Given these complexities and overlaps, a move to simplify the overall environment might have great appeal to many customers. Microsoft's Windows NT is aimed at addressing this problem. By providing server, LAN, and email functionality in a standard shrink-wrapped product, Microsoft hopes to drive at least two layers out of the system.

Eventually, by having NT available as a desktop operating system and by moving to enterprise versions of many key application products additional simplification is possible. Microsoft's Exchange product, although off to a slow start, is aimed at providing Notes functionality. Although the very high end may well be beyond Microsoft's current interest, the majority of the RDBMS market is vulnerable to its PC-style pricing as opposed to today's minicomputer-like RDBMS business model.

From a technology perspective, these trends strongly support the Microsoft approach at least for the server and network operating system levels. The inclusion of these into a single operating system seems natural and likely over time. The application and data management levels are less obvious, and Microsoft won't be able to dominate them unless its offerings are clearly superior in the market. Thus, the three-layered structure shown in figure 4-3 is perhaps the most likely near-term path and a highly desirable one for a significant share of the customer base.

Moreover, when the question is turned around, it becomes clear that both Lotus (now owned by IBM) and Novell have a strong interest in keeping the current highly layered structure intact. Since they don't control any other layers of the chain, any simplification is likely to work against them. Novell's efforts to spread into related areas such as DOS, Unix, and word processing have clearly failed. Although the chances for success in these three areas were never high, Novell clearly felt the need for a broader presence in the overall software value chain. With that avenue closed off, the company must now create networking value sufficient to justify the preservation of a separate industry layer. This is proving difficult.

As noted earlier, this is why the original plan for Lotus and Novell to merge would have made so much sense. The combination of Netware with Lotus's cc:Mail and Notes would have given the combined entity a powerful integration story, particularly if Novell could have convinced the industry to accept a standard version of Unix. However, for the next few years the user choice is clear: either accept the current highly layered system with its inherent trade-off between competition and complexity or increasingly move toward a Microsoft-dominated enterprise environment.

Since it appears they are choosing the latter, Microsoft software is poised to take on the role within the corporate information systems organization that IBM's MVS/CICS/IMS had in the 1970s and early 1980s. The implications of this for both Microsoft and the users are profound, particularly given that Microsoft's indirect model does not allow for the close support that IBM always offered. To truly dominate the enterprise, Microsoft will have to rely heavily on increasingly sophisticated partners such as Digital. This is a subject that will be addressed in depth in the subsequent section on evolving system vendor strategies.

Breaking Up the Triumvirate

The concept of mutually reinforcing monopolies between three different vendors—Intel, Microsoft, and Novell—was a rare and perhaps unique business phenomenon. Consequently, it is not surprising that it could not last forever. The changes within the hardware and software industry structures seem certain to change the relationship among the triumvirate's members. This conceptual change is depicted in figure 4-4.

That Microsoft and Novell are now direct competitors is clear.

Figure 4-4. Changing, competitive dynamic—Intel, Microsoft, and Novell.

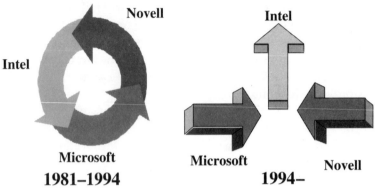

This had nothing to do with Novell's misguided and now divested acquisition of WordPerfect. This was mostly an extremely unfortunate sideshow. The real competition has always been between NT and Netware. Microsoft is attempting to make Novell's core offering essentially unnecessary, while Novell tries to preserve the existing order by staying ahead of Microsoft's network functionality. In theory it's a healthy competition, but so far the results have been one-sided.

From an executive standpoint, the situation is highly ironic. Back when both companies' success was largely synergistic, Bill Gates and Novell's Ray Noorda made their less-than-friendly rivalry highly public. Now, when Microsoft is essentially going for Novell's jugular, recently departed Novell CEO Bob Frankenberg and Bill Gates made a point of being publicly cordial and respectful.

If the rivalry between Microsoft and Novell is now clear, the changing relationship between Microsoft and Intel is less so. Since one is in the hardware business and the other in software, direct competition is highly unlikely. However, the mutual interests encapsulated in the phrase Wintel will likely weaken over the coming years, and although it may be a long time before the companies are truly indifferent to one another, the relationship can't be quite as close as it has been in the past for three main reasons:

Once the Intel-compatible chip market expands, Microsoft will have to work closely with these vendors as well. Intel will not like this, especially if, as forecasted in chapter 9, the compatibles start to get a large share of the business.

As NT becomes an enterprise server success, Microsoft will have a strong incentive to have its software run on other platforms, such as Digital's Alpha and IBM's Power PC. Intel won't like that.

Microsoft's and Intel's interests may well conflict in emerging areas such as network computers, PDAs, video conferencing, and 3-D graphics.

The net effect of this change in environment will be some strategic distancing, although since they will remain the two main industry leaders, significant cooperation will still be desirable. Suffice to say the relationship will deteriorate in proportion to the success of the Intel-compatibles or alternative microprocessor architectures. Over time, the outlook for both will brighten.

Services Industry Stability

Although, according to IDC, the support and professional services market, including consulting, design, contract programming, installation, systems integration, outsourcing, maintenance, and so on, comprises 35 percent of all customer spending with IT vendors, this critical part of the business has never attracted anywhere near the media or financial market attention enjoyed by hardware and software companies. Part of the reason is structural; since the business is inherently highly fragmented, it does not show the kind of de facto leadership patterns witnessed in product businesses. Companies such as EDS and Andersen may be the largest players, but they don't necessarily set clear patterns of behavior and competition. Furthermore, since no one company other than IBM has as much as 10 percent of the market, the great majority of users have had no relationship whatsoever with even the largest of services firms.

A second reason is technological. Since the IT industry has always been driven by innovation, it is hardly surprising that media attention focuses on the product side of the business where the overwhelming share of new technology occurs. Services firms certainly need to innovate in terms of business models, management practices, project leverage, and human resource management, but such improvements and even the occasional breakthrough are inherently less tangible, less likely to be widely or clearly communicated (often by design), and much less likely to immediately affect the behavior of others.

From a Wall Street perspective, services firms represent a completely different type of investment opportunity. Since there is no way they can ever attain the monopoly position of a Microsoft or an Intel, they can never provide those phenomenally rapid returns. On the other hand, since many services contracts are multiyear arrangements, the business is generally considerably more predictable, offering potentially solid returns over many years, as is evidenced by the great wealth created by companies such as EDS and ADP.

However, in the long run the influence of the services firms will grow. Over time, the IT business will become less technology and more application driven. Additionally, both the shift to the horizontal industry model and the diminished status of the traditional systems companies has created increased opportunities for services companies to improve their strategic position and market visibility. As will be shown in subsequent chapters, the network-centric era will accelerate the emphasis upon a service-driven industry.

The Current Services Structure Is Stable

As with hardware and software, as shown in figure 4-5, the services industry has its own functional layers. However, unlike the two product sectors, the service industry layers do not map cleanly to particular sets of vendors. Many vendors are involved in several or more of these activities; only the small companies tend to focus on just one layer.

Additionally, because there is clearly no underlying technology involved, there can be no homogenizing agent equivalent to the 32-bit microprocessor or Windows NT, and thus there isn't likely to be any major change to the current services industry value chain and resulting structure.

Over the first half of the 1990s, several major services firms, including EDS and Computer Sciences, have experimented with this sort of full range strategy, even to the extent of buying management

Figure 4-5. Services industry structure remains stable.

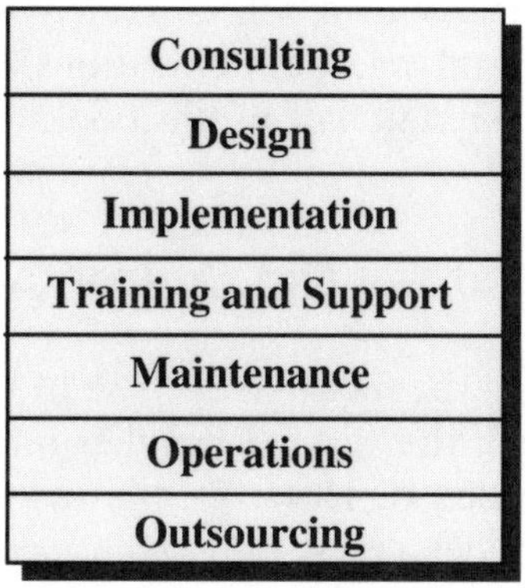

Consulting
Design
Implementation
Training and Support
Maintenance
Operations
Outsourcing

consulting and other necessary capabilities. However, these efforts, although moderately successful, have not resulted in an overall shift in competitive structure. Independent consulting, training, and programming firms, among others, continue to remain viable along with those who choose the full line approach.

This does not imply that services industry competition itself will not evolve. Certainly, the renewed focus on services by IBM and recently Digital will increase the pricing pressure for many bids. IBM, in particular, has seen its business grow rapidly in recent years. With their large multinational resources, the former systems companies are particularly well suited to take on global services projects. In contrast, although progress continues, nonproduct services companies have struggled to build up their global operations, resulting in frequent project partnering often on a country-by-country basis.

However, the most profound changes to this sector are likely to come from the steady and inevitable merger of computers and communications. As more and more activity goes on line, so-called processing services are becoming critical to communication suppliers. This has fueled frequent but as yet mostly fruitless discussions between the traditional service firms, local and long-distance telephone companies, Internet Access Providers, and even tradition on-line services firms such as CompuServe or America On-line. MCI's acquisition of SHL Systemhouse is the most important example to date.

However, as intriguing as some of these discussions may be, they are relevant only to those large services companies that are investing heavily in their own network infrastructures. The role of the typical small, professional services firm will be largely unaffected. The integration of computer and telecommunications services will be discussed in-depth in the second half of this book.

Rationalizing the Vertical and Horizontal Models

There is no questioning the fact that the rise of the horizontal model greatly diminished both the vertical supplier model and the systems companies that embodied it. However, the new did not destroy the old, and the vertical model has evolved and lives on in some important new ways.

This chapter examines how the vertical model changed to coexist with and, in fact, support the overall horizontal reality. As Microsoft moves up into more complex environments and as Internet-focused software companies such as Netscape target the enterprise market, this new synergy between the old and new orders has become increasingly important.

Supplier Rationalization

The most obvious affect of the move toward a horizontal model was to drive many of the weaker systems companies out of the hardware business. With the rise of so many new horizontal suppliers, there was no way that the declining vertical model could support all of the traditional vendors. By the early 1990s, the casualties had begun to mount—Prime, Wang, Control Data, Perkin Elmer, Gould, Modcomp, Computervision, and others all either went out of business or substantially refocused themselves. Others, such as Data General, struggled desperately to hang on.

Major mergers, alliances, and acquisitions became another means of supplier restructuring. Burroughs and Sperry merged to become Unisys. Honeywell sold all of its activities to Bull, which in turn got its mainframe hardware from the Japanese firm NEC. Apollo Computer was acquired by Hewlett-Packard. Hitachi absorbed its long-term PCM customer National Advanced Systems and renamed it Hitachi Data Systems. AT&T acquired NCR to replace its own struggling computer operations, only to spin it off again. Siemens absorbed long-term partner Pyramid.

In hindsight, this process looks quite efficient. By 1993, the major U.S. vertically integrated system suppliers who remained independent—IBM, HP, Digital, and Sun Microsystems—were clearly the strongest of the group. They were joined by the national champions of Europe—ICL in the United Kingdom, Bull in France, Siemens (which had also acquired local rival Nixdorf) in Germany, and Olivetti in Italy. A similar rationalization occurred in Japan. Previously minor systems players, such as Mitsubishi, Oki, and Toshiba, refocused on other segments of the IT business, leaving Fujitsu, Hitachi, and to a lesser extent NEC to compete in the traditional systems market.

Thus, within roughly a six-year period, the supplier structure went from more than forty significant general purpose mainframe and mini suppliers to roughly a dozen. With the exception of relative newcomer Sun Microsystems, all of the remaining vendors faced a similar set of strategic questions. Among some of the most daunting:

Legacy systems management. How much investment should go into their older, declining proprietary systems business?

PC strategy. Should they try and are they capable of competing in the fiercely competitive PC hardware marketplace?

Identifying core competencies. Which parts of their vertical enterprise legacy should they preserve and which should they jettison—disk drives, printers, terminals, software, and so on?

Unix strategy. Should they develop their own Unix hardware and software and play aggressively in that space or go with standard Intel and NT technologies?

Processor strategy. Should they try to develop their own microprocessors, pursue a joint RISC chip venture, or just sign on with Intel?

Services strategy. Is each supplier's field force designed to sell and support its own products, or should it take on a substantially broader, more independent mission?

In the face of such fundamental dilemmas, the system vendors (with the major exception of HP) all did basically the same thing. They froze.

In the late 1980s and early 1990s, the system vendors were in a continual state of indecisiveness and turmoil. Virtually all had at least one major reorganization and often more, and a great many—IBM, Unisys, Digital, Hewlett-Packard, AT&T, Data General, Tandem, Siemens, and Bull—changed chief executives at least once. In some cases, such as Digital, the entire upper management ranks were replaced.

More tellingly, the staggering financial losses were unprecedented in the IT industry's history. During the period of 1989 through 1993, the major U.S., Japanese, and European systems companies combined lost more than $25 billion. Clearly, only those with deep pockets could survive. Fear of financial collapse spread at various times to major players such as Digital, Unisys, Olivetti, and Bull. Even IBM had to worry about its declining debt rating and stock price.

The Market Intervenes

Despite these heightening pressures, system company strategic decisions were still often apparently too tough to directly face. In response to this inaction, the market once again took the lead, eventually dictating system company organization and strategy.

Figure 4-6 depicts two clear market messages to the systems com-

Figure 4-6. Market impact on systems company business model, 1982–1992.

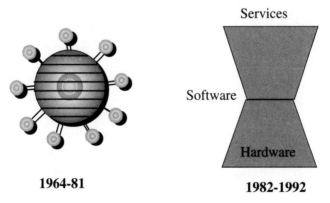

1964-81   1982-1992

panies: (1) that the hardware manufacturing and field service organizations were valued industry assets, and (2) that most of the systems vendors' software efforts were not. Each is explained below.

System vendors' hardware prowess in terms of quality, distribution, and product brand strength was demonstrated on several key fronts:

Proprietary systems continued to hold onto the high end of the market. Multi- and parallel-processing systems based on standard microprocessor designs made only modest high end inroads. After a few years of free fall, mainframe sales stabilized.

Traditional system vendors such as IBM, Digital, and HP successfully established strong positions in the Unix market, substantially surpassing in size the newer pure Unix system companies such as Sequent and Pyramid.

HP and Digital joined IBM as major players in the PC hardware market. Their large customer base provided an important market entry point. Globally, Olivetti, Bull (through its Zenith Data Systems acquisition), Siemens, Fujitsu, and NEC are all important PC players.

Perhaps, more important, the field forces of these organizations are still very important industry assets, particularly to the traditional management information system (MIS) customer.

As will be discussed in more detail in the analysis of enterprise computing in chapter 13, in recent years MIS influence within large customer organizations has been increasing after falling steadily through much of the 1980s. MIS has clearly been assigned the task of building the integrated enterprise information systems that many companies require. In addition, outsourcing, although popular within particular domains such as software development and wide area networking, is clearly not sweeping away existing in-house structures.

System vendors and MIS grew up together, and what is good for one often proves to be good for the other. To fulfill its mission, MIS needs to build adaptable client/server systems using technologies from many vendors. To do this, MIS needs a coordinated combination of platforms, tools, and support, and the system vendors are still often the simplest means of acquiring these capabilities. This is especially true in Japan where independent services companies are still not well established.

By 1994, the systems companies had finally begun to capture this new opportunity. IBM, Digital, Unisys, ICL, and others have since become important players in the services realm, emerging as serious direct competition to pure play services companies such as EDS, Andersen Consulting, Computer Sciences, and Cap Gemini Sogeti.

Software Is Another Story

The market took a decidedly cooler view of systems companies' software efforts. By and large, the market said the following:

- Forget about your database products; we like Oracle, Informix, and the like.
- Forget about your networking architectures; we're going with Novell, Cisco, Internet, and so on.
- Forget about your groupware and office products; we like Lotus Notes and/or Microsoft.
- As Microsoft strengthens NT, we might even drop your proprietary versions of Unix.

In short, system vendors' key software products were being soundly rejected. After an extended period of denial, this message began to be heard, and virtually all of the worldwide systems companies, with the major exception of IBM, began a broad retreat in terms of their software strategy. This crucial software decision has fundamentally recast and often reinvigorated system company business in the manner described in the next section.

Toward a Three-Part Systems Company Business Model

Figure 4-7 shows the evolution of the systems vendor business model from the pure vertically integrated approach to a more sophisticated three-part strategy consisting of legacy, discontinuous, and disintegrated activities. These three aspects are described in the following sections.

Figure 4-7. Systems company evolution, 1993–1996.

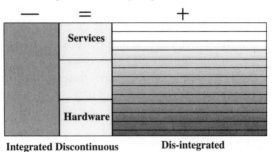

Integrated Legacy Systems

The traditional proprietary systems business, such as IBM's S/370 and AS/400 and Digital's VMS, remains in a general state of managed decline. Future investments are determined on a case-by-case, mostly profit maximization basis. Vendors with small legacy installed bases, such as HP and NCR, have tended to disengage themselves more quickly, while IBM and Digital continue to profitability milk the customer upgrade business.

Discontinuous Systems

This was the key innovation that responded to the software market realities described above. In this model, the system vendors would continue to make various hardware platforms that they would sell and service in the marketplace. However, the software for these systems would tend to be drawn from the Independent Software Vendor (ISV) community.

The obvious early examples were HP's and eventually Digital's abandonment of their own DBMS offerings in favor of those from the ISV community—Oracle, Informix, Sybase, and so on. An even more important example has been Digital's and increasingly other systems vendors' close cooperation with Microsoft to drive sales and provide support for Windows NT in large organizations.

This discontinuous model has also been chosen by virtually all of the major European and Japanese systems companies, most of whom are now aggressively supporting Microsoft technologies. Clearly, the bulk of the systems market has decided to switch rather than fight. And as Microsoft moves into the complex systems realm without a direct service force of its own, the global systems companies are becoming critical, cooperative partners, an important industry transformation.

Within this discontinuous approach, there are two main paths— Intel and non-Intel. As discussed earlier, the Intel systems are winning the majority of the market, particularly at the low end. Digital, Unisys, NCR, Sequent, and increasingly HP are all aggressively pushing Intel systems as is IBM for its OS/2 server products.

Two companies have resisted the discontinuous software strategy trend—Sun Microsystems and IBM. The case with Sun is clear. As a pure Unix systems company, Sun cannot aggressively adopt Microsoft technology without compromising its core business strategy. Of all the existing systems companies, it is the only one whose survival is so totally dependent on its Unix business. Sun, adeptly making a virtue out of necessity, takes pride in having such a clear and focused strategy.

The case with IBM is more complicated. Unlike all the other systems companies, IBM still prefers its own software, especially DB2, AIX, CICS, and OS/2. Its high-priced acquisition of Lotus for its Notes and cc:Mail products as well as the smaller, but still pricey, acquisition of systems management software vendor Tivoli should be seen as part of this larger overall software strategy. Given the high profits and market leverage attainable only in software markets, IBM's unwillingness to cede the software market to Microsoft is understandable. But is it realistic?

At this point, IBM seems to be losing many of its key bets. DB2, although still dominant on IBM's mainframes, has made little headway elsewhere and is thus steadily losing ground to the independent DBMS products; similarly, CICS is not really expanding beyond its existing mainframe base. On the critical operating system front, Sun is still the most influential Unix company, and OS/2 has lost the desktop and most of the server market to NT. IBM's bet on Lotus Notes has fared better and seems to be withstanding the challenge from both Microsoft and the Web.

IBM has the financial resources to compete for some time. However, if these software efforts do not pay off, they will hurt IBM's hardware platform and field services businesses as well. Consequently,

IBM's unique system vendor decision to essentially forgo the discontinuous model and to stay with its own proprietary offerings is one of high risk and high potential reward. Unfortunately for IBM, thus far it is the risks that are mounting, but one has to admire IBM's refusal to succumb to Microsoft, and clearly the battle for software industry leadership will continue well into the coming network-centric era. Given its success with Lotus and Tivoli, additional acquisitions, including Netscape, are a possibility.

Dis-integrated Businesses

Taken together, a declining legacy systems business and a moderately growing discontinuous opportunity provide a path for short-term system company survival and stability. Together, they have become the evolved form of the original systems company model; if effectively implemented, they are nearly sufficient to maintain and support large global sales and services divisions.

However, neither of these two models allows the systems companies to participate in the real growth sectors of the market that remain with the horizontal, dis-integrated business approach. These are products that are generally not sold as part of any larger systems solution. Rather, they are sold independently, usually through indirect channels. In short, they are separate stand-alone businesses.

Among all the U.S. systems companies, only HP had managed to have great success in this area. HP's dominance in the printer business helped put it on a rapid growth curve to eventually become the world's second largest computer company. Moreover, the brand power and good will developed in this consumer sector helped drive the sales of other HP products as the company found it increasingly easy to get on critical customer short lists. This ability of the dis-integrated mass market products to help drive higher priced, often proprietary systems is another manifestation of the now inverted industry order.

As the other systems companies witnessed HP's success, they too tried to compete in the dis-integrated side of the business. Not surprisingly, success to date has only been modest, since strong horizontal players are already entrenched in all existing sectors. However, as new sectors emerge, the old systems companies finally have in place a business model that will allow them to compete with more pure play rivals.

Sun's Java programming language for the Internet is proving to be the best example of this type of dis-integrated success. Digital's early and interesting work with various Internet products also typifies the overall business model rejuvenation. If the systems companies can consistently replicate this sort of success, they can have an exciting future. If not, the legacy and discontinuous business will still keep them around for quite a while. However, over time, success on the horizontal side of the market will be required to sustain product competitiveness and market brand power. In the future, the system companies will increasingly play by horizontal rules; they'll need to innovate and compete within their chosen layers in order to survive.

Reaching an Equilibrium

By the end of 1993, the rationalization of the vertical industry structure and its eventual adaptation to the horizontal model provided a sense of closure for the first two great waves of IT industry expansion—the systems and PC eras.

The horizontal market had clearly proved the more powerful, but the vertical approach had then evolved to address the real shortcomings of a pure horizontal approach. The result seemed to offer users the best of both worlds: the high innovation of the horizontal structure but with at least some of the service, support, and integration offerings of the older systems order, all within a highly competitive, unbundled pricing environment. This was a degree of choice, freedom, and clarity that customers had never seen.

From a customer's perspective, the unique position of Intel was simply not a worry. With so many vendors selling Intel-based systems and with Intel-compatible chips and alternative microprocessors waiting for any Intel stumble, users were assured of rapidly improving system price/performance. Hardware was in fact becoming an open system commodity. The price of processing power was now just a minor concern.

Microsoft's preeminence was only slightly more troubling. Certainly, many users were not eager to go back to the days when IBM's power was so unchecked in the marketplace. As Microsoft extended its reach up into the enterprise, the parallels with IBM appeared to be growing, even attracting significant antitrust attention.

However, since Microsoft does not sell any hardware or provide many services, the extent of Microsoft's power touches on only a very small share of the customer's overall IT budget. Even within that area, Microsoft, unlike IBM, has proved to be a very aggressive price competitor. Although this certainly causes problems for other ISVs, it is not something that customers themselves are going to complain about. Concerns about eventual monopoly pricing from Microsoft are very real, but still exist largely on a theoretical level.

These business model trends played themselves out on a global scale, bringing a degree of uniformity and consistency unavailable before. Large customers could begin to look forward to an increasingly interoperable and fully supported global information management capability, using established best-of-breed technologies. The industry seemed to have a smooth, if somewhat tame, path forward.

But just as waves one and two were reconciling themselves, a powerful third wave began to surface. By the end of 1994, talk of stability, clarity, and smooth paths forward had disappeared. Once again, the industry paradigm had suddenly shifted. The era of the desktop and the microprocessor was passing. In its place a network-centric world was rapidly emerging, opening up dramatic new possibilities, while comprising the first real challenge to the established wave two order.

CHAPTER 5
TIME OUT FOR SOME DATA

The following pages reinforce many of the previous themes from a quantitative perspective. They are also useful as a tangible base from which to begin discussions about future industry directions. All computer industry figures are from the International Data Corporation (IDC). All other data are from the U.S. Statistical Abstracts, published by the U.S. Department of Commerce.

The IT Industry in Perspective

How does the growth of the computer industry compare with that of
the other great technological advancements of the twentieth century?
Within the IT industry itself, there is often a sense that there has never
really been an industry like this one and that the great success and
proliferation of computers is a largely unprecedented phenomenon.

An examination of the available U.S. historical data shows clearly
that this is not the case. As figure 5-1 reveals, the pace of computer
deployment is neither dramatically slower nor faster than that for telephones, automobiles, or televisions. All four have taken off rapidly
and then slowed down as various demographic ceilings are reached.

Indeed, the small differences in the shapes of each curve are
readily explainable. Since it required the physical wiring of the American landscape, the telephone industry took the longest to fully emerge.
In contrast, since they could take advantage of broadcast technology,
televisions proliferated the fastest. Like automobiles, the computer industry has had to go through a long period of making its products
widely affordable.

Moreover, the growth of the computer industry has parallels with
all three of the other sectors. Like telephones, computers are used by
both consumers and business and need to be ubiquitously available.

Figure 5-1. U.S. installed bases of major devices.

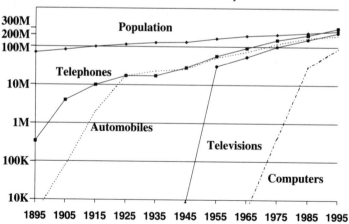

Note: The left-hand scale is logarithmic.
Sources: International Data Corporation and U.S. Department of Commerce.

Like automobiles, the PC is a highly personal productivity and life-style device that requires considerable investment and training. Like the television, computers offer instant access to a global community, often transcending time, distance, and even language barriers.

Over time, all four industries tend to reach their own different demographic ceilings. For example, between business, consumer, mobile, and public phones, the total number of telephones in use has now clearly surpassed that of the U.S. population. In contrast, since automobiles serve mostly an adult consumer market with only a small amount of additional business ownership, the total number of cars and trucks in use will always be less than the total population.

In the case of televisions, their durability and effectively zero cost of ownership has led to a virtually one-to-one relationship with the population despite having little incremental business usage. Finally, with computers, the combination of equal business and consumer usage, the occasional need for mobility, and the eventual desire for multiple PCs per home suggest that the total number of computers will ultimately fall somewhere between that of telephones and televisions, assuming much lower computer price points are eventually reached.

Understanding Today's Global IT Market

Whereas the previous section provided comparisons between the computer industry and other major technology sectors, the following section provides a quantitative view of the size, segmentation, and market shares of today's global IT business.

Figure 5-2 shows the IT market by product sector as of the end of 1995. The $530 billion figure includes all spending by customers with suppliers for general purpose hardware and software products as well as related professional and maintenance service.

It is important to realize that the size of the computer market can vary widely depending on the definitions used. For example, the $530 billion figure above does not include spending by customers on their own information systems personnel or spending on voice telecommunications services or equipment. It also does not include a variety of special purpose but still computer-based equipment such as check processing systems, automatic teller machines, electronic cash registers, mail sorting systems, and numerous similar devices. By including these IT-related markets, a market size of more than $1 trillion could easily be defended.

Thus, figure 5-2 shows the IT market from the typical computer vendor's perspective in terms of the available current opportunity for general purpose products and services. From this perspective, today's IT market is roughly half hardware and half software and services. The three hardware categories shown—single user systems, which consists of both personal computers and technical workstations; multiuser systems, consisting of mainframes, minicomputers, and specialized LAN servers; and data communications hardware, consisting of network interface cards, as well as hubs, routers, modems, and other specialized data communications gear—in 1995 accounted for 48 percent of user spending with vendors.

Packaged software products such as operating systems, tools, software utilities, and applications packages combined with professional services such as IT design, consulting, custom programming, systems integration, and outsourcing as well as various support, training, educational and maintenance services accounted for the remaining 52 percent of the market.

Over the course of the 1980s, the software and services sectors

Figure 5-2. 1995 Worldwide IT market by product sector.

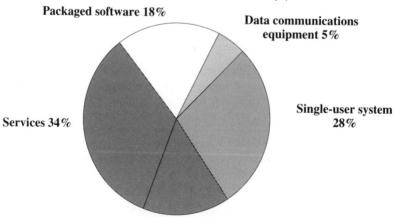

Packaged software 18%

Data communications equipment 5%

Services 34%

Single-user system 28%

Multiuser system 15%

$530 Billion

Source: International Data Corporation.

steadily gained in relative share. Indeed, by the late 1980s, many fore-casters were expecting software and services to account for two-thirds of the overall IT market by the end of the century. According to this view, hardware had become such a commodity that falling prices and eventual market saturation were inevitable.

However, over the 1992–1995 period, the hardware share has sta-bilized and has even edged up a bit. This has been primarily due to four factors:

> The emergence of the home market has opened up a major new PC growth frontier, allowing annual worldwide PC unit shipments to consistently expand by 20 percent or more. Con-sumer interest in CD-ROMs, sound boards, color monitors, large memories, and other high performance equipment has also helped stabilize average PC sales prices.
> The explosion of the Internet has led to dramatic surges in the still small data communications market, making this the fast-est growing of all major sectors. High speed modems, network switches, routers, and hubs have enjoyed particularly strong growth.
> A generally improved worldwide economy has helped bolster the still large mainframe market, which had gone into a free fall in the early 1990s.
> The services market has slowed some. There are real limits on spending increases in any people-intensive business. Addition-ally, the improved economy has slowed some of the frenzied, cost-cut driven outsourcing activity seen in the 1990–1992 period.

Looking forward toward the end of the decade, in an overall IT market expected to grow at 10 percent per year, the product composi-tion will continue to shift. According to IDC, software will be the highest growing segment, expanding at some 14 percent per year, but hardware will be second at 9 percent. Because a significant share of the services market consists of slow growing product maintenance, services will be the slowest growing sector at 8 percent. Overall, these forces will be somewhat countervailing, resulting in the hardware in-dustry share decreasing to 42 percent by decade's end, a decline of six points from 1995.

Today's Market by Region

Figure 5-3 shows the same 1995 global IT market, this time by the region of the consuming market. As with the product segmentation data, the changing regional composition of worldwide IT products and services consumption has caught many by surprise.

During the second half of the 1980s, the U.S. share of the worldwide IT market fell steadily. The U.S. IT business slowed while Europe, Japan, and emerging markets around the world, but especially in Asia, all surged. Many saw this pattern continuing through the 1990s. Some forecasted that the share of the worldwide IT market accounted for by the United States might fall to as low as 25 percent by the year 2000.

This, most emphatically, has not happened. Over the 1992–1995 period, the United States has been by far the fastest growing major IT market, dramatically outperforming both Europe and Japan. Today, the U.S. share of the global market stands at roughly 40 percent, not significantly different than a decade ago despite a generally falling dollar. There are three main reasons for this U.S. resurgence:

Figure 5-3. 1995 Worldwide IT market by region of consumption.

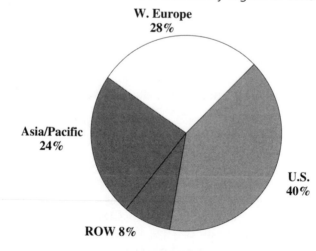

W. Europe
28%

Asia/Pacific
24%

U.S.
40%

ROW 8%

$530 Billion

Source: International Data Corporation.

1. *A strong U.S. economy.* As the base of technology users has broadened to include consumers and small businesses, domestic IT markets have become much more sensitive to overall country economic conditions. Over the last four years, the U.S. economy has been fundamentally much stronger than the major economies of Europe or Japan. The European economy was basically flat from 1992 to 1994. The situation in Japan, on the other hand, was much worse. The bursting of the so-called bubble economy in 1992 led to large drops in IT spending in both 1992 and 1993. Growth returned to the market in 1994 and 1995 but still at lower levels than in the United States.

2. *Aggressive technology adoption.* The U.S. market has consistently adopted new computing technologies faster than the major nations of Western Europe and Japan. (The smaller Scandinavian markets, particularly Sweden and Denmark, are often equally if not more advanced than the United States. Australia is another very developed but smaller market.) U.S. early adopter leadership has never been more obvious than with both the consumer PC and Internet markets. In both cases, U.S. domestic acceptance is several years more developed than in, for example, France, Germany, and Japan.

3. *Positive feedback loops.* The heavy U.S. IT investment patterns have coincided with greatly improved overall U.S. economic competitiveness. For the first time, many serious observers are making a direct link between the level of technological sophistication and overall economic competitiveness. This is fueling renewed enthusiasm for technology investments, further driving U.S. IT spending. If productivity gains continue, this could mark the beginnings of a powerful virtuous circle that could drive the U.S. economy and U.S. IT spending still further. More likely, the business cycle will eventually reassert itself; nonetheless, the overall U.S. economic and technology outlook is widely believed to be positive.

In sum, the strength of the consumer market and the rapid creation and acceptance of cyberspace continues to bode well for the U.S. market over the rest of the decade. Over the long term, a country with 25 percent of the world's GDP and just 4 percent of the world's population won't be able to hold 40 percent of the world's IT market. But as long as different stages of development persist, such discrepancies can continue. The U.S. market probably won't begin to significantly decline in relative IT importance until the end of the century at the earliest.

Today's Market by Type of Customer

Figure 5-4 shows the same 1995 market, this time segmented by type of customer. Some simple definitions are in order. In this chart, small businesses are defined as those companies with one hundred or fewer employees. All other organizations are classified in this chart as large businesses. Consumer spending is defined by purchases of information technology by U.S. households, including those for work at home and other job-related spending.

As the data show, large businesses are still by far the largest market for IT products and services. However, their share has fallen significantly over the last decade. For instance, in 1980, these same businesses would have accounted for roughly 90 percent of all U.S. IT spending. The consumer market at that time was in its infancy, and most small businesses made little use of the existing minicomputer technologies.

Figure 5-4. 1995 Worldwide IT market by type of customer.

Small businesses 34%

Homes 7%

Large businesses 59%

$530 Billion

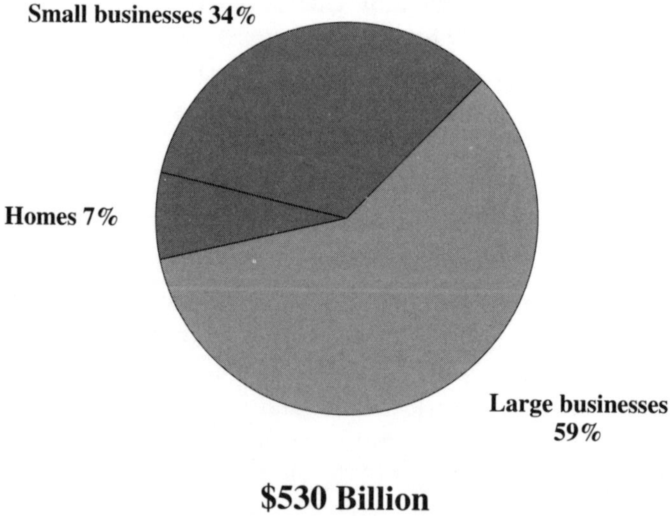

Source: International Data Corporation.

It was the PC and the PC LAN that really opened up both the small business and consumer markets. Today, in the United States, more than 90 percent of businesses with ten or more employees have some sort of computer on-site. On the consumer front, roughly one-third of U.S. households now have at least one PC.

Looking ahead to the end of the decade, the share of the U.S. IT market accounted for by small businesses will likely level off. Although still less computer intensive than large businesses, the gap has significantly narrowed. Perhaps more important, the labor-intensive nature of many small business service jobs—restaurants, home services, taxi drivers, landscaping, and so on—often does not lend itself to heavy IT investment. Most likely, the small business share of the IT market will move in line with the small business share of the U.S. economy, recognizing that this is a notoriously difficult share to accurately measure.

Not surprisingly, more significant market share gains will occur in the consumer sector. In 1995, the entire worldwide consumer market for hardware, software, peripherals, upgrades, and on-line services was approximately $37 billion, or some 7 percent of the global IT industry. Given uncertain consumer tastes, demographics, applications, and technological innovations, forecasting new consumer markets is always difficult, but IDC expects that consumer spending will account for 15 percent of overall spending by the end of the decade.

This is an admittedly conservative figure that will be reached if consumers in other economies start to use home PCs at the rate the United States already does. A major technological breakthrough in available bandwidth or an important application innovation in either entertainment or transaction services could lead to significantly higher spending. The prospects for such market driving applications will be discussed in subsequent chapters. Nevertheless, the consumer IT market will remain smaller than that for both large and small businesses for the foreseeable future.

Today's Market by Region of Vendor

The final market view in this series of pie charts uses the same $530 billion figure but this time segments it by regional vendor market share, providing a high-level view of the current global competitive

environment. More than any of the others, this figure requires care-
ful definition.

The main purpose of figure 5-5 is to show which country's (or in
the case of Europe and Asia, which region's) vendors are getting the
worldwide IT business today. In other words, the data show that companies whose headquarters are based in the United States currently
get 62 percent of the global IT business, Europe-based firms get 15
percent, and so on.

The data say nothing at all about where a product is made or
sold. In other words, if Compaq actually makes some of its PCs in
Taiwan or sells them in Brazil, all Compaq sales still count in the U.S.
total since Compaq is a U.S.-based company.

The data also do not deal with value added at a component level.
In other words, the market share accrues to the vendor under whose
name the product is sold. In the case of hardware, this usually means
the name on the box. Thus, the fact that the DRAMs and CD-ROMs
in a Compaq PC were actually made in Japan or Korea does not alter
the data in any way. The finished good is branded under Compaq, and
since Compaq is a U.S.-based company, it becomes credited to the
U.S. share.

Figure 5-5. 1995 Worldwide IT market by region of selling vendor.

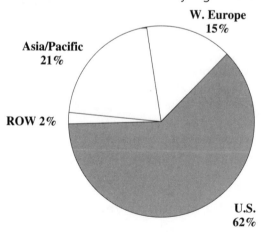

$530 Billion

Source: International Data Corporation.

The alternative data views described above would result in different pictures of today's global market share, particularly the view of where products are physically made. However, none of this changes the fact that from an end user and brand awareness perspective, the United States has nearly two-thirds of today's IT market, a share that continues to slowly rise.

In some ways, the current share is actually understated. The two-thirds figure is for all global hardware, software, and services offerings. As discussed earlier, the services business has always had a strong local component, and thus the U.S. share of the services business is only in the mid fifties. (U.S. companies have almost 100 percent of the U.S. domestic market services business but only about 25 percent of the rest.) In contrast, U.S.-based vendors' market share in the hardware and software product business is now actually more than 70 percent, a remarkable figure given the diverse and rapidly expanding nature of the industry.

The reasons for and implications of this current dominance are explored more deeply in the global competitiveness chapters. At this point, it is sufficient to note that the shift to a horizontal supplier model has been led almost exclusively by U.S. firms—Compaq, Intel, Microsoft, Seagate, Oracle, and others. As the information industry becomes not only among the world's largest but also perhaps the most strategic, current U.S. leadership is a frequent cause for concern in many world capitals. The sustainability of this position is one of the most important industry questions for the second half of the 1990s.

CHAPTER 6

UNDERSTANDING THE
NETWORK-CENTRIC ERA

*This chapter provides an overview of the
key aspects of the network-centric era
that more than justify the term* paradigm
shift. *It then looks back to explain the
peculiar suddenness and power with
which the Internet arrived. Unlike the PC
era, the Internet was built upon and drew
much of its strength from previous computing investments.*

It is convenient to mark IT industry progress by certain key symbolic events. Seventeen years passed between the introduction of IBM's S/360 family in 1964 and the arrival of the IBM PC in 1981. Although one can debate when exactly the current network-centric era began, the arrival of the Mosaic interface in late 1993 and the subsequent explosion in use of the Internet and Worldwide Web is perhaps the most commonly cited. It was this graphical interface that made the mass market possible, launching a high-growth phase in a manner precisely analogous to the IBM PC in 1981. In this view the PC era lasted approximately thirteen years.

Figure 6-1 is presented again to highlight the current period, showing the changing centers of gravity as the IT industry expands and becomes increasingly pervasive. It is now clear that just as the system-centric world gave way to a PC-centric one, so too is the PC era passing in favor of a network-centric IT industry. Each previous wave has been characterized by roughly an order of magnitude increase in the total number of worldwide users and a huge expansion in industry revenues. As will be described over the remainder of this book, the current wave seems certain to continue this pattern.

Within this new world, ubiquitous and mass market connectivity is the prevailing dynamic. The bandwidth of these connections will clearly increase over time, but the more important task is to make connecting computers as simple and as common as telephone connec-

Figure 6-1. Stages of industry growth.

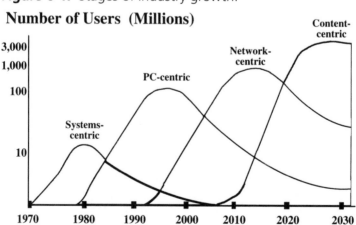

tivity is today. Put simply, the mission of the current era is one of getting the world wired, with the popular and aptly named magazine *Wired* capturing the spirit of the times.

Indeed, an easy way of seeing the current period is that it represents the true and long awaited merger of computers and communications, a world where computers can routinely call upon each other and interact. It is this marrying of the worldwide communications infrastructure with the power of general purpose computers that defines the new network-centric era. To cite just one obvious example, today a simple laptop computer can send and receive messages from perhaps 40 million people all over the world no matter where that laptop is located. By the end of the period, the number of people connected should reach 1 billion or more.

But it is important to keep in mind that connectivity is not an end unto itself. From a longer term perspective, the current period should be seen as just the third major phase of the industry's growth and evolution. A decade from now, when ubiquitous, high bandwidth, device connectivity is a given, then from a user's perspective the network can recede into the background and eventually become so commonplace as to become almost invisible. In this sense, one of the great goals of the network-centric era will be to make itself largely transparent. At that point, a magazine named *Wired* will likely seem as strange and as antiquated as a magazine called *Dial Tone* would today.

Once the ubiquitous network is in place, the focus and energy of the industry can shift toward the multimedia content that runs on top of this network. It is this future, content-centric industry that will both mark the end of the network-centric era and become the real basis for the much talked about information society. Speculation on what this content-based era world will look like comprises the final chapter of this book.

Understanding the Current Paradigm Shift

In this book, the term *paradigm shift* is deliberately used sparingly. It is chosen only to describe those rare times when multiple aspects of a current system are inverted, reversed, or fundamentally altered in some way. As was demonstrated earlier, the shift to a PC-centric industry was clearly one such period; this chapter shows why the network-centric era should be considered one as well.

Figure 6-2 summarizes the major issues involved:

From PC-centric to network-centric. This top-level change has already been sufficiently discussed, but consider the shift in language alone. In the late 1980s, most of the industry talk was about PC hardware, PC software, PC printers, PC storage, and so on. Today, the dominant phrases all begin with Internet or Web—Internet usage, Internet access, Internet pricing, Internet stocks, Web servers, Web sites, Web design, and Web development. The share-of-mind battle has clearly been won.

From microprocessor to communications bandwidth. In the PC era, the industry followed Intel's lead, with the introduction of the 286, 386, 486, and Pentium all becoming major industry events. In the network era, although Intel chips will still be key components, they will no longer be the critical technological enabler. Discussions of the upcoming Pentium Pro are not nearly as pervasive as other Intel product introductions.

Communications bandwidth has now replaced processing power as the scarce industry commodity. The graphical capabilities of the Worldwide Web are clearly restricted by the cost and availability of communications capacity, especially in consumer markets. With all

Figure 6-2. Summary of network-centric paradigm shift.

1981–1994	1995–2005
PC-centric	Network-centric
Microprocessor speed	Communications bandwidth
Moore's Law	Metcalfe's Law
Local area networks	Wide area networks
Graphical interfaces	Internet browsers
Indirect channels	Online channels
Standalone products	Bundled products
Client/server	Electronic commerce
Individual productivity	Virtual communities
Horizontal computer industry	Converged industry value chain
Global products	National services

due respect to Intel, an easy way to understand the current shift is to recognize that, today, a doubling of modem speed would do more to move the industry forward than a doubling of microprocessor performance. The implications of this for Intel and the overall PC hardware industry are explored later and are, in the long run, likely to be profound.

Of course, the communications bandwidth providers plan to do much more than merely double communications speeds. Technologies to be discussed later, such as ISDN and more dramatically the cable modem, promise great increases in network access speeds. Indeed, a primary goal of the current period is to transform bandwidth from a scarce resource to a surplus one. This was one of the great accomplishments of the microprocessor era. Inexpensive MIPS (millions of instructions per second) are now routinely exchanged for improved performance in other areas such as graphics and ease of use, making today's modern software possible. Transforming bandwidth into a surplus commodity will take a decade or more.

From Moore's law to Metcalfe's law. The economics of networks have replaced the economics of silicon as the principle industry driver. Moore's law that semiconductor density would double every eighteen to twenty-four months still holds true, but its preeminence has been replaced by what is now often referred to as Metcalfe's law, named after Bob Metcalfe, inventor of Ethernet and founder of 3Com. Metcalfe's law states that while the cost of a network expands linearly with increases in network size, the value of a network increases exponentially. Thus, as networks expand, they become dramatically more cost effective. The implications of Metcalfe's law are described later in this chapter.

From local to wide area networks. From a networking perspective, the 1980s were clearly the decade of the LAN, with Novell becoming the dominant local area network software player. Additionally, network interface cards and LAN servers, as well as LAN-based network routers and hubs emerged as important new hardware markets.

In the coming era, attention has clearly shifted away from internal company LANs to wide area network services, particularly the building of so-called Intranets, internal networks using both Internet technologies and the Internet infrastructure. The key competition is now between on-line network providers such as America On-line, Internet access companies such as UUNet, and increasingly the traditional telephone companies. On the software front, LAN companies such as Novell are trying to position the traditional Network Operating System (NOS) as the underlying foundation of an Intranet, while Microsoft and Netscape, among others, argue that given the power of their servers and application software a separate NOS is no longer required. In many ways, the Intranet provides a new and even higher stakes competition between the various generations of software technologies.

From graphical user interfaces to Internet browsers. Even the Windows interface itself is challenged by the new paradigm. Products such as Netscape's Navigator should be viewed as a window into the Internet. In this sense they are a direct challenge to the heart of Microsoft's power. The core, unique position of Microsoft has always been its direct intimacy with each machine and each user through the DOS and then Windows interface. As on-line activity accounts for a greater share of overall PC usage, the network browser might well take on much of this function. Microsoft's handling of the Internet and Netscape is a direct parallel to the situation that IBM faced in the early years of the PC business.

From indirect to on-line channels. The shift from the systems world to the PC era coincided with a major change in IT product distribution channels from a predominantly direct sales and services model to an increasingly indirect approach. In the network era, direct supplier sales and service will return, this time through on-line media. This will be particularly true for software as well as many forms of customer support. The extensive use of on-line freeware from Netscape, Sun, Adobe, and others is the most important new example of this change. On-line delivery will eventually spread into numerous other business sectors, especially those with a high information content. This last topic is explored in detail in the customer directions and on-line publishing chapters.

From a stand-alone product to a bundled service mentality. The PC era was characterized by discrete product sales. Increasingly, the network era will subordinate products to a higher value service offering. Internet terminals, ISDN adapters, cable modems, and CATV set top boxes will all likely be sold, at least initially, as part of a bundled service. This changed marketing emphasis will have profound implications for the way today's products are sold, used, and serviced.

From client/server to electronic commerce. Historically, computer systems have been mostly used to improve internal efficiencies through internal automation systems. As the network-centric era emerges, this emphasis will steadily shift toward an external focus. In this sense the current focus on Intranets can be seen as either a temporary diversion or perhaps the final phase of the traditional internal orientation. Future application priorities will involve connecting directly to customers, suppliers, and other important parties for sales, marketing, service, order processing, and other key applications. Current security issues will be overcome, and electronic commerce will emerge as one of the core applications of the Internet.

From individual productivity to virtual communities. One of the great benefits of the PC era was its empowerment of individuals and eventually small groups of people within a single enterprise, providing unprecedented tools and capabilities at affordable prices. This trend will surely continue. However, the main contribution of the network era in this regard will be to eliminate time, distance, and even organization barriers between people. This will lead to the establishment of countless virtual communities—groups and individuals with common interests, goals, or needs. These communities will exist primarily within the emerging cyberspace. Over time, their influence in business, the arts, the sciences, politics, religion, and other key societal domains is likely to be profound.

From a horizontal computer industry to a converged industry value chain. The structural changes in the network-centric era will exceed those of the PC revolution. Over the next fifteen years, today's separate computer, telecommunications, consumer electronics, and publishing/media industries will merge into an increasingly unified IT industry value chain. The markets for devices, software, transmission, and eventually content will be reshaped as today's overlapping markets are rationalized. As with the PC era, changes in underlying industry structure are likely to have the most profound effects on long-term global competition. This issue will be addressed at length in chapters 7 through 11.

From a global to a national industry center of gravity. Core PC products such as X86 microprocessors, Windows, Excel, Compaq PCs, and so on have all tended to be sold in similar ways for similar purposes all around the world. In the network-centric era, national infrastructures, national network services, and national content will lead to a much more multinational, multicultural industry orientation. This will greatly facilitate changes in global IT industry power as well as vendor sales and marketing strategies.

Using the Present to Fix the Past

Perhaps the final test of a true paradigm shift is whether the new order can solve the main problems of the previous era. Despite its many great successes, the PC era had its share of shortcomings. To cite just three: PCs are still too expensive for the mass market and for true ubiquity; PC technology is still far too complex for most consumers and arguably getting more so; and finally and perhaps most annoyingly, the constant need to upgrade both hardware and software is expensive, complicated, and contrary to a typical consumer product experience.

As will be explored in detail in the following chapters, the network-centric approach can, at least in theory, make significant progress in all three of these areas by moving cost and complexity away from the desktop and out toward the network. Internet terminals, longer PC product cycles, lower PC price points, and bundled network services will be the most important manifestations.

Perhaps even more important, the power of this third wave is now widely recognized both within and outside of the IT industry. In many ways, it is this deeply shared vision of where the technology is heading that has helped restore the IT industry's sense of mission. Ever since computers began to be used, there has been talk about building a wired world and a true information society. With the arrival of the Internet, the path toward that goal suddenly looks much more straightforward, tangible, and realistic. This shared vision is the source of both the industry's current unprecedented excitement and the accompanying but understandable levels of hype. It's easy to see why many would hope that, just as a turbocharged PC was, to many, an irresistible symbol for the individualistic 1980s, the Internet might come to embody the emergence of a more communal future.

Sources of Third Wave Power

Much of the power of the network-centric era comes from combining the unique economics of both software and networks as depicted in figure 6-3. Software economics are now well understood. Once developed, the marginal cost of an additional copy is that of a diskette, a CD-ROM, or, in the case of electronic distribution, nearly nothing at all. This results in virtually infinite supplier economies of scale, and an asymptotic average cost curve.

Calculating network economics is somewhat more complex but equally powerful. Through a concept that has come to be called Metcalfe's law, it can be easily shown that although the cost of expanding a network tends to increase linearly as additional nodes are added, the value of the network can increase exponentially. Consider the following simplified example that considers only the number of possible two-way network connections:

Figure 6-3. Software and network economics.

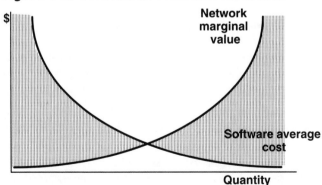

Number of Network Nodes	Number of Additional Two-Way Connections per Node Added	Incremental Network Cost per Node	Average Additional Value per Additional Node
2			
3	2	X	2/X
4	3	X	3/X
5	4	X	4/X
6	5	X	5/X
7	6	X	6/X
8	7	X	7/X
100	99	X	99/X
1000	999	X	999/X
1,000,000	999,999	X	999,999/X

Thus, the larger a network becomes, the more potential value it has, and the more units of software that are sold, the cheaper each unit theoretically can become. The two forces become mutually reinforcing, resulting in enormous value creation opportunities. From a broader social perspective, there is nothing new here. The principles of Metcalfe's law are much the same as those that drove the expansion of the telephone industry. However, from a computer industry perspective, network economics have emerged as a new and often overwhelming force.

The Internet—Why Now, Why So Strong?

Perhaps the most remarkable thing about the current period is not that computers and communications are merging. This after all had been predicted for decades. The most remarkable thing is the way it has all happened. Why has the main driving force, the Internet, sprung up so quickly and independently, indeed almost by accident—created, owned, and managed by essentially no one? Try to find any other industry whose center of gravity is so distant from the major players involved. This is a truly unique industry development, and the reasons behind this tell us much about the current period.

First, let's look at the easy part. Why has the Internet grown so suddenly? To help explain this, I will again draw on the concept of Metcalfe's law. Figure 6-4 shows the basic principles in graphical form, indicating that at some number of nodes, N, a network's value will exceed its cost. However, once that point is reached, the gap between costs and value can increase rapidly (and virtually infinitely) as the number of nodes increases. This appears to be the period the industry entered in 1994–1995.

Before the Internet, IT vendor network strategies left us in the shaded period. Telephone companies with mail services (such as MCI mail), on-line services (such as CompuServe), and computer messaging systems such as IBM Profs all had the same fundamental problem. Each limited their service offerings to their own subscriber universe, and thus each deliberately constrained the number of nodes on their networks and thereby greatly, if unwittingly, reduced their value. Frequently user requests to build links from one vendor's messaging system to another were generally ignored.

In effect, these vendors were doing what computer vendors had always done. They were building closed, proprietary, minicomputer-like systems that they could control. Unfortunately for customers and for the largely unprofitable on-line service vendors themselves, the value of networking required telephone-like interconnectivity or PC-like interoperability. Imagine if subscribers to MCI's long-distance ser-

Figure 6-4. Market effects of Metcalfe's law.

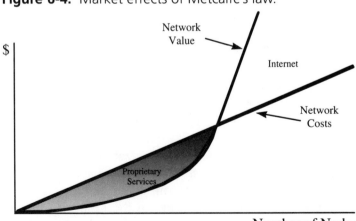

vices could call only other MCI customers. The idea just wouldn't sell, no matter how good the service.

This is why the wide area networking market and on-line services in particular moved disappointingly slowly in the 1980s even as the local area network market exploded. As the number of PCs in use continued to soar and as the value of email became more widely recognized, these largely artificial market constraints became increasingly bothersome. From a more positive perspective, enormous pent-up network demand was accumulating.

Enter the Internet

The history and evolution of the Internet have been recounted in detail many times. As a largely government-driven initiative, the early public record is quite clear. The following brief summary provides only the background needed for this book's purposes.

The roots of the Internet go back to 1969, when the U.S. Government's Advanced Research Projects Agency (ARPA) began to address the problem of maintaining computer communication in the event of nuclear war. Eventually, their networking research led to the development of ARPANET, an early packet-switched network that was originally used to link the diverse computers of government research sites, military facilities, and key military contractors.

By the early 1980s, after considerable and often heated debate and experimentation, Transmission Control Protocol/Internet Protocol (TCP/IP) had become the standard ARPANET communications software, eventually adopted by all computer vendors doing extensive U.S. defense-related business. Over time, the research needs of the military led to the inclusion of a number of key university sites as well.

Once the academic world started to enthusiastically use the network, the defense-only mentality steadily faded. By the mid-1980s, the U.S. Government's National Science Foundation had essentially taken over the old ARPANET, opening it up to basically any "noncommercial" purpose. Schools and research organizations quickly became by far the biggest users. A great deal of "free" information began to be stored on this growing network of computers.

Finding and sharing information on the network soon became a problem. In 1989, a major breakthrough occurred at CERN, the

European physics lab in Switzerland. For strictly internal convenience, Britain's Tim Berners-Lee developed the "hyperlink" technologies that helped tie together documents and sites in a weblike fashion. His work, of course, soon became the foundation of the Worldwide Web.

However, accessing this growing web of information required the mastery of many cryptic computer commands. In 1993, programmers at the University of Illinois, led by Marc Andreeson, developed an easy to use, graphical interface to the Worldwide Web, which they called Mosaic. Mosaic would do for the Internet what the Macintosh and eventually Microsoft Windows did for PCs.

By 1994, various versions of Mosaic (such as Netscape's Navigator) had become commercially available, dramatically improving mass market access to the Internet's full range of messaging, file transfer, and news group services. Demand for Internet access surged, and hundreds of new Internet Access Providers sprang up to make connection simple for any personal computer user. As the commercial market took off, the government slowly and quietly got out of the Internet backbone management business altogether. The third wave had clearly begun.

Demand for Internet connections soon spread to all of the on-line services vendors who could no longer resist the now overwhelming momentum. The TCP/IP protocol became a simple way of linking these large, existing on-line islands together. Once one email or on-line service provider began to offer an Internet gateway, the others had to quickly follow suit. This effectively broke the proprietary bottlenecks, allowing Metcalfe's law to kick in and the huge pent-up demand to be finally satisfied.

That so much could be done with such a relatively simple technology proves how natural computer communications really is. But, simple as the technology may be, the implications of the Internet are enormous, eventually leading to nothing less than the reinvention of the telephone system itself.

Key Lessons from the Early Days

In terms of this book's main themes of technology adoption, industry structure, and supplier market power, the history of the Internet is fundamentally different from that of the systems and PC eras. Consider that:

The Internet wasn't created by and isn't owned by any single vendor or group of vendors. The Internet Engineering Task Force (IETF) is as close to a governing body as currently exists, but its processes are informal and it does not control any company's actions. It can suggest, but it cannot guarantee a clear path forward. Its long-term effectiveness is likely to diminish greatly.

In other words, the historical IT industry pattern has been reversed. In the past, the computer business has always had strong leaders who set clear directions, and, because of their privileged position, these same leaders also made most of the money. With the Internet there is no clear leader and no one currently positioned to make an inordinate share of the profits. In short, industry power has almost overnight gone from being tightly controlled to being almost nonexistent. This inherently unstable situation will surely change.

Indeed, one of the great competitive questions going forward is whether the industry will go back to its old habits and allow certain vendors to dominate, trading off equity for leadership, or whether a new type of truly more open competition has arrived thanks to this largely accidental, one-time leveling of the playing field. This issue will be addressed at length in subsequent chapters.

Unlike the PC era, all of the key enabling innovations—packet-switching, TCP/IP, Worldwide Web, Mosaic—came from the government and university communities and are therefore available at little or no cost. Future innovations, such as Java, 3-D imaging, audio, video, and so on, will of course come from the private sector. The era of public sector leadership and stewardship is over. This transition will coincide with the establishment of new power bases.

The government provided initial seed funding but has now fully turned the business over to the private sector, thus far without any obvious effect. In a time of much government criticism, all of this was done remarkably smoothly. The overall role and contributions of government are the subject of chapter 15.

The Internet is not just a computer industry phenomenon. The telecommunications, media, and eventually consumer electronics industries will also be heavily involved. In particular, the computer and telecommunications industries both see the Internet as "their issue." Converging industries will be introduced in chapter 7 and discussed in detail in chapters 8 through 11.

In sum, we have already seen how so much of the defining characteristics of both the systems and PC eras can be traced back to their earliest beginnings. In the end, it was the drive of Thomas Watson, Sr., that defined the way the systems business would work and the Pandora's box effects of IBM PC strategy that determined so much of the PC era. Similarly, it is the unique roots of the Internet that will shape global competition in the network-centric era. As with the PC era, the network-centric era will once again bring about its own changes in the very structure of the information technology industry.

CHAPTER 7

TOWARD A CONVERGED INDUSTRY VALUE CHAIN

As was discussed at length in chapter 2, one of the great changes of the PC era was the movement toward a horizontal industry value chain. It was this change in underlying industry structure that helped overturn both the previous generation of suppliers and the global balance of IT market power. As the following chapters show, even more traumatic structural transformation will occur during the network-centric era, challenging the global supplier hierarchy once again.

For more than a decade, industry observers have been talking about convergence among the 4 Cs—computers, communications, consumer electronics, and content using graphics (shown in figure 7-1). Until recently, however, most of this discussion proved to be frustratingly premature, with each industry making few inroads into the other despite many high profile attempts by industry leaders such as IBM, AT&T, Sony, Time-Warner, and others.

Ironically, just as many were getting tired of waiting for or even talking about industry convergence, along comes the Internet, which for the first time demonstrated exactly what convergence was, why it was important, and how quickly it could come.

Stripped of all the hype, what is the Internet, other than the merger of computer and telephony industries? What is the cable modem or cable set top box other than the early signs of a merger of the computer with the cable TV and consumer electronics business? Finally, and perhaps most important, what is the Worldwide Web other than the first great manifestation of the intersection of computers, telecommunications, and content? Just as it has with convergence, the Web has also given real meaning to the another term of the late 1980s and early 1990s—*multimedia.*

It is, of course, digital technology that has brought these sectors together. All four industries are increasingly based around the idea of using ones and zeros to encode their information. In contrast, just a few years ago only the computer business was truly digital; the others were primarily using either analog or physical media formats. Today, as all four increasingly come to share a common digital foundation,

Figure 7-1. Changing IT industry structure.

<table>
<tr><td>**Vertically
Integrated**</td><td>**Horizontal
Computer
Industry**</td><td>**Converging
Information
Industries**</td></tr>
</table>

these sectors can now interact in a way that simply wasn't possible before.

Given the vast differences in structure and leadership between these industries, it should not be surprising that the convergence process is proving and will continue to prove chaotic—with joint ventures coming and going and much talk about major mergers and acquisitions. After all, one could hardly find four industries with such different structures and patterns of leadership.

Consider that the computer industry is largely unregulated and dominated by U.S. vendors. The telecommunications business is heavily regulated and dominated by national, often government-controlled carriers. The consumer electronics industry is largely unregulated but dominated by Japanese or other Asian companies. Finally, there is the content, or media, business that is sometimes regulated and sometimes not, with both strong global players, mostly based in the United States, and strong local country players as well. About the only thing the four sectors have in common is that they are all large, highly visible, and fiercely competitive. Additionally, all four seem to believe that the changes of the coming era will work to their own industry's advantage. In a competitive market, this seems unlikely.

The Internet is the first real manifestation of this convergence. The Internet was developed and built by the computer industry (with government support and direction), but it largely runs over the existing telephone network and works much like an asynchronous version of the telephone system. Much of the content currently on the Internet comes from the traditional publishing and media industries, who see this as a natural extension of their established broadcast activities. Finally, the consumer electronics companies, having missed most of the PC market, see the Internet as a second, and perhaps last, opportunity to get into the computer business—whether it be through cable set top boxes, Internet appliances, video game upgrades, smart phones, or PCs themselves.

The next several chapters examine the interplay of these sectors. In particular, the probability of a converged information industry value chain is assessed and forecasted. One of the key premises of this book is that if the eventual structure of the industry can be ascertained, it becomes much simpler to understand the implications for users, suppliers, and other interested parties. Understanding the likely industry structure is also the first step in identifying potential leverage points and other sources of industry market power. The next few chapters are designed to show why the structural changes now beginning will over a ten-year period prove to be at least as significant as the shift from the vertical to the horizontal model in the 1980s.

A Converged IT Value Chain—What Is It?

From a structural perspective, this book's main hypothesis is that over the next decade or so, the four key industries—computers, communications, consumer electronics, and content using graphics—will be restructured in a manner that smoothes away many of today's market and competitive overlaps. The result will be an eventual clarity of market segmentation equivalent to that which exists within each of the individual industries today. One could then draw a simple chart showing the key industry segments, their underlying business models, and how they relate to one another in terms of a functioning overall supplier value chain. Given the many existing overlaps and discontinuities that exist today, such a model clearly does not currently exist and will likely become even more difficult to describe in the short term.

From a practical perspective, knowing where the overall industry structure is heading can be very helpful in understanding and interpreting current issues and challenges. The market's daily turmoil can be viewed against the backdrop of the movement toward a converged industry value chain. From a supplier perspective, companies can more accurately position themselves and define appropriate segmentations. This can be critical in understanding which companies are potential competitors and which potential allies. Historically, neighboring positions on the industry value chain have been where the most important developments have occurred.

Because this restructuring should, according to theory, run concurrently with the network-centric era, the model should have a useful life of at least ten years. Ideally, the converged value chain theory will prove as useful in understanding and forecasting this third industry wave as the movement to a horizontal model was in analyzing the second wave. Figure 7-2 provides a simple picture of what such a chain might someday look like.

It is critical to realize that, overall, a horizontal IT industry structure will be maintained. The hardware, software, transmission services,

Figure 7-2. Establishing a converged, horizontal structure.

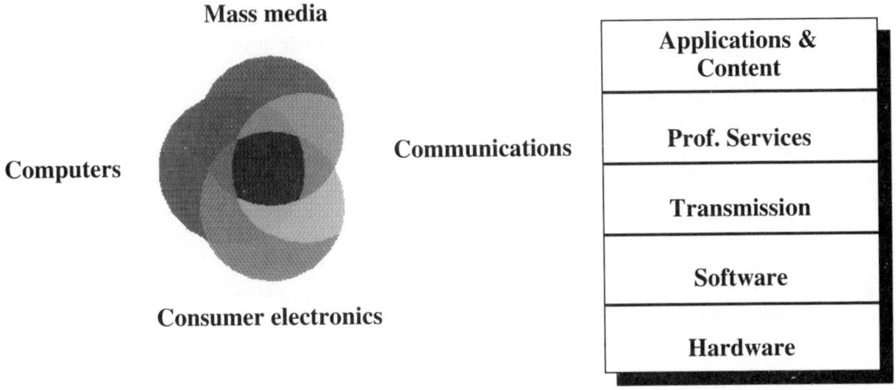

professional services, and content businesses will remain largely separate. What is different is that within each of these five broad categories elements of each of the 4 Cs will overlap, compete, merge, and eventually be rationally structured. It is this process of creating a new converged horizontal structure that will define the information technology industry evolution of the early twenty-first century.

The issues in terms of developing a converged structure for each level of the emerging industry value chain are outlined in the following sections. Subsequent chapters will address the implications of this shift for the hardware, software, and telecommunications services industries along with their likely effects on IT supplier market power and the global competitiveness of nations. The brief discussion that follows, and is summarized in figure 7-3, is primarily designed to flesh out the overall concept and to provide a sense of the enormous stakes involved.

A Converged Hardware Market

There are two main areas of possible convergence: end user devices and backbone network equipment. The former has certainly attracted most of the publicity.

Even the general public has been blanketed by discussions regarding the potential integration of PCs, smart TVs, cable set top boxes, so-called network computers, smart phones, PDAs, and potentially VCRs, CD players, and stereos. This convergence is finally hap-

Figure 7-3. Layers of a converged industry value chain.

Content & Applications	Information, entertainment, transactions
Professional Services	Consulting design, implementation, maintenance, operation
Transmission Services	Twisted pair, fiber, cable, satellite, wireless
Software	Operating systems, tools, utilities, routing directory, security, network management
Hardware	Input, output, display, processing, datacom, etc.

pening. Established vendors such as Gateway and Compaq have shown interest in bringing the Internet experience into the family entertainment room. Perhaps more important, start-ups such as WebTV are already bridging the gap between the Internet and the television. Content providers are clearly anticipating increased device integration. Be it the Olympics, the political conventions, or the daily news, the connections between television and the Web are rapidly rising.

The network equipment story has understandably received less attention and publicity. To date there has not been much of a convergence story. Computer vendors have built the modems, routers, switches, and hosts that drive the Internet, while the telephone industry has provided the handsets, PBXs, and central office switches that support voice telephone services.

However, with the arrival of Digital Simultaneous Voice Data (DSVD) modems, ISDN adapters, cable modems, Internet voice telephony, and in the future hybrid real-time/packet-switched systems, Internet broadcast capabilities, and other important new technologies, the distinction between computer and telephone networking gear will steadily erode. Additionally, as data traffic begins to dwarf voice transmission volumes by orders of magnitude, the traditional voice communications equipment vendors will have little choice but to attempt to dominate in the larger and faster growing data side of the business.

A Converged Software Market

There are two main aspects of software industry convergence, one of which has attracted far more attention than the other.

First, some terminology must be clarified. Throughout this book, the word *software* is used primarily to refer to specific computer programs—operating systems, tools, applications, interfaces, protocols, and so on. It is generally not used to refer to what this book labels *content*—music, video, text. Software consists of a set of instructions; content revolves around some form of information, be it text, images, sound, video, or a combination thereof.

Historically, from an analytical perspective, it has generally been a good idea to assess software and content separately whenever possible, since the two businesses often have some fundamentally different market characteristics. Software markets tend to be broadly horizontal in nature, whereas content markets, although sometimes broad, are often quite fragmented and highly driven by individual consumer tastes. Software markets tend to have monopoly leaders; content markets do not.

However, on the Web, and increasingly in the converged industry that is evolving, some of this distinction will break down. There will continue to be many areas where program instructions and information content will be clearly separate, but there will also increasingly be many times, especially in interactive applications, when the program instructions and the content itself will be so interwoven as to be essentially one. Microsoft, among others, often uses the phrase "rich content" to describe this new information form. It is a useful phrase signaling a new information form.

This new form implies new competition. Who should develop rich content—existing software vendors, existing content companies, a joint venture between a software and a content company such as that between Microsoft and NBC? Or will new rich content start-ups emerge to take on the established players? Convergence will clearly restructure much of the industry.

While the issue of rich content has attracted the same sort of media attention that the PC/network computer/set top box discussion has in the hardware segment, as with hardware, equally tumultuous changes will likely take place behind the scenes as the software that manages the overall network infrastructure experiences its own version of convergence.

While the importance of computer software companies and the major content providers is easily understood, it is often forgotten just how much software has been created to drive the global telephony industry. Consider the extent to which current computer software deals with structuring information—user names, directory services, addresses, updating procedures, security, metering, billing, and so on. These are also all critical and well-established functions of our current telecommunications system. For many years, the telephony industry has invested heavily in network software that will very much overlap with future computer network management software, particularly as integrated voice/data applications and complex payment, billing, and security systems start to emerge.

Once again, as user applications converge, competition will change. Whereas the computer industry has thus far dominated the software discussions in forums such as the Internet Engineering Task Force, as the telephone companies begin to become major Internet access providers they will bring their software know-how and ambitions with them.

A Converged Transmission Services Market

This is likely to be the biggest change of all. As described in chapter 6, one of the major technical goals of the network-centric era will be to transform bandwidth from a scarce to a surplus commodity in a manner analogous to what the microprocessor did for computer processing power. Intel was, of course, the great beneficiary of this change. However, as will be explored in chapter 11, no one company will dominate the bandwidth industry (at least not in the United States). It is not surprising that many will try.

Internet access providers, on-line service companies, cable companies, and most important, the regional and long-distance phone companies have all grown up separately, performing different functions for particular sets of customers. Over the next few years, the overlaps will greatly increase as all of these vendors begin to carry voice, audio, video, graphics, and text-based information. The competitive situation is further complicated by critical but often unresolved regulatory environments in many countries, although the recent major telecom reforms in the United States should prove to be a big step forward.

As voice becomes a more important part of the Internet, telephone companies that continue to miss out on the Internet market will do so at their own peril. Similarly, as the Internet begins to require faster transmission speeds for graphics and video, the cable network also becomes a real threat to the access provider and telephone businesses. Competition, mergers, and acquisitions will all be part of the rationalization process.

This process will likely vary greatly by country. But one outcome is almost certain. Since communications bandwidth is now the critical industry bottleneck, telecommunications companies will move to center stage in terms of moving the industry forward. Computer companies accustomed to leading the technology industry are in for a harsh awakening.

A Converged Professional Services Market

Since services markets are the least dependent on particular technologies, this segment tends to be the industry's most stable, a pattern likely to hold true through the network-centric era. Most professional services firms will need to learn the new skills of the network era, and of course some will do this better than others. But much of the current business services industry model will remain intact. There will continue to be independent consultants, value-added resellers mostly serving small and medium-size customers, and systems integrators working mostly with large corporations and government agencies.

However, there is one area of potentially significant change. Although historically it has generally been useful to distinguish "professional services" (consulting, programming, system integration) from "communications services" (mainly analog and digital transmission), over the next decade some convergence will happen here in a manner analogous to the "rich content" discussion above.

To meet their customer's requirements, large processing services firms (those companies that actually provide computer processing services as part of their service offerings) will be drawn ever deeper into the networking business. This is already the case for EDS, IBM, and MCI today.

As these companies are currently structured, networking services will continue to require large infrastructure investments that may be difficult to justify solely for their own internal usage. This may well necessitate partnerships with some of the major network carriers. EDS has been looking at this issue for some time, thus far without results. However, eventually some significant linkages between telecommunications and professional services firms are likely. Communications services and professional services will always be markets sufficiently distinct to support many separate vendors, but a number of companies are likely to try to participate in both. It's an optional but interesting opportunity.

A Converged Content and Applications Market

The evolution of the content industry was discussed earlier in regard to the increasing role of the software industry and will be discussed in more detail in chapter 16. At this point it is sufficient to note the obvious—television, music, newspapers, magazines, sports, and all other forms of entertainment are coming together on the Internet using the same mix of multimedia technologies. Products that are completely different in their native media all tend to look alike on the Internet. Already, the movement of talent between different media is becoming commonplace. Consider the highly regarded political commentator Michael Kinsley moving from print (*New Republic*) to television (CNN) to a Web-based magazine (*Slate,* owned by Microsoft).

The network-centric era will also restructure the content business via the effects of sheer volume. In the past, content delivery was greatly limited by channel issues. There were only so many TV and radio licenses, and the cost of putting out a newspaper or magazine was considerable. The Web offers virtually limitless digital spectrum, and by stripping out printing, postage, and distribution costs, it greatly lowers the barriers to entry. The result, of course, will be an enormous increase in content creation, much of it being given away for marketing and advertising reasons.

Thus, today's content creators face heightened competition from other content providers that previously relied on different media; they will also face competition from entirely new providers of all shapes and sizes. The emergence of multimedia players and products along with new rules for subscriptions, advertising, and editorial customs will result in a radically restructured global content industry.

Assessing the Market Opportunities

IT industry history suggests that each wave of industry expansion tends to be bigger and more powerful than the last. This is ironic since for first PCs and now the Internet much of the conventional wisdom has focused on how small the current business is. Just as many once said there is no money in PCs, the same words are now said about the Internet and the Web.

As the number of users and the range of technology applications swell and as consumer electronics, telecommunications, and even content spending become available to the IT marketplace the potential size of the business is almost unimaginable. Substantial new opportunities exist within each of the major parts of the converging industry value chain. The evolution of each sector is analyzed at length in subsequent chapters.

Hardware

Although there will always be cyclical patterns to the hardware business, growth rates should continue to stay strong through the network-centric era. On the computer side, one can expect that within the next five years the great majority of all businesses within developed nations will have one or more servers connected to the Web. This implies worldwide server sales in the tens of millions. Today, most of these servers are based on either Intel or Sun platforms, although IBM, HP, and Digital all have a share. Specific vendor hardware success over the next few years will likely be tied to the operating systems competition.

Communications hardware sales should be equally if not more robust. Certainly, the near term outlook for fast 28K modems is outstanding. However, modem technology seems likely to top out at about 56K bits per second, still far too slow for many graphics and multimedia applications. This is opening up demand for ISDN adapters, which operate much like a digital modem, but can offer up to 128K bps that can also be split between multiple voice and data applications. ISDN speeds are also sufficient for low-quality video transmission.

For high-quality video, much faster speeds are required. The most likely candidate for this today is the cable modem, which allows a direct connection between a PC and a cable TV network, offering speeds up to 10 megabits per second, nearly a thousand times faster than typical modem speeds today. Cable modem products will be in the market during the late 1996–1997 time frame. If the cable companies can in fact successfully integrate this technology, they could revolutionize the Web. Countries with large cable TV infrastructures—such as the United States and Germany—will have a big edge over

those that do not—such as France and Japan. However, cable companies have a tremendous amount of preparation to do, so the overall
rate of migration will likely be slow. ADSL, which hopes to deliver
high bandwidth over existing copper wires, is another, though less
likely, possibility.

All of the communication equipment sales relate to increasing
the speed of the end user connection, and this will clearly be the communications industry's primary area of focus. But while this investment will be highly visible, tremendous investments will also be made
in the backbone network switching systems, which will continue to be
expanded and upgraded at an aggressive rate. As network transmission volumes soar, the demand for ever faster network switching gear
seems certain. However, the basic underlying fiber backbone's capacity can be expanded relatively easily, making this the first area of surplus bandwidth capacity.

Software

Opportunities on the software front are equally exciting. The 1996
public offering that eventually valued tiny Netscape at as much as $7
billion shocked many observers, but it is representative of the huge
software opportunities expected. The unique, largely infinite scale
economies make Netscape uniquely positioned to capitalize on the
upcoming mass market era. The potential for profits is extraordinary.

As mentioned above, sales of server system software and related
tools in the tens of millions of units are likely, with Microsoft, Netscape, and various freeware offerings such as Apache being the main
players today. Virtually all of these servers will also need so-called
firewall security and encryption software. At a desktop level, the numbers get much larger. Consider that within just a few years, virtually
every PC will have a network browser and probably related search,
email, and eventually encryption software. This implies literally hundreds of millions and eventually even billions of copies and upgrades.
This is one reason why giving away browsers today makes perfect
sense.

Similar numbers are possible for languages. Sun's Java has been
the prominent example of a programming language suited for the
Web; it allows applications and data to be transmitted together to
any device that runs the Java language, greatly increasing applications
portability and developer freedom. Again, it's possible for products

such as Java to be sold, either directly or as part of a bundled offering, in the hundreds of millions of units. Much talked about software agents that provide additional specific customer services are farther off in the future but clearly hold great long-term promise.

Network Services

The simple task of getting people connected remains an enormous opportunity. Consider that today, roughly one-third of U.S. households have a PC and about 50 percent of those have a modem. However, many of these modems are not used very much if at all. In fact, by the end of 1995 there were only about 6 million U.S. homes connected to the Internet or any kind of on-line service. Since there are roughly 100 million U.S. households, this means that only some 6 percent of U.S. homes are on-line today, and the United States is the world leader. Clearly, the connectivity era has really just begun.

Today, typical Internet access charges average about $10 to $20 per month. Although basic access prices will fall, the addition of higher performance cable or ISDN services should be sufficient to keep average prices relatively stable. As the number of users grows into the hundreds of millions, the Internet access market (or more likely, its next phase of development) will easily generate billions of dollars in annual revenue.

Professional Services

The five professional services categories listed in figure 4-5—consulting, design, implementation, operations, and outsourcing—are not coincidentally the same types of opportunities that defined the professional services business in the PC era. In other words, for services firms, the Internet is really just another issue, another opportunity, just as mainframes, PCs, and LANs were in their day.

This business model continuity is by no means meant to diminish the scale of the market opportunity. Consider that as early as January 1995, IDC research showed that roughly 25 percent of all companies with more than two hundred fifty employees were looking to hire Internet-related expertise. The inevitable personnel shortages will prove a boon to services firms set up to leverage such skills.

Services firms also tend to prosper during times of high confusion. Given the many uncertainties regarding Internet strategies, designs, and implementation, the market for consulting type services should remain strong. Indeed, a running industry joke is that during the early years of the Internet, the consultants, the venture capital firms, and companies who have had their initial public offering (IPO) have been the only ones making any real money at all.

From a longer term perspective, the outsourcing market looks especially intriguing. Consider that in the future many businesses will exist totally in cyberspace. If the management of these network-based businesses is outsourced, the services firms essentially run the businesses on behalf of their owners. This creates the quite real possibility that many small, medium, or even large companies could be built that have very few actual employees, another example of the increasing leverage characterized by the network era.

Content

As noted in the introduction, it is the author's view that the real content revolution will not come until after a ubiquitous network infrastructure has been put into place. Much of what is being done today is merely migrating existing content onto the on-line media. As often as not, the results have been disappointing.

Nevertheless, on-line content is already and will continue to be a critical part of this third wave value chain. The list of existing and planned content offerings is well known and expanding. Among the most prominent are news, information, sports, entertainment, shopping, investing, voting, gambling, on-line experts such as lawyers and doctors, and special interest topics of all variety.

Today, this business is largely running at a loss. However, advertising revenues on the Web have begun to grow quickly and will be the largest source of Web funding over the next few years. With so much free content and service available, content subscription revenues have been hard to develop, but in the end there is only so much advertising available. Expect for-fee content to begin to gain momentum in 1997–1998.

The Movement Toward a Converged Industry Value Chain

In sum, major progress toward a converged IT value chain seems highly likely over the next decade. This is by no means meant to imply a complete market integration. Just as technologies integrate, they also can fragment, and there will always be highly specialized products and services. After all, the old vertical model still lives on fifteen years after the horizontal movement began. The important lesson of the past is that early alignment with the dominant new structural trend is likely to prove to be a critical success factor.

Indeed, another great lesson of the past is that the stakes are often higher than generally understood. Competitive systems usually produce clear winners and losers. Despite much talk about mainframe, minicomputer, and PC coexistence, in the end, the horizontal model either humbled or eliminated just about all of the old vertical players. This next wave of change should be expected to do the same thing. In other words, not all the existing players will successfully make the transition.

Ten years from now, in contrast to today's world of separate, highly successful cable, telephone, Internet, and on-line service companies, there will be some dominant broad-based network transmission providers and some surviving legacy specialists. Similarly, a decade from now, it is unlikely that American PC companies and Japanese consumer electronics companies will coexist so nicely in the home. One or the other or perhaps some new players altogether will have gotten the clear upper hand. The next few chapters will try to forecast the most likely scenarios for this long-term structural movement.

But It All Takes Time

Without trying to downplay the current excitement, it is critical to keep in mind that these changes will take a long time to fully emerge. Even though the paradigm is shifting away from the PC-centric world, it is this existing PC business industry that will be paying the IT industry's bills for at least the rest of the century. The actual current spending on Internet-related products and services remains a tiny fraction of the global IT marketplace. As was the case with PCs, it will likely take from five to ten years for the full economic power of the new era to emerge.

Consider that it was not until 1990 that the worldwide PC hardware business equaled that of the supposedly long obsolete mainframe and minicomputer businesses. Even today, in terms of revenues, the

mainframe software business is still larger than the PC software industry. Perhaps more ominous, during the systems to PC era transition,
the overall IT market performance was often weak, especially in the
1985–1991 period in the United States. This seven-year stretch exhibited a "death valley" syndrome. Despite rapid growth, the new PC
market was still too small to carry the overall industry. However, interest in PCs was sufficient to stall or eliminate much mainframe and
minicomputer spending. The result was an extended period of single
digit U.S. market growth that didn't end until 1992.

The health of the existing PC-centric businesses is especially relevant to this particular paradigm shift. In its early days, the PC industry existed largely independent of the existing mainframe and
minicomputer companies, creating a false sense of system vendor security. In contrast, PCs are the critical access devices to the Internet.
A growing PC industry is very much in the overall Internet industry's interests.

More broadly, because of the impact of industry convergence, the
entire issue of forecasting overall market growth will become greatly
complicated. All of the data presented in chapter 5 was for the traditional computer hardware, software, and services industries. Clearly,
by the end of the network era, such measures will be inadequate.
Spending on various transmission services, new network access devices, and even content itself will need to be included in order to accurately assess the full IT opportunity.

In this sense, over the next decade, the information industry will
grow at an unprecedented rate as analog, paper, and other media are
transformed into part of the digital domain. This growth won't always
reflect new customer spending, but it will nevertheless present a real
opportunity for suppliers of various IT products and services. In other
words, whereas most of the growth in the PC era came from new IT
investments, in the next decade, there will be two main drivers. As
devices and services proliferate, incremental growth will continue. In
addition, the convergence of today's computer industry with other
major industry sectors will provide a second even more powerful push.
Taken together, the expansion of the IT industry over the next decade
should equal or even exceed that of the PC era.

Chapter 8
Applications Drive Structure

The applications available for today's Internet and future network infrastructures will be as diverse and complex as society itself. More than any other aspect, applications determine technology's popularity and use. They also simultaneously shape its development and influence the willingness of private firms to make investments. Applications also vary greatly in their demands upon network bandwidth and software complexity. It is this interplay between desired applications, their technological requirements, and related supplier business strategies which will drive much of the network-centric era.

From the very beginnings of the personal computer market, two applications—word processing and spreadsheets—provided the clear utility necessary to trigger rapid growth. They were soon joined by a handful of additional functions—graphics, desktop publishing, and database management—that provided a relatively complete set of personal productivity tools. By the mid-1980s, these individual packages began to be supplemented with various group-oriented programs, first local area networks that allowed print and file sharing, then email and fax, and finally sophisticated database sharing and groupware products such as Lotus Notes.

Although this history is now so clear as to seem obvious, it is worth remembering that during the 1980s there was often considerable debate about what PCs would actually be used for or where PCs would go "beyond spreadsheets," to use a then common phrase. As the network-centric era emerges, once again there has been active discussion about what will be the driving application of the Internet and what the overall rollout of applications will look like.

Although the applications focus of the coming era will clearly be completely different than in the PC era, once again we will likely see a pattern of a few applications being sufficient to drive the early years of the market. Over time these initial functions will be supplemented by increasingly sophisticated tasks. Whereas it is impossible to predict precisely what these new applications will be, it is relatively easy to describe the basic types of applications that are likely to emerge and endure. As this chapter shows, each of these types will have their own implications for the structure and evolution of the IT industry.

Classifying Network-Centric Applications

There are basically four major users of computer network services—businesses, consumers, governments, and educational institutions. Although today, much of the industry's attention is rightly focused on the huge business and potentially huge consumer markets, the role of government and educational organizations in the evolution of the networking industry has been critical, and it would be a mistake to believe that this influence has suddenly come to an end. This is particularly true for the U.S. university community, within much of Europe, and in other countries with an activist public sector, such as Singapore. A specific analysis on the changing role of government is provided in chapter 15.

Figure 8-1 provides a representative list of typical network applications for three of the four main user groups. The five categories—messaging, information access and retrieval, transaction processing, audio, and video—can either individually or in combination define the great majority of significant applications. Within figure 8-1, they are also listed in rough order of both likely market timing and bandwidth requirements. In addition, each application category tends to have its own set of technological demands, allowing this simple classification scheme to help define the necessary network infrastructure. Each of the five main application categories and their inherent technological requirements are described in the following sections.

Electronic Mail

In the United States at least, market analysts and many IT suppliers often use the phrase "killer application," or more commonly "killer app," to describe the search for a single application that can drive a broad new market in a manner similar to that of word processing and spreadsheets. (Given the violence in today's society, many, including the author, find this to be an unfortunate expression; however, it is in such wide use and describes such an important function that it is a difficult phrase to avoid or ignore.)

As with PCs, there are once again two "killer apps"—email and the Worldwide Web. These applications account for the great majority of traffic on today's Internet. Indeed, development of an essentially public domain email system is still, at least arguably, the Internet's

Figure 8-1. Network-centric application taxonomy and examples.

	Business	Consumer	Government
Messaging	E-mail/forms	E-mail/chat	E-mail
Information Access	Search/retrieval	Education/training	Info distribution
Transactional	Electronic commerce	Shopping/banking	Voting/taxes
Audio	Industry news	Audio-on-demand	Speeches
Video	Events/presentations, customer service	Video-on-demand, video publishing	Speeches, citizen service

single most important industry and social contribution. Pervasive e-mail for the first time demonstrated the potential for a telephone-like utility. Additionally, it was the desire to be able to send and receive Internet email and the potential embarrassment of not being able to that spurred many individuals and organizations to obtain their initial Internet access.

From an industry perspective, delivering global email was a relatively small step. The PCs were in place, and standard telephone lines and existing modems were more than adequate. The main steps needed were in software, principally the TCP/IP protocol and the necessary naming and directory issues. It remains the case that virtually the entire world could be linked through an email system without any great changes in existing technologies. As with word processing in the PC era, the most widely appealing and perhaps most important and ubiquitous application turns out to have relatively small technology requirements. Even more evolved forms of email such as chat rooms and other discussion groups require relatively little new technology and bandwidth.

Information Access and Retrieval

Whereas email has provided the biggest initial utility, the information access and retrieval capabilities of the Worldwide Web have caused the early excitement and mass awareness. In this sense the Web is playing a role analogous to that of spreadsheets in the PC era. Whether it was Visicalc or Lotus 1-2-3, spreadsheet products consistently generated more fascination and cachet than word processing ever could or did, despite much higher overall word processor usage levels. Similarly, although far more people have access to the Net's email capabilities than to the Worldwide Web (although this gap is clearly closing), it is the Web that has captured the hearts and minds of the world IT community.

Information access and retrieval accounts for the great majority of traffic on the Worldwide Web. The majority of Web sites are designed to essentially deliver information to whomever asks for it. Overall interaction between site visitors is usually quite limited, often impossible. There may be a thousand people simultaneously accessing a popular site, but the only way an individual visitor would know this is by the slowness of the response. So-called MUD (Multi-User Domain, originally Dungeon) technologies may eventually allow interaction of this sort.

Although, like email, most of the early years of the Web have been based on existing technologies, this has proved to be problematic with the Web. The steadily increasing use of graphics on the Web has already pushed traditional modem technology beyond its limits. Many Web users have become frustrated at the long processing delays even with top-of-the-line 28K devices. Since many of these graphics have little or no practical purpose, there has been a real backlash among consumers, many of whom would gladly accept a text-only site in exchange for the faster response times it would offer.

Nevertheless, given the desire to build attractive sites, the trend toward increasing Web graphics will almost certainly prevail, pushing many applications beyond what modem technology can adequately manage. In contrast, today's 14K or 28K modems should remain perfectly adequate for text-based email systems for the foreseeable future.

This divergence is compounded by the fact that many businesses will have access to much faster T-1 or higher Internet connections. This has put the Web community into a bit of a bind. Should a company design a site for high bandwidth customers and effectively snub consumers who only have a modem connection? Or does it address the entire market but thereby leave out certain bandwidth intensive features? For those seeking a middle ground, is it even possible to cost effectively design hybrid sites that can optimally serve both customer bases?

In short, the Web provides the IT industry's first clear example of how communications bandwidth has already become *the* driver of the IT industry. In the search for new consumer bandwidth, the critical technologies are ISDN, ADSL, and cable modems. The first two are largely within the domain of the telephone companies, the third clearly not. These issues will be discussed in more detail in chapter 11. At this stage it is sufficient to note that be it phone or cable companies that eventually deliver the bandwidth, it needs to be recognized and understood that this crucial part of the advancement of the Web is largely out of the computer industry's hands.

Although, as the subsequent discussions on transaction processing and audio and video support will show, the computer business clearly has plenty of Web-centric work to keep it busy, it is fair to say that, with the arrival of the Web, the existing computer hardware and software companies have begun to lose control over the overall pace of industry advancement.

Transaction Processing

Just as local area networks brought the PC industry into an entirely new era, transaction processing should prove to be the next great frontier for the Internet. Once the Net can reliably handle electronic commerce between businesses and consumers, its overall impact on society will greatly increase. Whereas messaging and information access define today's Internet, transaction processing should emerge as the major new application category over the 1998–1999 period.

Some of the major possible types of transaction processing are shown in figure 8-1. Predicting which of these will be most successful is all but impossible. However, since their underlying technology requirements are often similar, the impact of increased Internet-driven transaction processing on the IT industry should prove predictable.

Compared to messaging applications, transaction processing systems clearly have higher requirements for response times, security, reliability, and auditability. A reservation system must be able to change or confirm transactions instantaneously, and obviously all monetary transactions need to have special security and data integrity arrangements.

These are features not historically associated with the Internet or other public on-line services. For some twenty years, major banks and insurance companies have invested heavily in building secure, on-line transaction processing systems. They are understandably reluctant to expose these systems to the relatively open world of the Internet. However, the potential for cost savings and expanded market access is too great to ignore. This is driving the strong demand for technologies such as password protection, data encryption, and digital signatures. Once these capabilities are in place, entrepreneurs and consumers will determine what can and cannot be sold electronically.

Thus, unlike the Web, the key technological requirements for transaction processing will have little to do with increasing bandwidth. Rather, they will have to with the Internet's ability to evolve in a manner that produces levels of reliability, response times, and data integrity comparable to traditional on-line transaction processing expectations. In this sense, there is yet another parallel to the LAN phase of the PC industry. LANs were often assessed in terms of their ability to match the functionality and reliability of older, usually mini-computer-based approaches.

The requirement to build a high integrity transaction processing capable Internet has three main components: the network, the software, and business oversight.

Network Integrity

Here the most obvious requirement is for reliability. Internet "brown-outs" or even total losses of service for extended periods are unacceptable if serious transaction processing systems are to be built. The Internet's challenge is to become as reliable as the telephone system. A second problem is response time. The Internet's underlying packet-switched approach is inherently less predictable than a system using direct, real-time, or virtual circuit approaches.

A predictable consequence of the need to offer transaction processing services will be that the very small Internet access providers that still provide the majority of U.S. consumer Internet services are likely to be even further squeezed. As the world moves toward one of increasingly wired consumers, having small, inherently unstable businesses within the network system will likely prove unacceptable. A big corporation trying to reach its customers nationwide wants to be able to deal with other big organizations should any problems occur. In short, transaction processing will bring big business to the Net, and in this world the Internet's decentralized, grass-roots network structure will no longer be appropriate. This restructuring has, of course, already begun, but the demand to build and use serious transaction processing systems should help complete the process.

Software Integrity

Just as one of the great accomplishments of the PC era was the establishment of a functioning horizontal industry value chain, one of the great challenges for the coming era is to build a fully functional network software infrastructure through the Web's open systems culture. Transaction processing software touches on most of the critical areas:

security, authentication, encryption, database updating, transaction acceptance or denial, and so on.

History suggests that unless a multivendor approach can generate this sort of system integrity, eventually a single vendor solution will emerge. Chapter 10 examines this issue and forecasts that this time the multivendor approach is likely although not certain to prevail.

However, history also reminds us that that just about everything being said about Internet security today was said about credit cards in their early days. Perhaps more important is that even today's credit cards are not particularly secure. However, they are secure enough that the merchants and credit card companies are willing to absorb the cost of any misuse. Once consumers are confident that any problems with their transactions will be borne by some other party, they will feel confident using the new systems. Until then, why should they?

Business Oversight

Although the antiregulatory culture of the Net has generally made important and positive contributions, once money begins to be exchanged new levels of government oversight will be required. Reasonable protection against fraud and tax evasion will have to emerge. If new forms of exchange such as digital cash and smart cards catch on, a whole new level of monetary supervision will be required. As businesses begin to exist solely within cyberspace, issues of regulation and jurisdiction will inevitably emerge. Until these new institutions and practices emerge, the potential for abuse, confusion, and anxiety will be high.

Thus, there are two highly likely structural implications of the forecasted rise in transaction processing: a more concentrated and tightly managed network service infrastructure and a steadily more supervised business environment. The main wild card is whether a competitive software market will emerge or the single vendor Microsoft-type model will triumph. This is the subject of chapter 10.

Audio

As recently as late 1994, the idea of delivering audio over the information highway was generally overlooked, as telephone and cable companies became nearly obsessed by the allure of video-on-demand. After all, between voice telephony, radio, and music CDs, how much unmet consumer audio demand could be left?

However, as the Internet replaced the cable industry as the early information highway model, audio has emerged as an important new application. There are two main types of products: (1) software to enable voice, telephone-like service, offered by companies such as VocalTec and the Internet Telephone company, and (2) audio-on-demand end user and server software from companies such as Progressive Networks.

The voice products are today more symbolic than fundamental. The fact that one can use packet-switched technology to carry on a virtually free international phone call is evidence of the huge gap between the Internet's flat rate pricing and the usage-based metrics of the telephone industry. It is not that the Internet-based approach is technically superior; in terms of quality it clearly is not. However, it does point out the currently irreconcilable differences in the Internet and telephone company pricing mechanisms. Successful resolution of these conflicts will be a good indicator of the emergence of a truly converged transmission value chain. Until then, consumers and some businesses will increasingly experiment with using the Internet to get around artificially high telephone company prices, particularly for international calls. However, for reasons of equipment, overall compatibility, and convenience, use will be limited.

Whereas the voice products essentially offer lower prices for a standard telephone call, the audio-on-demand products from Progressive Networks and others enable a whole new range of services. Potential popular applications include broadcasting political, musical, or other events; enabling callers to dial in to hear news, sports, and other programs from other cities or countries; the ability to search and retrieve archival audio broadcasts; and a variety of Web-based graphics and audio multimedia offerings. Pay-per-listen might well become an interesting early market for digital cash. A Chicago Bulls fan living in Florida might well pay a small fee to listen to particular Bulls game. Similar small fees could be collected from Bulls fans all around the country or even the world.

Archival audio services are also likely to emerge. Whereas video-on-demand is in retreat due to huge technological hurdles, audio-on-demand, although still much less heralded, is technically far more feasible. In particular, the ability to listen to music on demand will likely fuel interest in higher performance PC sound equipment and eventual integration with high fidelity stereo equipment.

All of the above will likely emerge as popular multimedia forms well before high-quality video-on-demand is available. Perhaps the most significant reason for this is that these products can run sufficiently well at 28K modem speeds. ISDN or cable modems clearly would help but are not required.

Like email, the Web, and transaction processing, audio will make its own mark on the technological evolution of the Web. Perhaps most prominently, many audio applications have a real-time broadcast requirement. The current Internet routing approach was not designed with this in mind and therefore can be highly inefficient. Given that neither Microsoft nor Netscape is involved in this side of the business, audio broadcast standards evolution will be an important test case of the relative strengths of computer and communications companies in establishing major Internet enhancements.

From a structural perspective, the potential for real-time audio and audio-on-demand provides a smooth and predictable steppingstone to a more converged hardware industry. As the range of audio services becomes more attractive, the desire to have higher fidelity speaker and recording equipment will logically follow. This consumer and business demand provides a natural path for the integration with the stereo, tape deck, and CD player industries. This integration is in fact easier to predict than much higher profile video applications; it should be readily visible within two years.

Video

Whereas the expansion and requirements of the previous four major application categories will principally facilitate the convergence of the Internet and telephone infrastructures, video applications will drive the additional integration of the high bandwidth cable infrastructure as well as the eventual convergence of the PC and consumer electronics industries.

Of all the application areas, it is video that is the least predictable, most controversial, and if it is to be realized requires the most investment. It is also the area that is likely to take least advantage of the personal computer technology. The success of digital video is the final, critical part of the development of a truly converged IT industry value chain.

Today, there are three main classes of video applications: video conferencing, video-on-demand, and interactive video. All three require more bandwidth than is currently available to many consumers, although it is often available to businesses.

Video Conferencing

Video conferencing technology has now reached levels of reliability, image and sound quality, and low cost that permit wide use in businesses, many of which now have sufficient bandwidth. Adoption, however, has been slower than many expected, largely due to the initial expense and inconvenience of equipping the necessary facilities. Nevertheless, because of increasing global cooperation and continued business cost pressures, eventual strong business video conferencing growth still seems likely.

It will be several more years at least before the devices, transmission speed, and related costs improve to the level necessary to reach most consumer markets. If video conferencing is restricted to face-to-face images, blackboard presentations, and conventional static slides on both ends of the circuit and if a relatively small, jumpy image is acceptable, a midrange bandwidth technology such as ISDN is sufficient.

However, higher transmission capacity is needed if the conference involves moving pictures or real-time action (for example, looking at a piece of equipment in operation). These higher transmission speeds will likely require cable or fiber-optic technology, although attempts to achieve these speeds over regular twisted pair wires continue. Even with the technology in place, there are real doubts about the appeal of video conferencing services to the typical consumer rightly concerned about a potential loss of privacy. The most likely near term home market success will come in niche markets such as those for geographically dispersed families and certain home office businesses. Overall, video conferencing is unlikely to have sufficient consumer appeal to drive major bandwidth investments.

Video-on-Demand

In the early 1990s, consumer video-on-demand was often presented as the signature application of modern information infrastructures, obscuring many other valuable uses. This was especially true in the United States where both telephone companies and cable TV providers used the requirements of video-on-demand as part of their push for more rapid regulatory reform.

Over the last few years, the rise of the Internet, the lukewarm response from consumers, and the steep technical and financial challenges presented by video-on-demand have cooled most players' enthusiasm. Many of the major alliances of the early 1990s have been either canceled or significantly scaled back, and the prospects for large-scale consumer initiatives over the next few years remain uncertain even in the United States. In most of Europe and Japan, where cable TV is much less pervasive, there has generally been much less publicity and activity.

In contrast to the lowering consumer expectations, video-on-demand within the business community is quietly and steadily gaining momentum. Potential business applications include executive presentations, product descriptions, education, and training. The ability to quickly retrieve and view selected video material has these modest but worthwhile benefits. With their existing local area networks and leased line backbones, many businesses have sufficient bandwidth in place. Progress is also being made on the server side, as hardware companies such as Digital Equipment and Sun Microsystems and software vendors such as Oracle fine-tune their offerings to efficiently broadcast streams of video information.

From a structural perspective, at least in its early years, business video-on-demand will be largely driven by the computer industry, with PC/LANs and lease T-1 type lines being the primary network infrastructure. However, as cable channel capacity expands, the use of this technology for private company video is certainly possible, especially for covering important live events. Imagine a hundred private channels of essentially C-Span-like offerings for particular business niche audiences, each delivered directly to each user's desktop PC. Conference presentations, stockholder's meetings, product announcements, and various other demonstrations are the most likely areas of focus. Once cable capabilities are brought inside the corporation, usage could quickly take off.

From a consumer perspective, video-on-demand awaits the major upgrading of the overall cable infrastructure. In advanced markets such as the United States, significant usage will likely begin by around the end of the century.

Interactive Video

There are two types of interactive video. While most video-on-demand or home shopping plans envision a high bandwidth channel to the home but perhaps a relatively low, telephone-like connection channel back from the consumer, truly interactive video, necessary for any sort of high-quality face-to-face applications, will require high two-way bandwidth.

A second, less publicized but potentially more significant two-way application would allow consumers to produce and broadcast their own videos. Given the pervasiveness of low-cost video cameras and recorders and the rapidly improving video creation and editing capabilities of the personal computer, consumers and small businesses will soon be able to produce video output at quality levels once reserved for only large businesses.

The ability to transmit these images out across the network could radically transform the nature of program content as everyone could conceivably become a video content producer. This is already happening on the Internet in the text/messaging area; should it move on to include video it could become a substantial driver for the need for high two-way bandwidth as well as a driver of home digital technology. Consumer videos are another potential application for digital cash.

Hybrid Models

As the computer and consumer electronics industries come together, various hybrid products have already begun to emerge. Perhaps the most notable of these are efforts to use the television set to access the Internet. Currently, the most prominent of several vendors taking this approach is WebTV Networks, which uses a low-cost adapter box made by Sony and Philips to allow a standard television set to receive and display Web pages. The devices are based on a microprocessor made by MIPS, Inc., currently owned by Silicon Graphics. By offering an unlimited access fee of $20 per month, WebTV hopes to market its Internet/Web service in a manner similar to cable TV.

Broadcast Services

The integration of the television and the computer is more than just a hardware issue. As "broadcast" services such as Pointcast rapidly catch on, it has become clear that computers will be used to receive both broadcast and narrowcast information. Indeed, the ability to efficiently send the same message to millions of users across the Internet will be one of the key areas of required technology evolution.

Overall Effect on Structure

In sum, each major type of application will likely leave its own mark on IT industry structure and evolution. Electronic mail provided the initial utility and still drives the push toward telephone-like ubiquity. The Web has provided the mass market sizzle and long-term inspiration. Transaction processing will force the Web to improve itself in terms of its overall performance and reliability. Audio will eventually force some reconciliation between the telephone and Internet industrys' currently conflicting pricing schemes; it will also spur important new broadcast transmission schemes. And, finally, video will first in business and eventually in the consumer market bring about a blurring of the lines between cable and wire, PC and TV.

CHAPTER 9

GLOBAL HARDWARE COMPETITION IN THE NETWORK-CENTRIC ERA

As with previous paradigm shifts, the network-centric era will change global competition in two ways. New technologies will allow new vendors to enter the market and evolving market requirements will alter the global competitiveness of nations. After a brief review of previous patterns of vendor competition, this chapter describes why the network era threatens U.S. dominance in current PC hardware and component marketplaces. It also shows how the highly horizontal supplier model that characterizes today's U.S. PC-centric industry will likely prove to be inappropriate for an increasingly diverse IT market consisting of PCs, Internet appliances, cable TV set top boxes, personal digital assistants, and increasingly smart TVs and video game machines.

The lessons of the IT industry are clear. Major new generations of technology have almost always been pioneered by new generations of vendors. In the 1960s, while mainframe vendors were focused on building bigger and ever more complex, batch-oriented systems, researchers at the Massachusetts Institute of Technology were experimenting with smaller computers of simpler, less costly, and more interactive design.

One of these engineers, Ken Olsen, raised some venture capital money and started selling the industry's first really successful minicomputers through his new company Digital Equipment Corporation. Digital's success eventually led to a whole new wave of minicomputer vendors, including Data General, Prime, and Wang. Although mainframe companies such as IBM, Burroughs, and Honeywell eventually had their own successes with small systems, the minicomputer suppliers consistently maintained the technological and market edge. IBM, which enjoyed nearly 60 percent of the worldwide mainframe business in 1980, had only about 15 percent of that year's market for minicomputers and other small business systems.

The birth of the personal computer industry entails a similar story. Before the IBM PC arrived in 1981, companies such as Tandy, Commodore, and Apple had already developed the field. Even after the IBM PC reshaped the competition around the DOS standard, yet another wave of new companies moved into the market. That list included Compaq, Dell, Gateway, AST, and countless others, many of whom, of course, are now long gone. Until quite recently, with the major exception of IBM, none of the other U.S.-based mainframe and minicomputer players had any real PC success.

This failure to anticipate and take advantage of new opportunities seemed to hold regardless of top executive backgrounds. IBM's chief executives, following in the Watson family heritage, almost always came up through the sales and marketing side. In contrast, many minicomputer vendors, including Digital, Data General, Wang, and Prime, were founded by some of the industry's most brilliant engineers—Ken Olsen (Digital), Edson DeCastro (Data General), William Poduska (Prime), and, of course, An Wang.

Moreover, this pattern of changing leadership has not been just a hardware phenomenon. Consider the spreadsheet market where each generation of technology has had a clear new winner—Visicalc in the 8-bit world, Lotus 1-2-3 in the DOS era, and Microsoft's Excel in the

Windows phase. Similar patterns are found in networking. Today's LAN-centric vendors such as Cisco, 3Com, and Bay Networks have long since passed companies such as Codex and Telex that were strong in the older terminal connectivity businesses.

Thus, as the network-centric era begins, industry anticipation and anxiety has been running high. Certainly, there is evidence that new vendors are rising once again. Whether the market be for Internet access, graphical browsers, Web server tools, security software, or cable modems, many of the network wave pioneers are start-up companies. Indeed, the current venture capital market is so strong that there are some seventy-five significant new Internet-related market entrants and countless other firms too small to be easily noticed.

However, there is good reason to think that there might be some important differences this time around. Virtually all of the leaders of the second wave—Intel, Microsoft, Compaq—lived through the transition from the mainframe to the PC era. They saw first hand how the established systems companies arrogantly and foolishly refused to acknowledge the potential of both minicomputer and then PC technology; they were the ones who eventually prospered from the systems companies' long periods of denial and inaction.

PC-era companies also have witnessed, through the example of Hewlett-Packard, that if an existing company can manage to catch a second wave, it can ride it to unprecedented levels of success. Perhaps an even more important lesson from HP is that it is in fact possible for an average player in the existing order to become a major player in the new. HP's PC printers are far more successful than its minicomputers ever were. HP by itself proves that it is not inevitable that only new players will dominate a new era. The fate of today's leaders is largely dependent upon their own decisions and their own behavior.

As industry leaders such as Microsoft's Bill Gates and Intel's Andy Grove see the network wave rising, they have become very wary of not repeating the mistakes of the past. Beyond their obvious business concerns, there is also a strong personal dimension to their determination. Since both Intel and Microsoft were given a huge head start in the PC industry courtesy of IBM, making a successful transition to the network era is a means of indisputably demonstrating their individual managerial and strategic reputations. Should they fail, historians may well see their companies' great success as being largely one of inheriting an accidental empire, effectively exploiting it but ultimately letting it slip away. The real challenge is to preserve a monopoly through the transition into a new era.

In the PC companies' favor, it is worth nothing that many of the PC-era executives are still relatively young and open to new technology. They are also much closer to the actual marketplace than were their counterparts in the comparatively bureaucratic mainframe industry. Nevertheless, the explosion of the Internet caught Microsoft and most of the rest of the PC industry completely off guard. Perhaps the biggest difference is that major PC-era players have not gone into a long period of denial; rather, they are quickly, perhaps even desperately, trying to transform themselves to take advantage of the changing market reality. Microsoft has already shown a remarkable willingness to fine-tune and sometimes even reverse its own Internet strategies.

Bill Gates captured the overall issue well when he said in his recent book *The Road Ahead** that when he first founded Microsoft he worried that someone else *might* have the same idea he had regarding the potential for PC software. Today, he worries because he *knows* that fifty thousand people all do have the same idea. Everyone sees the power of the network-centric era, which is why technology stocks and Internet stocks in particular surged so mightily over the course of 1994 and 1995.

Finally, from a historical perspective there is the whole issue of power. We have shown that the sources of IBM power go back to the 1920s and 1930s when it aggressively grabbed a near monopoly position in the market for accounting machines. This power was successfully passed on to the computer business through IBM's S/360 family; it was then unintentionally bestowed upon Microsoft and Intel, which both took full advantage of the opportunity presented.

As the industry goes forward, new questions of power emerge. Will it stay with Microsoft and Intel? Will they wittingly or unwittingly give it away? Will a new company come in and take the power away? Or has the industry reached a level of maturity where no vendor can maintain a special status that has always characterized the IT industry? After all, in today's Internet, at least arguably no one really has any power at all.

To answer these and related questions, this chapter as well as the

---

* Bill Gates, *The Road Ahead* (New York: Penguin, 1995).

next two examine the competitive implications of the current era for the hardware, software, and network services markets by using key criteria—technology impact, emerging supplier business models, and related industry structure. As in the PC era, fundamental changes in global market advantage should be expected.

The Impact of Hardware Subordination

One of the unique attributes of the personal computer, in sharp contrast to televisions and telephones, is its ability to perform both stand-alone and networked functions. In the 1980s, most PC use for applications such as word processing, spreadsheets, database, desktop publishing, presentation graphics, and so on was in the stand-alone mode. As discussed in chapter 6, the principal impact of the network-centric era on the PC market is to make network-based usage the dominant, although certainly not the universal, pattern. This conceptual shift in overall PC marketing is shown in figure 9-1.

In order to further enable this stand-alone device, since its beginnings in the late 1970s, PC industry emphasis has been geared to stuffing more and more power and features onto the desktop. While this has dramatically increased PC functionality, it has also resulted in relatively high prices and increasingly complex device management issues—application and operating software versions, sound boards, fax boards, scanners, network hardware and software interfaces, disk back-up, memory upgrades, and so on. Perhaps Oracle's Larry Ellison

Figure 9-1. PC usage trends over time.

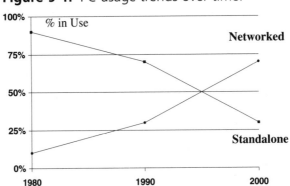

has gone a bit far in labeling today's PC a "ridiculous device," but it is certainly true that current personal computers have foisted complex systems management issues on tens of millions of users who are neither qualified for nor interested in such tasks.

High prices and complexity have been further compounded by rapid product obsolescence. In today's market many customers see PCs as having only a three or four year useful life cycle. This has been great for the PC industry, which has enjoyed a huge and growing replacement market. It has also been a boon for Intel, which uses short microprocessor product cycles as one of its primary barriers to PCM competition. For customers, however, it has been an expensive but largely unavoidable problem.

The underlying metaphor of the "Network Computer" or "Internet appliance" is that at least some of this rapid pace of upgrading will shift away from the PC and out toward the network. In this manner, technology development can still proceed freely but without constantly destabilizing the individual desktop environment. Perhaps more important, like the telephone and television, the PC itself will become increasingly subordinate to higher value network services. Some of the key ramifications of this change follow.

Slowing Growth in Microprocessor Requirements

In the PC era, the hardware industry followed Intel's lead, with the introduction of the 286, 386, 486, the Pentium microprocessors all becoming major industry events. In the network era, although Intel chips will still be important components, they will no longer be the critical market mover. Put simply, the Web experience for most customers is not greatly affected by the processing power of the PC. Not surprisingly then, mass market interest in the upcoming Pentium Pro is not nearly as pervasive as for previous Intel microprocessor introductions. Today, the real need for processing power improvements is not on the desktop but on the server, a significant but much lower volume market.

Longer Product Cycles

The reduced emphasis on microprocessor speeds is symbolic of a broader slowdown in PC technology evolution. As PCs become more dependent on network resources, the need to pack ever more technology into the PC itself will diminish. This will almost certainly have the effect of lengthening product life cycles, an important business and critical consumer concern. Although it will likely be decades before computers offer the ten year or more life cycles of cars, televisions, stereos, and other major consumer purchases, even a move to a five to six year replacement cycle would dramatically change current PC market dynamics.

The great test of this concept will come within the next couple of years. When Microsoft rolls out a mass market desktop version of NT, will today's huge base of 486 and Pentium machines upgrade to the complex NT environment with its 16MB or more memory requirements? Or will they keep their current machines running either Windows 95 or quite possibly Windows 3.1? For those customers who use a PC mainly to communicate—email, search/retrieval, bulletin boards—the need for device upgrades may be quite limited. In these cases, incremental investments in network upgrades may well offer superior returns. The limited impact of Windows 95 may be an early signal of the slower hardware and software upgrade cycles to come.

As product cycles lengthen, global PC competition will change dramatically. Consider that today effective time-to-market is the most important source of U.S. vendors' competitive edge in the global PC hardware market. It is the ability to quickly get the right feature mix to market at the right price that has distinguished U.S. suppliers from their many Asian rivals. Should speed become a less important competitive factor, much of the U.S. edge would likely vanish.

It is, thus, not surprising that Japanese, Korean, and Taiwanese firms are gearing up for another major run at the worldwide PC market. Once customer adoption rates slow significantly, Asian PC vendors will likely start to gain share. Samsung's acquisition of AST and NEC's large stake in the combined Packard Bell/Zenith entity should be viewed from this perspective. As discussed in chapter 3, changes within the Japanese domestic market are also rejuvenating the major Japanese PC suppliers.

Longer product life cycles will also substantially change microprocessor competition, making it much easier for the Intel-compatible chip vendors to keep pace. The net effect should be to squeeze a considerable share of the leverage, profits, and power out of this now globally dominant sector. Over time, although the total number of microprocessors sold will increase enormously, the gap between Intel's special position and that of the other great world semiconductor companies will substantially narrow. Despite its first rate management, there is probably little that Intel can do to prevent this.

Renewed global interest in the Intel-compatible market should accelerate these changes. It seems almost inevitable that a major Japanese or Korean semiconductor company, either on its own or in combination with an AMD or Cyrix, will enter the Intel-compatible chip market. Fujitsu, NEC, and Samsung or perhaps a joint effort among several global vendors are the most likely candidates. Asian financial and manufacturing muscle combined with slowing PC product cycles could put significant new pressure on Intel. These changes should become visible within the next twelve months and increase substantially quickly thereafter.

Lower Price Points

Even as PC product cycles lengthen, technology will continue to move forward at a steady rate. Vendors clearly will not stop offering systems with faster CPUs, higher capacity storage devices, more memory, and so on. There will always be a large segment of the market that will want these advanced new platforms.

However, within the network-centric era, an increasing share of the customer base will not need to pay for these latest technologies. As technology advances and product life cycles lengthen, development and amortization costs can be spread over a longer period of time, lowering overall system prices. For example, used 486 and Pentium machines are likely to prove much more valuable than their 286 and 386 predecessors, which quickly became almost worthless because of their inability to satisfactorily run Windows-based applications. Used 486-based business equipment will prove to be particularly attractive to certain segments of the global consumer market.

The predictable result is that new, less than state-of-the-art PCs with prices in the $500 to $1,000 range as well as both used PCs and network computers in the $100 to $500 range will become commonplace. The net effect will be the creation of a much broader hardware marketplace, covering a price spectrum of roughly $100 to $3,000. Such a range of choice is needed to expand the home market beyond today's limited demographic profile of the relatively young, the relatively well educated, and the relatively affluent. A broader price spectrum is also the first step toward the establishment of a more uniform hardware industry value chain.

These lower price points will also bring new opportunities for Korean, Taiwanese, and Japanese suppliers, even if U.S. vendors continue to control the market for leading edge devices. As the overall price spectrum broadens, at least initially it will be very difficult for any one vendor to effectively compete in all major market segments. Pricing, positioning, branding, and other marketing considerations will prove challenging.

As the television, VCR, stereo, DRAM, and other industries suggest, if product features become stable and predictable, it can be very difficult for U.S. vendors to maintain competitiveness with Japanese, Taiwanese, and Korean firms. Once their products become fully competitive, the diversified giants of Asia would then be capable of using aggressive, perhaps even predatory, pricing to gain market share against their low-margin, nondiversified rivals. In this environment, the purely horizontal structure that has been such a great asset in the high-speed PC world could increasingly become a liability. All the mid-1980s fears of an Asian takeover of the global commodity PC business may well return late in this decade. We will return to this theme in the industry structure section of this chapter.

Bundled Mentality

Cable TV set top boxes, Web TV, cable modems, and network computers will in many cases, at least initially, be part of a bundled product/service offering from a cable TV or telephone company. This bundling may well be necessary to launch new services, maintain quality, lower initial price points, and reach mass market audiences. Although it is unlikely that PCs will ever be marketed this way, the mind set may well become an important way of seeing the industry, particularly as advanced cable TV and cable modem based services emerge. Increasingly, the consumer will be buying a service, with the underlying hardware only a minor consideration.

The marketing and channel implications of such a shift are likely to be dramatic. Rather than selling mostly to the end user, vendors of these products will be selling mostly to large service providers. In contrast to today's PC industry, which consists of thousands of channel partners and millions of customers, a vendor of hardware destined to be bundled seeks only a few critical OEM supplier relationships. Obviously, within these markets, the importance of product image and brand would decline markedly, whereas customer service, reliable delivery, staying power, and overall company reputation would become increasingly important.

Decreasing Hardware Advertising Share

Advertising for television shows and telephone services is much greater than for televisions and telephones. Correspondingly, spending on network services promotion should eventually surpass that for PC hardware and software. Today, most IT industry brand loyalty is for hardware and software products. Over the next decade, network services brand loyalty will assume equal and eventually greater importance. Where significant competition exists, service brand name establishment—AT&T versus MCI, ABC versus NBC versus CBS, American versus United Airlines—tends to require very large marketing investments. Since some countries will have much more competitive and diverse communications environments than others, marketing practices should vary much more widely than in the more homogenous global PC industry.

Extending the IT Hardware Value Chain

Thus far in this chapter, we have mostly examined the effect of the network wave on existing markets and players. Clearly, however, the coming age will create new markets to at least as great an extent as it changes existing ones. For more than a decade, the PC market has been basically the only high-volume IT sector. Over the next decade, this will cease to be the case. The addition of several new high-volume hardware markets suggests profound changes for long-term component and end device supplier structure. Some of the most prominent new opportunities are summarized in figure 9-2 and explained as follows.

Figure 9-2. An expanded range of hardware devices.

- Technical workstations
- Personal computers
- Network computers
- Enhanced video games
- Cable TV set-top boxes
- Web TV adapters
- Personal digital assistants
- Smart phones

Network Computers

These, of course, have recently received a tremendous amount of both trade press and general media attention. Although they will not replace PCs for most users, these products still should eventually sell in very high volumes. In addition to frequently mentioned consumer markets, network computers are ideal for libraries, airports, hotels, bars, cafes, gambling facilities, sports arenas, shopping malls, and other business centers. When customized, they are also likely to be extremely popular in stores, kiosks, banks, and government offices. They will likely prove to be critical in making network access ubiquitous. As will be discussed in subsequent chapters, network computers might become particularly attractive in country markets that lack a strong cable industry, especially those with a strong commitment to universal service.

Video Games

Current and future video game machines from Sega, Nintendo, Sony, and others are now using 32-bit microprocessors and will move to 64-bit chips over time. Some of these vendors will seriously try to move up into home computing or at least into Internet access markets. Their low prices and strong appeal to children make it likely that they will continue to sell in high volumes, almost certainly opening up a non-Intel high-volume microprocessor market. Today, there are more than 30 million video game players installed in the United States and some 100 million worldwide.

Cable TV and Web TV Set Top Boxes

Although TV set top boxes and cable modems have received most of
the media attention, noncable set top boxes from vendors such as
WebTV may well have most of the near term market impact. Current
products, manufactured by consumer electronics vendors such as
Sony and Philips have the potential to marry the Web with the home
television/entertainment system, bringing large-screen, high-quality
Web access for an initial investment of just a few hundred dollars.

In the United States, this Web/cable set top market could have
volumes comparable to those of the PC business by the end of the
decade. Consider that there are 60 million U.S. households with cable
service today, and other major countries are rushing to install cable
technology. As with video games, most of the set top box projects
are based around non-Intel processors. WebTV uses microprocessors
from MIPS.

PDAs

Although sales of so-called personal digital assistants such as the
Apple Newton have been disappointing so far, vendors have not given
up. Although ever smaller laptops will meet some of the demand, there
is certainly demand in the market for a personal communications device that is smaller, lighter, and cheaper than today's portable computers. Today, there are many traveling workers who carry around both a
cellular phone and a laptop, and the laptop is often used almost exclusively for email. A low cost, lightweight, highly portable device with
wireless fax, email, and Web/Internet capabilities looks like the most
likely market winner. (Given the continued shrinking of cellular
phones, the integration of cell phone capability is probably not a major requirement.) Such a wireless network product could certainly be
sold in the millions of units range, opening up the volume market for
lower power consuming components.

The only real question is when and how such a device will be
built. There are few greater challenges for today's small device manu-
factures with major problems in both keyboard and screen size, along
with less daunting but still considerable obstacles with software complexity, battery life, and price. However, significant progress is likely.
At this time the most probable device would weigh about a pound, be

roughly the size of a small paperback book with perhaps a 6-inch diagonal color screen, have no disk drive, and use an alphabet ordered keyboard with keys sufficiently large to do comfortable two or four finger typing. Numbers and other commands would be handled through shift functions. Such a device should be feasible within a few years.

Noncomputer Devices

The amount of computational power in the average automobile will continue to increase at an extraordinary rate. The long product design-in cycles of cars, trucks, and similar embedded systems markets can provide a stable source of high-volume semiconductor business. The list of imagined and as yet unimagined possibilities is long and growing, currently including smart TVs, appliances, cameras, and sensors as well as next-generation telephones, home security systems, electronic wallets, and more.

Impact on Industry Structure

As the market for IT products broadens, the pure play specialization of today's U.S. PC companies such as Compaq, Dell, Gateway, AST, and Packard Bell will likely cease to be the dominant industry model. The market will come to dictate a more diversified hardware approach such as that taken by the Japanese and Korean consumer electronics companies or U.S. companies such as HP and Motorola.

Since most of these products will eventually take on commodity-like status, it will be difficult for small, stand-alone players to withstand the pressure and dangers of a globally competitive marketplace. Today's pure play PC companies are totally dependent on the PC market and because that business is characterized by very thin margins, the fundamental financial base of many of the PC companies is not strong—witness the need for Packard Bell to take money from NEC and Bull and AST from Samsung, with other similar deals likely to come. As described in chapter 2, the unique, largely assembly-based structure of today's PC industry makes it inherently a low-margin business.

Therefore, as the hardware market broadens, U.S. PC vendors

will need to broaden with it. Unfortunately for them, most simply do not have the financial resources to invest heavily in emerging sectors. Look at the damage the Newton caused to the then relatively cash-rich Apple. Even the major IBM-compatible companies have taken few large risks; recall how quickly market leader Compaq abandoned the printer business in the early 1990s and how cautiously it is approaching networking today. Looking forward, either these companies will stay with their current narrow focus and try to cope with the brutal financial challenges this will bring, or they will come to align themselves with a bigger, richer, and more diversified partner. Some of these partners may well be other U.S. firms but the majority are likely to be major Asian players.

In short, over time the network-centric era will likely put an end to the idea of the highly specialized horizontal end user device market. Such a model could work well when speed and focus are the key to competitive advantage. However, it has never been well suited to making the large investments necessary to move the market forward. Additionally, as the network era reduces the importance of time-to-market issues, the survivors will be those companies that can both stand up to a bruising price battle and invest in the many new opportunities of the twenty-first century. Most of the current PC players aren't in a strong position to do either.

As the range of volume IT markets expands and as the highly horizontal supplier model breaks down, a more diversified and increasingly integrated computer and consumer electronics marketplace should begin to emerge.

Can Intel's Monopoly Be Sustained?

Thus far, the hardware analysis has focused on the end user equipment side of the business, suggesting that the U.S. leadership in this sector will soon be significantly challenged. Some might argue that this would not be such a big deal, since after all the core U.S. source of great hardware value-add is not with the PC products that can be assembled by almost anyone but with the underlying semiconductor components. Since Japanese and Korean firms already dominate the global DRAM market, this analysis is largely based on microprocessors. Most of the cost of PC hardware comes from the microprocessor, the DRAMs, the disk drive, and monitor. Although significant markets for specialty semiconductors exist for graphics, video, audio, and other tasks, even their combined market, although growing, is still relatively small.

Consequently, perhaps the single biggest hardware question is whether the network-centric era can challenge Intel's currently overwhelmingly strong position. Today Intel is not only the world's largest semiconductor company but also one of the world's most profitable corporations. For fifteen years it has held a near monopoly position in what was the single most important technology of the PC era. Clearly, the future of Intel can be seen as a bellwether of the overall health of U.S. hardware companies.

In the preceding discussion of network computers, cable television (CATV) set top boxes, and PDAs, it was shown that many of these new product efforts will not be based on Intel microprocessors. There are both business and technical reasons for this, but in the end it is clear that unless there is a compelling need to use Intel, most hardware companies will decline. Since Intel's products are general purpose in nature and of an older design, there are often sound technical reasons for choosing another microprocessor; however, the additional, widely shared, business desire to rein in Intel's power should not be underestimated.

Thus, the emergence of other mass market IT products, in and of itself, will tend to put Intel's great success into a broader market perspective. Even if Intel holds its position in PCs, if other sectors emerge to become comparable or even nearly comparable markets, one vendor's dominance in one major area would not be viewed as such a defining industry presence. The real question is whether Intel can hold on to the PC position it has in what will continue to be a strongly expanding PC market.

There are basically two main challenges to Intel—alternative processors and Intel-compatible chips. In terms of alternative technologies, RISC microprocessor vendors have received most of the attention. The strategies and prospects for the RISC chip vendors were covered at length in chapter 4: To quickly summarize, unless the link to Microsoft software can be broken, prospects for RISC chip vendors in the mass PC market are limited. Microsoft's Windows NT offers the possibility of true platform independence. Should it become the desktop standard, the RISC vendors may get their chance to compete chip-to-chip with Intel. For RISC vendors such as IBM, Digital, and HP, the challenge is to survive in the microprocessor business long enough to see if the NT or an equivalent option becomes a reality. There will clearly be a big market for these so-called fat clients.

So-called media processors are perhaps a more likely alternative technology threat. These chips are specially designed to handle audio, video, telephony, and 3-D images, with the implicit understanding that it is these new multimedia applications that are driving the need for more PC computing power. They can run either independently in a non-PC device or as a coprocessor with an Intel CPU.

A number of vendors, including IBM, MicroUnity, NEC, Philips, Samsung, and Chromatic Research, are already building these chips, which should begin to hit the market in 1997. Even Microsoft is researching this area, recently announcing that it plans to license its Talisman 3-D graphics architecture to interested chip makers. Should these chips prove valuable, they will allow PC makers to use less powerful and less expensive microprocessors and/or force Intel into even more aggressive high end microprocessor pricing. In this sense, the multimedia nature of the network-centric era threatens to obsolete the general purpose technologies of the PC era.

In contrast to these speculations about alternative architectures, real opportunities in the so-called Intel plug-compatible manufacturer (PCM, sometimes also referred to as program compatible) market have existed for more than a decade. Until the simultaneous arrival of its own Power PC chip and the Intel Pentium, IBM made most of the microprocessors in its own PCs. In the mid-1980s, NEC was a major player in the 286 market, again mostly for its own use. Outside of these two captive markets, however, the history of this business so far has been fairly unimpressive. Despite a number of ventures, only Advanced Micro Devices (AMD) has become a significant player, and even it has a small share of the Intel-compatible segment, mostly at the low end of the market.

Looking Back at PCM History

The industry's past suggests that high-investment PCM efforts can take a long time to take off. From virtually the day that the original S/360 machines were announced, talk of compatible products from other vendors was commonplace. (In fact, the first truly program-compatible product was the Honeywell Liberator series introduced in 1963 and aimed at IBM's then large 1400 series base. This machine's rapid success was one of the reasons IBM introduced its new S/360 family as soon as it did. The announcement of the S/360 stopped the Liberator's momentum cold.)

In terms of developing a real plug-compatible mainframe business, however, the first S/370-compatible machines from Amdahl did not reach the market until 1975, and the first significant successes did not come until roughly 1978. Over the next decade, despite fits and starts, PCM mainframe market share gains were steady. By 1990, compatibles had nearly 50 percent of the worldwide IBM-compatible processor market (assuming that the near IBM-compatible systems sold in Japan by Fujitsu and Hitachi are counted). However, getting to this point took some twenty-six years.

The state of the Intel-compatible market fifteen years after the introduction of the original IBM PC is remarkably comparable to where the IBM-compatible mainframe companies were in 1978. A few smart vendors have a viable idea but desperately need cash and credibility to fight a powerful market leader. Even the names of the two main PCM players—Amdahl and AMD—are remarkably similar, and the Japanese giant Fujitsu still owns a stake in each. Numerous smaller, often unsuccessful vendor PCM attempts were also a common aspect of both periods. As discussed in chapter 3, the overall role of Japanese vendors and the near-compatibility aspects of the Japanese domestic market are additional striking similarities.

The final key similarity has been Intel's attempts to make life difficult for compatibles through various legal challenges. However, as was the case with IBM, although these cases certainly harassed competitors, delayed products, and drained resources from both sides, in the end the right to make compatible hardware products has always prevailed, the results of particular cases notwithstanding. Nevertheless, for both IBM and Intel, the courts have proved to be a formidable competitive weapon, especially against the Japanese, as Fujitsu and Hitachi (vs. IBM) and NEC (vs. Intel) can all attest.

Perhaps the main differences between now and then is that Intel CEO Andy Grove is heavily market share driven, while IBM management at that time, perhaps because of antitrust concerns, often seemed to take much more of a profit maximization strategy, particularly in the mid and late 1980s when the big PCM gains were made. Whereas Intel constantly seemed to do things more aggressively than the market expected, IBM often appeared to be holding back, with many of its mainframe product announcements of the 1970s and 1980s characterized as disappointing.

(IBM's 4300 series of small mainframes was a notable exception; its industry leading price/performance shocked the industry and wiped out much of the third party leasing industry. However, for whatever reasons, IBM never extended this level of price competitiveness to its high end machines, leaving room for high end PCMs to expand.)

Intel has also aggressively accelerated product cycles in a way that IBM did not. Of course, since IBM also controlled the software environment, it could control the overall pace of innovation in a way that Intel couldn't. In the end, IBM's strategy created a price umbrella under which compatible vendors such as Amdahl and its partner Fujitsu and eventually Hitachi could generally but not consistently profit. Intel doesn't want to let that happen. So far it hasn't.

On the other hand, a second key difference tends to work in favor of today's PCM players. In the mainframe era, the decision to buy a compatible machines was made by the actual end user, who risked the wrath of IBM, whose support was still needed for the required IBM mainframe software. IBM's attitude toward PCM procurements was so negative that it even had its own expression, FUD, standing for fear, uncertainty, and doubt. It was often highly effective with the highest levels of customer management.

In the PC era, the decision to use a compatible part is made primarily by the presumably much more technically savvy PC manufacturer. Intel FUD efforts at the manufacturer level take their own form in terms of chip access, chip pricing, and the controversial Intel-inside campaign. Despite Intel's efforts, end users have shown only modest interest in knowing who manufactured a machine's microprocessor. Overall, Intel's version of FUD has also been quite effective but slightly less so that IBM's.

In conclusion, the expanding global PC market, the renewed competitiveness of Japanese PC manufacturers, the forecasted slowing of PC product cycles, and IT industry history itself all suggest that the Intel-compatible market will significantly increase in importance over the next decade. There is probably room in the market for several such vendors, which combined might, over a number of years, be able to obtain 40 to 50 percent of the market.

Given the forecasted microprocessor market growth, this will still leave Intel as a huge and profitable supplier. However, its position as near monopolist with such tremendous leverage over the major PC hardware vendors will likely erode. Given that customers will likely resist ever shorter product cycles, advanced technology will be insufficient to control the market, especially given increasingly viable advanced technology alternatives. Once other vendors reach large manufacturing capacities, Intel will increasingly need to compete on price. If the lessons of the mainframe era teach anything it is that it is best to start to trade profitability for market share early in the cycle. Intel, and especially Andy Grove, shows every sign of fully understanding this. From a long-term perspective, it hopes to continue to lead the industry by focusing on the integration of computers with conventional television.

Devices vs. Components

One of the most frequently asked questions of the PC era is whether the microprocessor business and the end product business would remain separate or eventually reunite, with product vendors making their own microprocessors in the way that an automobile maker usually builds its engines. Clearly, there does not have to be a universal answer to this, and given the industry's complex roots, a mix of models is quite likely.

However, the network-centric era will make its own mark on this long-term hardware industry issue. The emergence of new high volume device markets—network computers, PDAs, cable set top boxes—seems certain to create substantial markets for non-Intel microprocessors. Many of these end user devices are likely to be provided by diversified global electronics firms. If these firms could use a single microprocessor across all of these platforms, they would almost certainly do so and would be tempted to make it themselves.

However, each of the above product markets is likely to have significantly different technology requirements. PC chips need powerful general purpose processors; network computers will focus on low cost and rapid communications processing; PDAs will focus on low power consumption; and cable boxes will need high-performance video processing. These underlying requirements tend to support the view that each device will define its own processor, which in most cases will come from a merchant semiconductor company.

In the end, however, from a traditional computer industry perspective, the key question is whether the industry can shake off its long history of closely linked processor and operating system selection. The development of a totally horizontal value chain requires the clean separation of the system hardware and its operating system. In the systems era the processor and operating system were largely inseparable; in the PC era, "Wintel" has defined a fundamental but seemingly inherently unstable hybrid status. The following chapter discusses how this critical software issue is likely to evolve throughout the network-centric era.

CHAPTER 10

GLOBAL SOFTWARE COMPETITION
IN THE NETWORK-CENTRIC ERA

Software has been and will continue to be the single greatest area of U.S. IT leadership. However, the ongoing network-centric paradigm shift will challenge virtually all of today's PC-driven software leaders. From a software industry perspective, the uniquely powerful combination of software and network economics should reinvigorate supplier competition, eventually moving much of the market away from its long-standing pattern of de facto monopoly vendor leadership. As software products become increasingly subordinate to higher value network services and content offerings, the relative overall IT market power and influence of packaged software vendors will decline even as software sales surge mightily.

Fundamentally, the outlook for selling software could hardly be better. As described in chapter 6, virtually every aspect of the network-centric era brings with it demands for ever more powerful and flexible software. In addition, software and network economics are highly synergistic from sales, marketing, distribution, and unit cost perspectives. The volume and complexity of software sold during the network-centric era will dwarf that of the PC age. Over the next decade, whole new areas of new functionality and value-add will emerge as literally millions of multimedia Web sites are designed, built, and enhanced.

From a global perspective, the software business has been a double win for U.S. vendors. First, the very nature of software with its marginal costs of virtually zero and therefore its virtually infinite scale economies has historically tended to create a series of highly concentrated markets. As described in detail in chapter 2, it is no accident that Microsoft has such high shares in desktop operating systems and core applications. Consider IBM's dominant position in mainframe operating systems, Novell's in LANs, AutoCAD's in computer-aided design software, Adobe's in print format software, and Netscape's in browsers. Strong de facto supplier leadership has been the industry rule, not the exception.

This market reality has been compounded by U.S. vendors' overwhelming dominance of the global software industry. With the minor exceptions of the German business software company, SAP, and the video game industry where Japanese and U.K. firms have a strong presence, U.S. suppliers control virtually all major market segments. The reasons for this leadership are generally well understood and, if anything, even overexplained. The key factors include a creative and entrepreneurial business culture, an aggressive venture capital industry, ready access to the huge U.S. market, and the English language itself. Despite the rise of India, Ireland, Israel, and other potentially important international software players, most of these global advantages should continue to hold through the network era.

Nevertheless, despite this underlying market and supplier optimism, global software competition will change dramatically over the next decade. These changes are described in the following sections.

Software Product Subordination

As with hardware, software products will become increasingly subordinate to higher value network services. This change may prove to be even more difficult for software vendors to absorb and accept. Throughout the PC era, packaged software products often have been the final organized step in the overall IT industry value chain. Once an application is installed, additional levels of services tend to be provided by VARs, consultants, or internal IS staff. None of these groups have been organized sufficiently to influence software vendor behavior in any meaningful way. Thus, the U.S. software industry has become the main driver of many IT industry standards. This has given certain software companies tremendous freedom and leverage in the overall IT marketplace.

In contrast, the emerging network services industry will be highly organized in two important ways. First, network service providers themselves will increasingly be large corporations. Today's extremely fragmented Internet access industry will eventually consolidate around a few major players in each country. These vendors will have significant influence in regard to how underlying software products are supported and even marketed. They will have little incentive to allow any software vendor to gain the market control necessary to extract monopoly rents on an ongoing basis. Figure 10-1 summarizes the key changes from the PC and network eras.

Second, and perhaps more important, network content providers see the underlying software as something to be bundled or even given away as part of their offerings. These content-focused companies will include most of the world's largest corporations—Citicorp, Federal Express, Time-Warner, Disney, and others. None of them are about to allow any software product vendor to dictate their offerings. Microsoft's inability to get Visa and Mastercard to jointly use its proprietary security technology is an excellent example of this changing market standards process. The two U.S. credit card giants forced a compromise between the competing Microsoft and Netscape proposals. Large non-U.S. customers will likely prove to be even more reluctant to accept standards driven solely by U.S. software companies.

Figure 10-1. Software product subordination.

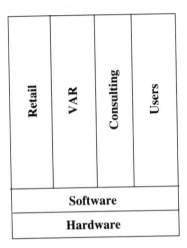

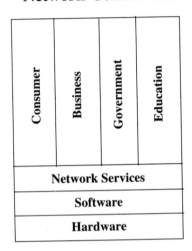

Impact on Existing Software Markets

Obviously, the key technological change is that most of the existing PC software base will over time become network-enabled. Given that the great bulk of PC software—word processing, spreadsheets, databases—was designed primarily for stand-alone use, this is not a trivial issue. Old products will either have to be substantially reengineered or risk becoming quickly obsolete.

Consider the example of word processing, by far the single most popular PC application and considered by many to be a stable commodity product. Yet despite its long history, for many users word processing today continues to exist in an awkward, divided, and unsatisfactory state. In reality, the product is about to go through its own network-driven revolution. Over the course of the network-centric era, the distinction between word processing and email will likely go away.

Today, just about every PC user has a powerful, multifeatured word processor such as Microsoft Word. However, a substantial share of many users' word processing is actually done for email purposes. Although most email systems have methods of importing popular word processing files, it is often more convenient for both sender and recipient for the message to be prepared directly within the email software, even though that software is almost always substantially less functional than a true word processing package.

An obvious solution is to have powerful word processing capabilities within the email system, ideally callable directly from the email interface or network browser. At a minimum, such software should be able to move easily between MS-Word, HTML, and other popular document formats so that information can be directly loaded onto or retrieved from the Web and other systems. It would also merge email and word processing filing systems. However, although there is little doubt that the market will move in this or a similar direction, this simple technology shift poses great challenges for the current word processing software leader, Microsoft.

History shows that retrofitting old software for new purposes is almost never easy, especially given backward compatibility requirements. More important, complex competitive conflicts can arise between systems software and application vendors. For example, since Microsoft ultimately would like to take the browser market away from Netscape, it will always think twice before making any of its key application products, such as MS-Word, complementary with its main system software rival. However, if it does not do so, it risks creating a new word processing market opportunity for others, be it a Netscape, a specialty email company such as Eudora, or a groupware leader such as Lotus.

Put simply, just as in the past the needs of IBM's PC operation conflicted with those of its small systems groups, over time the needs of Microsoft's word processing division may well diverge from those of its Windows and browser units. For Microsoft, such conflicts are new. Since its overall strategy has always been fully aligned with the momentum of the PC industry and since it controlled the underlying PC systems software, Microsoft has never had to face this type of major internal positioning decision for its core products.

However, if non-Microsoft system software environments such as Netscape become permanent, mixing applications and systems software strategies will become strategically much more complex. Virtually everything said here concerning word processing software could also be said, although to a somewhat lesser extent, for spreadsheet software, as on-line links to products from vendors such as Intuit start to expand spreadsheets usage beyond today's mostly stand-alone mode.

If an increasingly hybrid, multiplatform, network-centric market emerges, the current clarity, focus, and aggressiveness of the overall Microsoft vision will become much harder to maintain. It will begin to face some of the same conflicting, seemingly no-win product positioning issues that IBM faced between its PC and small systems businesses. However, Microsoft shows every sign of being able to deal with these issues both faster and more effectively than IBM, an issue dealt with in more detail near the end of this chapter.

These conflicting interests will likely become a daily topic of debate over the next few years as Microsoft tries to reconcile its PC-centric and network-centric strategies. The December 1995 decision to support Sun's Java language has thus far been the most prominent example. While much of the industry applauded Microsoft's willingness to incorporate an increasingly popular product, Bill Gates could not help but be aware that much of the industry also applauded IBM's decision to use Intel and Microsoft products in its PCs. If Java takes off, it could revolutionize many types of applications, and this may very well work against Microsoft's business interests. Microsoft's endorsement may well prove to have been a half hearted one, but even that approach might create more problems than it solves. Microsoft is not known for doing anything halfheartedly. Microsoft clearly hopes to marginalize Java.

All these risks and challenges are not unique to Microsoft. However, since Microsoft has such a strong share in so many key applications areas and because only it also has the systems software issues to manage, Microsoft does face the most complex challenges and clearly has the most to lose. The control of both operating systems and applications has always been Microsoft's great strength; in the network era this is already showing signs of becoming a potential weakness. On the other hand, should Microsoft be able to overcome these obstacles and pass on its current monopolies into the new era, the potential returns are virtually boundless. This issue will also be addressed later in this chapter.

Outside of Microsoft, perhaps the next most prominent example would be Lotus Development, which was acquired by IBM in 1995. With its Notes product, Lotus has developed a strong internal network groupware franchise, popular with many advanced information customers. However, this powerful, if relatively high cost software was suddenly put at great risk by the ubiquitous and low-cost Worldwide Web, a fact that IBM began to realize virtually days after its expensive acquisition. In this case, the challenge is to take the valuable replication and reliability aspects of Notes and marry them to the Web and to do so before Web-centric approaches have time to emerge. Thus far, Lotus seems to fully understand this and is responding well. It is a classic example of the Web being simultaneously a grave threat and tremendous opportunity.

New Software Markets

The preceding applications discussion looked mostly at the effect of the network-centric era on existing software markets. However, clearly new opportunities and requirements will define the main impact of the network-centric era. These tend to fall into three basic categories:

1. *New software packages.* Browser, web server, audio, encryption, search engine, and other forms of network and multimedia software will all become important new market segments. However, from a broad industry perspective, all of these can be defined as traditional packaged software products. Here the main competitive battle is whether new firms and products such as Netscape and Java will unseat the current market leaders.

2. *Hybrid "rich content" products.* This is a largely new category that the Web has brought into being. Products where software is so embedded as to be almost indistinguishable from the content itself, are a potential new market for software companies in much the same way that CD-ROM titles have been. In this case, the main question is, What role, if any, will software product vendors play in developing this content? This issue will be explored more deeply in the structural implications section of this chapter.

3. *New device opportunities.* As discussed in chapter 9, during the network-centric era, the range of important hardware markets will expand to include network computers, cable set top boxes, PDAs, and so on, all of which will require some type of operating system software. Here, the critical question is to what extent these operating sys-

tems will come from a different set of vendors. Although Microsoft is actively participating in many of these markets, it is likely that, just as many of the hardware suppliers of these devices would prefer to use non-Intel microprocessors, there will also be a strong overall market inclination to not use Microsoft operating system software. This is especially true in the network computer and TV-based products.

Thus, over time, as device variety increases, multiple operating systems are also likely to proliferate, diminishing the importance of any one environment. More important, the network will become accustomed to dealing with these diverse devices in an increasingly intelligent and platform-independent manner. It is this overall market broadening that is likely to be the most effective means of minimizing any one software vendor's power.

New Software Supplier Business Models

The changes in software supplier business models are likely to prove every bit as great as in key products and technologies. These changes are of a more fundamental nature than the hardware business model shifts described in chapter 9, although aspects of bundling or even giving products away are common to both. The unique economics of both software and networks have combined to fundamentally alter standard software marketing techniques. Essentially, there are six key assumptions simultaneously at work:

1. The software market tends to have strong de facto leaders, and therefore establishing an early market share is critical.
2. Once developed, the marginal cost of producing an additional unit of software is effectively zero.
3. When software is delivered on-line, the marginal unit cost of distribution can also be effectively driven down to zero.
4. The more people use a piece of software, the more it attracts support from related industry sectors, further increasing its overall utility and market value.
5. Once customers successfully adopt a certain piece of software, loyalty rates tend to be very high, leading to a steady upgrade business.

6. Once a de facto leadership position is established in a mass market segment, the potential profits can be extraordinary, significantly higher than for either the hardware or services sectors.

Putting these six assumptions together produces the current network-centric software business model: develop an innovative product; give the initial versions away to the early adopters; establish mind share leadership; then sell upgrades and related products to the installed base and new versions of both to the emerging mass market.

This has been the model used for Netscape's Navigator, Sun's Java, Progressive Network's Real Audio, Adobe's Acrobat, and countless other "freeware" products sold by new and existing companies alike. Freeware represents an extraordinarily innovative market response to one of the software industry's biggest traditional problems—getting people to use a new and unfamiliar product. Network technology makes it all possible. In the PC-centric past, no reseller channel would have any interest in stocking and providing freeware. Even if they did, the costs of physically distributing shrink-wrapped software would have been prohibitive. Over a network, downloading software files can be done directly by the vendor without significant cost.

The freeware model can potentially neutralize several of first IBM's and now Microsoft's greatest competitive weapons. First, freeware diminishes the impact of FUD (fear, uncertainty, and doubt). As there is no financial cost in trying out a new product, barriers to user experimentation are greatly lowered. Once a customer becomes familiar with a product, FUD is far less effective. Having received their first copy of, for example, Netscape's browser at no cost, many satisfied customers don't mind paying a small amount for the latest version.

Additionally, at the server end, the cost of Web server software is a relatively small percentage of the overall server management cost, and therefore many Web managers will be willing to pay for a product that they believe to be superior. In the end, the freeware model cannot provide the support that serious customers require; witness the move away from the leading free Web server software product, Apache. This need for supplier support provides a natural bridge from the free to for-fee business model. However, Microsoft has responded aggressively with its own freeware and bundling strategies. When combined with its great financial power, Microsoft freeware can make life very difficult for a start-up such as Netscape.

Structural Implication 1—Diminished Monopolies?

The software supplier de facto monopoly patterns of today will be challenged from two directions. Powerful network services and content companies can impose discipline and control over software product vendors in a way that services companies in the PC era never could. In addition, network technology has enabled the software industry itself to find new means to compete with established monopoly players.

The net affect should be a faster moving and more competitive industry. Both are extremely important. Since the 1960s, conventional industry wisdom has maintained that improvements in software productivity have consistently failed to keep up with the rate of price/performance on the hardware side of the industry. Freeware and on-line distribution have enabled the software industry to surpass the rate of hardware change.

The strategies of Netscape, Sun, Adobe, Microsoft, and others have taken several years or more out of the traditional software product adoption cycle. In addition, on-line upgrades offer the possibility of improving existing software on a regular basis in a way that cannot be done for hardware. Whereas the network era should slow many PC-era hardware product cycles, the pace of software evolution will almost certainly accelerate.

The development of a more competitive software industry is perhaps more controversial. Software scale economies still argue for fewer, larger players, but there is now less reason to think that "fewer" will necessarily translate into "one." As software unit volumes soar, most market segments will be large enough for several vendors to operate at highly efficient volume levels. With software sales in the tens of millions of units, the near zero marginal cost situation can easily be enjoyed by several vendors.

More important, the network content and services industry will grow increasingly capable of accepting and incorporating several software vendor offerings. If there are areas where a single standard is required, as in the case of credit card security, lead customers will play a major role in setting it. This is the crucial difference compared to the past. Although it has become clear that standards bodies such as the Internet Engineering Task Force will find it difficult to keep up with rapidly changing network software extensions, organized market forces will begin to impose discipline on competing products, driving them toward more interoperability. This can limit any one software vendor's power and make it easier for compatible products to remain viable in the market.

Ideally, both the Web server and browser markets will follow this pattern. Given today's diverse hardware installed base, no vendor is likely to monopolize the Web server system software market. Even as it evolves, the Internet should continue to be largely hardware platform independent, implying that multiple server operating environments will be capable of supporting the required tools and client software.

Perhaps more symbolically, there will likely be more than enough room in the market for at least two network browsers. The technology is relatively simple, and most network and content players will not want to become dependent upon any one vendor. If even a duopoly market pattern emerges, the influence of any one vendor won't be anywhere close to what Microsoft has in PC software today.

Whereas in the past, as the Unix workstation and Japanese PC markets evidence, the lack of a single standard has slowed overall market growth, the network's ability to smooth over underlying incompatibilities should allow overall network usage to expand largely unimpeded. In the long run, competitive software markets should drive industry growth, not hinder it. The ability to encompass real and ongoing software product competition will mark a major step forward in the maturation of both the software and overall IT industries. It should have an enormous effect on pricing. With marginal costs of close to zero, real competition could force software product pricing down to almost unimaginable levels.

Beyond the freeware examples already cited, perhaps a more tangible example of this potential price collapse is shown with Corel. Having bought Novell's application business, Corel has wisely started marketing an entire suite of word processing, spreadsheets, and so on for as little as $10 per machine. With new PC shipments eventually going over 100 million per year, this level of price aggression is easily sustainable.

As the industry looks out at a browser market of perhaps a billion installed units early in the next century, it is easy to imagine competitive market pricing of, say, $1 per copy or less. When we compare this to monopoly pricing of perhaps $20 per machine, it is easy to see the tremendous stakes involved in terms of whether a competitive software industry develops or not. Carry this logic forward across a wide range of software products, and it becomes clear why a competitive structure is capable of substantially accelerating overall industry growth.

Structural Implications 2—Premature Value Chain Consolidation

From a software industry value chain perspective, the initial Web software industry began as a replay of the early years of the PC era. Most of the key network-centric products—browsers, Web development tools, server software, security—all came from different vendors. As in the past, this structure helped speed innovation but tended to make integration and decision making complex.

However, the ambitions of the major players and the huge stakes involved have led to much more rapid attempts by both Netscape and Microsoft to simplify the market by incorporating key functions into a standard system package. It is unclear whether an integrated, broad-based approach is appropriate for the early stages of the network era. The market may well decide to mix and match for a considerable period of time. The full-line solution approach may well be precluding cooperative arrangements that otherwise might have made sense. Consider that a joint Netscape/Novell browser, server, NOS, directory approach might have been a much more powerful front against Microsoft than a full-line approach by either company. Conversely, Microsoft may well find that it must fully support Netscape's Navigator if it is to fulfill its Web server ambitions.

Structural Implication 3—Sharing the Stage With Telecom

To date, computer companies, especially software companies, have defined most of the critical architectures of the Internet. Although these companies will continue to play a key role, they will have to share certain areas with their telecom rivals.

This pattern will likely begin within the internet infrastructure as the current router based system increasingly moves toward ATM and other switched services. These new architectures will have to be supported by the main Internet backbone carriers, which will increasingly be the main telecom carriers. These carriers will also bring with them their own software and practices regarding network management, security, and customer billing. Over time, this influence is likely to spread into closely related areas such as addressing, naming, directories, and protocols. As the telephone companies begin to control many of the Net's Points of Presence (POPs), they will be well positioned to provide much of the software (sometimes known as Popware) these sites will need. These issues will be explored further in chapter 11 covering the evolution of the communications architecture.

Global Competitive Implications

From a global perspective, since virtually all of the software market power today belongs to U.S. firms, a less monopolistic and increasingly subordinate software industry translates into reduced U.S. software company influence on the global IT industry, this despite the likely tremendous financial success of many U.S. software vendors and overall continued U.S. software leadership. Much of the power that Microsoft has today will migrate toward the owners and providers of network services and content. Since it is impossible for an industry to have multiple leaders, there is, in effect, only so much power to go around. In terms of industry influence, the gains of the network providers necessarily come at the expense of today's PC-centric leaders.

In addition, the global reach of the Net and the power of freeware should make it much easier for non-U.S. firms to reach large customer audiences. There has clearly always been a great deal of very good non-U.S. software that largely for lack of marketing and distribution clout has often never gone beyond the originating country's borders.

A number of countries, including the United Kingdom, Ireland, India, Israel, Australia, Hungary, and Russia rightly believe that they can make an important contribution to global software development and are gearing up for the necessary marketing efforts. Given the virtually unlimited demands for new and varied software products and services, the addition of these highly skilled and relatively inexpensive human resources should further accelerate software industry innovation.

However, although network technology will fundamentally level much of the playing field from a distribution perspective, the United States is still likely to continue to lead in overall product innovation, development, and time-to-market. As the work of Michael Porter suggests, being close to the industry's most demanding customers brings critical competitive advantages. The sheer scope and volume of today's Internet-driven software activity in the United States bodes extremely well for continued U.S. software product leadership.

The most likely scenario is for existing and emerging U.S. software vendors to increasingly act as both developers and publishers, freely drawing on the talents of the worldwide market. In contrast, the great powers of Asia seem likely to continue to sit out of most of the global software industry competition. However, as their home markets expand, the domestic software opportunities will eventually become substantial. This may in time lead to a more competitive global posture.

Impact on Microsoft

Few IT issues have attracted more attention than the impact of the Internet on today's software industry leader. Unfortunately, given this industry's fast moving pace of events, there are limits to how deeply this book can examine the prospects for any one vendor. However, there a number of basic forces that are likely to hold true for each of Microsoft's core businesses.

PC operating systems. Microsoft will almost certainly hold its monopoly position here for at least five years, probably much longer. Even if it loses the operating systems opportunities in network computers or TV-based systems, these products are unlikely to challenge the preeminence of the PC. As the industry moves toward a marketplace with as many as 1 billion PCs in use, the profits to be made in PC operating systems are almost unimaginable. Microsoft's main challenge is to continue to provide sufficient functionality to get its base to upgrade. In this sense, it is mostly competing with itself.

PC applications. Although Microsoft currently has an overwhelming position here, it is not a monopoly one. The combination of aggressive pricing from vendors such as Corel and competition from new network-enabled applications will pose real challenges. The upgrade business might slow, and new package pricing might well collapse. Nonetheless, the outlook for profits here is again outstanding unless the company stumbles badly.

Internet software. Given the large lead that Netscape established in 1995, building competitive products would probably not have been sufficient to allow Microsoft to dominate in browsers and server software. This is why Microsoft has aggressively used other weapons such as product bundling, free browsers, and even free access to various content services. These practices will continue to trigger serious antitrust concerns that may well shape the eventual competitive outcome. Left unchecked, Microsoft's financial muscle alone might prove sufficient to crush weaker competitors or at least force them to align themselves with players with equivalent financial muscle. Should the pressure on Netscape become unbearable, an acquisition by IBM or another IT leader would not be surprising. Another major Microsoft monopoly would clearly not be good for the industry.

Legal issues aside, Microsoft deserves tremendous credit for the speed with which it has become a major Internet player. The most probable outcome is that Microsoft will develop a major but not monopoly position. However, any combination of a major slipup from Netscape, lack of resolve or support from key industry players such as IBM, Sun, and Oracle, or lack of vigilance by the United States or other governments could once again lead to a major Microsoft victory. This is the single biggest issue facing the software industry.

Rich content. Given its riches and ambitions, it is understandable why Microsoft would invest in high-stakes business such as TV news

(MS-NBC) as well as high-profile on-line publications (such as *Slate*). In these areas, Microsoft will face serious competition from new and existing competitors alike. It may succeed or fail, but it will almost certainly never get the sort of monopoly shares and profits it gets in its core businesses. It will, at best, be one of many players in a huge market. Profits are almost certainly years away. Overall, the risks are high and the rewards, by Microsoft standards, somewhat low. The company will almost certainly feel a backlash from content companies who don't want their software supplier to be a content competitor.

In sum, because the network-centric era is inherently such a fertile one for software companies, Microsoft should grow mightily even if it fails to extend its monopoly into major new categories. The lasting legacy of its PC position is so strong that it will continue to be a major player in just about any software category it chooses.

From a larger industry perspective, Microsoft's great riches also allow it to play a major role in IT industry research and development. Just as IBM pioneered many of the great technologies of the 1970s and 1980s—including DRAMs, RISC microprocessors, disk drives, relational databases, and flat screens—so Microsoft will be expected to make important innovations in areas such as speech recognition, 3-D processing, and software architectures. Bill Gates seems fully aware of this opportunity and obligation.

Why does it seem that Microsoft will fare better in the network-centric era than IBM did through the PC wave? The answer is simply one of management. In less than a year, Bill Gates refocused virtually his entire company around the implications of the Internet. In contrast, IBM and its fellow systems companies spent the better part of the decade pretending that the PC market would not have any significant impact on their existing businesses. As shown with Intel in chapter 9, Microsoft has seen what has happened in the past and is determined not to repeat it.

CHAPTER 11

TRANSMISSION SERVICES

A fundamental premise of this book is that communications bandwidth will be the single greatest driver of the network-centric era. Communications infrastructures will vary greatly by country and be largely dominated by national entities, each of which needs to be analyzed individually. In this chapter, we examine the evolution of the U.S. telecommunications industry, with emphasis on the process of developing a rational and integrated transmission services industry. Chapter 12 will then contrast this U.S. situation with that of the other major industrialized nations.

Nowhere is the movement toward a converged IT industry value chain more obvious and more important than in the broad area of information transmission services. It is clear that the Internet represents the beginning of the true integration of the computer and the telecommunications industries. It is also certain that within the telecom sector, telephone, Internet access, cable TV, satellite, and wireless services businesses will become increasingly more cooperative and competitive. Today's almost entirely separate supplier structures will likely fade away, and a new era of diversified transmission carriers will emerge. Over the next few years, the emphasis will be primarily on the integration of the Internet with the telephone industry. Later in the decade, the focus will shift to the inclusion of cable and wireless systems. This chapter discusses both developments.

Skeptics will note that the merger of computers and telecommunications has been predicted for decades and has been consistently proved wrong. They would use this argument to caution against expecting radical changes in existing telecommunications markets any time soon. A brief review of the past suggests that there are certainly a number of lessons to be learned.

Perhaps the clearest example of the dangers of accepting the conventional wisdom began on January 8, 1982, when the Reagan administration announced both the agreement to break up AT&T and the decision to drop the Justice Department's thirteen-year antitrust suit against IBM. At that time, it was the nearly unanimous view of the marketplace that with these momentous decisions in place, the 1980s would witness a titanic struggle between the two U.S. giants as the computer and telecom industries invaded each other's markets.

In retrospect, of course, no such battle happened. The conventional wisdom was half right; both IBM and AT&T did rush into to each other's backyard. In addition to its establishment of Satellite Business Systems in the late 1970s, just two months after the government decision, IBM made headlines by establishing its IBM Information Network; it then went on to acquire Rolm, a leading vendor of telephone PBXs. It even bought a minority stake in MCI. It certainly appeared that AT&T was being put on notice.

AT&T made similar noises. In the summer of 1982, it announced with great fanfare its Net 1000, a processing services network that would, according to a top AT&T executive at the time, "do for data communications what the switchboard did for voice communications.

It is the cornerstone of our corporate strategy." In addition, over the course of the 1980s, it repeatedly tried to enter various aspects of the computer hardware business, selling PCs, terminals, handheld devices, modems, and even minicomputers. It developed partnerships with computer firms such as Olivetti, Convergent Technologies, and Fujitsu and often did little to dampen rumors that it planned to acquire Digital Equipment Corporation. In a direct challenge to IBM's traditional systems leadership, it even tried to control the Unix systems software standard. After all, Unix was originally developed at AT&T's Bell Labs.

Obviously, the results of most of these efforts were enormous losses for both IBM and especially for AT&T. In the end, not only didn't the computer and telecommunications industries merge but there proved to be remarkably little synergy between the two businesses. IBM's strength in computers was not much help in selling increasingly uncompetitive Rolm PBXs. It eventually sold Rolm as well as its share of MCI and abandoned its plans for Satellite Business Systems. Although its infrastructure remains in use, the IBM Information Network never developed a strong industry identity.

Even more clearly, AT&T's telecom reputation did little to help it sell its PCs, 3B2 minicomputers, and other computer products. It eventually gave up on its partnerships and own in-house computer plans. In the early 1990s, it decided to acquire NCR, only to spin it back off again in 1995. It also sold off all of its interest in the Unix software business. As of the time of this writing, having lost billions, it is largely out of the computer hardware and software business.

Yet despite the near total collapse of IBM's and AT&T's grandiose plans, data communications was in fact rapidly becoming a critical computer industry requirement. The overall importance of networking was best evidenced by Digital Equipment, whose simple but powerful peer-to-peer systems architecture DECNET became one of its main competitive advantages during the mid-1980s.

During that period, most computer networking consisted of proprietary computer vendor architectures such as DECNET and IBM's SNA. In a similar fashion, Burroughs, Sperry, Honeywell, Fujitsu, Hitachi, and the other systems companies each developed its own networking technology, which usually could talk to another vendor's system only through specially constructed communications gateways.

Third-party network service providers (often referred to as Value

Added Networks, or VANs) generally using the same packet-switched technologies used by the Internet today also carved out a small market niche. Companies such General Electric's Information Service Company (GEISCO), Telenet (eventually acquired by GTE), and Tymnet were among the leaders, but although their offerings seemed promising, their overall base of business remained relatively small.

The net result was that, between the mainframe and minicomputer proprietary architectures, the increasing number of LANs, and the independent VANs, various mostly incompatible islands of computing proliferated. As discussed in chapter 6, much of the great initial strength of the Internet came from its ability to quickly tie together these existing systems.

Perhaps the great irony is that while giants such as IBM and AT&T spent billions trying to force the computer and communications industries together, the Internet sprang up and succeeded without any major vendor's conscious effort and with a remarkably small amount of additional spending. If someone had told the executives at IBM or AT&T in 1986 that, in fact, most of the world's computers would within a decade be hooked together without major vendor leadership, the reaction would likely have been one of disbelief, hostility, or more likely laughter.

Few members of the telecom industry paid any attention to the development of the Internet in the 1970s and 1980s. In fact, it really wasn't until the usage explosion of 1994 and 1995 that the Internet and the Web became a key area of focus. In contrast, although computer industry vendors certainly did not anticipate the extent of the Net's success, many vendors were at least closely involved. This was especially true for the Unix systems and software suppliers as well as much of the industry's research and development community. Sun Microsystems was perhaps the systems vendor most directly associated with the emerging Internet industry.

However, although they understood the technology, the computer vendors did virtually nothing to spread Internet usage to a wider mass audience. Much of this work came from the grass-roots efforts of so-called Internet Access Providers (IAPs). Most of these companies started off very small, often operating banks of modems out of homes. By and large, theirs was a hacker culture, with many of the early entrepreneurs having their roots in the free-wheeling computer bulletin board industry. By 1995, there were well over a thousand such IAPs in the United States alone. Although most of these individual IAPs had computer networking backgrounds, they had clearly infringed on telecommunications industry turf, leveraging existing phone company local and high speed lines.

In addition, the IAPs along with on-line services vendors such as CompuServe, Prodigy, and America On-line had accomplished what the giants of the industry could not; they had made it clear why the computers and telecommunications industry would need to converge. As the Internet expanded, the use of a single phone line for consumer on-line usage meant the loss of voice services for extended periods. Clearly, this would not be acceptable to many consumers. Moreover, it soon became clear that many potentially useful future network applications would require both voice and data capabilities. Voice and data services would need to be provided as part of an integrated system. This would require an expanded definition of what is meant by telephony service.

Reinventing the Telephone

From a structural perspective, the Internet and the telephone industry could hardly be more different. Perhaps, the two main things they have in common are the existing copper wires they use and their similar attitudes toward content. Clearly, the phone company has little knowledge or interest in the content of individual telephone conversations. Similarly, the IAPs (current political pressure notwithstanding) don't want to be responsible for the content that they transmit to their customers. In contrast, for key issues such as technology, ownership, access devices, pricing, regulatory climate, and geographic scope, they are virtually mirror images of each other. The key differences between the two industries are identified in figure 11-1 and described in the following sections.

Technology

Most voice transmission is still analog in nature. In contrast, all Internet services are digital based. This underlying technology is reflected in the primary Internet and telephone service access devices, the digital PC and analog telephone, respectively. Analog technology

Figure 11-1. Key differences between Internet and telephone industries.

	Telephone	Internet
Technology	Analog	Digital
Transmission mode	Dedicated circuit	Packet-switched
Pricing	Usage-based	Flat rates
Responsible for content	No	Sometimes
Regulated	Yes	Not yet

is fine for voice conversations but obviously greatly limits enhanced voice processing applications. ISDN technology now allows both voice and data to be managed by a single digital line.

Transmission Mode

Internet traffic is based on packet-switching technology; all data streams are broken up into individual packets that are routed through the network and reassembled at the receiving node. More fundamentally, all Internet traffic is asynchronous in nature, which means that there is not an ongoing real-time connection between the sending and receiving points. In contrast, telephone traffic is synchronous, with a dedicated virtual circuit provided continually between the communicating parties.

Because of the variabilities of asynchronous delivery, the packet-switched technology used by the Internet cannot guarantee precise delivery timing and thus is inherently not suitable for continuous, real-time, and interactive streams such as voice, audio, video, and transaction processing (although remarkable progress has been made in partially overcoming these built-in problems). Similarly, the switched circuit structure of standard telephone service is rarely fully utilized and is thus inherently inefficient for data transmission when compared to a packet-switched approach.

Pricing

Again, the differences couldn't be more stark. Most local telephone service pricing has almost always been based on an initial flat rate coupled with additional charges based on usage. This additional usage pricing has traditionally been based on a combination of duration, time-of-day, distance, and geographic factors. Long-distance phone service pricing is almost entirely usage based but again with a heavy reliance on time and distance factors.

In contrast, Internet pricing has relied heavily on a basic flat rate with some incremental charges for heavy users. A typical IAP might charge $20 per month for thirty hours of usage, with perhaps $1 per hour for additional time. Distance and geography are irrelevant. Access to a computer halfway around the world costs the same as access to one across the street.

As Internet-based voice/data applications emerge, these discrepancies will become increasingly untenable. Perhaps more than any other single issue, the future models for telecommunications services pricing are complex and highly controversial. Comments about some of the possible options are included at the conclusion of this chapter.

Regulation

Here the contrasts are so sharp as to be ironic. Telephone services have traditionally had regulated rates and unregulated content. With the Internet, rates are totally unregulated, but there are many politicians and social groups who want to regulate content. The telephone industry is moving steadily from a regulated to an unregulated business. The Internet risks moving in the opposite direction. However, as the two industries merge, an integrated regulatory framework will be required. It's a daunting bureaucratic challenge.

Network Service Area

Clearly, most telephone systems are either regional or national in nature. In contrast, the Internet currently does not recognize any national borders. One consequence of this difference is that telephone companies have a pretty clear picture of what their overall traffic patterns look like, but no such global picture exists for the Internet, although some interesting traffic modeling work has been done.

More tellingly, today's telephone services have complex access and settlement fees that compensate for service between overlapping phone systems. For example, when an AT&T customer makes a long-distance call, AT&T pays for access to any necessary local telephone service links, whether they are within the United States or another country. These settlement charges are then, of course, passed back to the consumer. They make up a significant share of the cost of long-distance service.

One of the key market dynamics of the Internet is that there are essentially no settlement charges. If an Internet user at Stanford wants to send a message to an America On-line (AOL) subscriber at Harvard, AOL does not get any money for providing access to its individual subscribers. Similarly, if that same Stanford student sends a message to a friend in Paris, French Telecom receives no direct payment. Each part of the network collects payments only from its own subscribers.

Since access fees provide a huge source of telephone industry revenue, the lack of similar Internet settlement systems comes as a major cultural change and, at some point, will likely meet fierce resistance from certain players or more likely certain countries. Given the literally thousands of IAPs involved today, a telephone-like settlement scheme would be impossible to implement. However, as the IAP industry consolidates, the issue becomes more manageable and may well be revisited.

The Telephone Industry Reacts

The events of 1994–1995 understandably triggered alarms in the executive offices of the major regional and long-distance telephone providers. For decades, these companies had patiently waited for the marriage of computer and telecom technology and the exciting opportunities it would bring. However, now that it was all finally happening, they found themselves sitting on the sidelines while the new IAP and existing on-line services industry were dominating the business. Perhaps more worrisome, the whole Internet enterprise followed rules and patterns developed by the government, university, and computer communities. Traditional telephone systems management, pricing, and usage patterns had been generally ignored.

Since it is now clear that eventually there will be roughly as many computers as there are people (and even more computer-enabled devices) and since it is also clear that computers can and will generate far more transmission traffic than people ever will, a failure to become a major player in the computer communications business would doom the telephone companies to an increasingly marginal and vulnerable role. They simply cannot afford to fail in this area. This concern is compounded by their long history of failure in most computer-related ventures.

Nevertheless, the Internet business is still in its infancy, and the telephone companies still have ample time to reestablish their position. Beginning in 1996, technology and market momentum began to shift in their favor. The following section outlines seven key reasons why today's telephone companies, both the Regional Bell Operating Companies (RBOCs) and the major long-distance players, should come to dominate the U.S. consumer Internet access business, essentially taking it away from today's entrepreneurial IAPs.

Bandwidth ownership. The simple fact is that the phone companies own most of the underlying telecommunications infrastructure. From a value chain and industry structure perspective, there is little reason to have a separate business for installing and owning bandwidth and another industry essentially geared toward using and selling that bandwidth. Pure bandwidth resellers such as the IAPs are inherently vulnerable.

ISDN. Most consumers will not want to pay for a second telephone line to be installed. They will, however, want to mix voice and data applications. Despite all the talk about cable modems, ISDN is still the most likely technology to fulfill this mission in the next few years, although the window is closing. The RBOCs are uniquely well positioned to offer ISDN installation, service, and support. Indeed, RBOC ISDN pricing policies will be perhaps the key determinant of overall ISDN usage. In contrast, many IAPs will find it difficult to move up and support more complex ISDN connections. Despite serious, and given the stakes inexcusable, delays in taking advantage of this opportunity, the RBOCs' position remains fundamentally very strong.

Transaction processing. As the Internet begins to be used for various transaction processing tasks such as banking, investing, shopping, reservations, and so on, a highly secure and reliable end-to-end system will be required. Key application drivers such as Citicorp and Visa will not want to have a lot of small, inherently unstable, vendors within the overall network system. Large companies will feel much more comfortable with other large companies that can, at least eventually, take full financial and legal responsibility for service delivery and problem resolution.

Lower pricing. AT&T, MCI, and Sprint are already used to bruising pricing and marketing battles, and already they are bringing this mentality to the Internet. Although the RBOCs are certainly not traditionally associated with aggressive behavior, they have little choice but to respond. Consider that the RBOCs are already paid for the telephone line for local service; they also have most of the necessary billing in place. Additionally, much of the cost of the typical small IAP goes to buying equipment and leasing T-1 or higher capacity lines to connect directly to the Internet. These high-capacity lines are then used to support multiple consumer subscribers. The RBOCs already have most of the required equipment and high-speed capacity. This should provide a considerable cost advantage.

Size and branding. Obviously, both the long-distance carriers' and the RBOCs' existing customer relations and powerful consumer brand recognition are important assets to build on, especially for reaching less sophisticated users. This advantage should further increase if network computers become an important part of the service mix. Today's IAPs are not equipped to provide the support and financing that the major phone companies can, particularly if bundled hardware and service offerings prove popular.

More open regulatory climate. With the passage of the recent telecom reforms, more aggressive RBOC behavior will likely be tolerated. With strong future competition expected from long-distance, cable, and wireless providers, the elimination of many small IAPs will be seen as inevitable. RBOCs will argue that only by controlling local Internet service will they be in a position to cope with the strong, new challenges to come.

Content controls. Politicians concerned about the possibility of illicit content on the Internet will find it much simpler to work with a small number of phone companies than with a large number of fiercely independent, often countercultural IAPs. Many will look on an telephony takeover of consumer Internet service as natural and as being in society's best interest. The telephone companies, obviously, have very close relations with much of the federal, state, and local political establishment.

In short, if they can overcome their tendency to be slow, stodgy, and unresponsive, there is little reason to doubt that within a few years the telephone companies will be the dominant providers of consumer Internet access, especially if ISDN usage takes off. Small IAPs will either be driven out of the business or evolve to provide more specialized related professional services such as business Internet support, Web site setup, and maintenance. Many of the larger regional and national IAPs either already have or will likely be acquired or specialize in business networking services. The telephone companies could certainly use the skills, knowledge, and entrepreneurial culture of the IAP community.

Implications for Internet Evolution

Should all this come to pass, the results will not just be brighter prospects for the phone companies and a more stable Internet industry. As the Internet access provision business gets more formally organized, a new source of industry power will emerge, one which will increasingly be capable of shaping the evolution of the Internet itself.

Imagine an environment where most consumer Internet access comes from either an RBOC or a national network provider such as CompuServe, AOL, AT&T, MCI, or Sprint. In this scenario, perhaps a dozen network carriers would dominate the Internet market. It is only a small step to the conclusion that these new market leaders will want to play an increasing role in the technological evolution of the Internet itself.

It has now been more than a decade since the breakup of AT&T. Since then, AT&T and the RBOCs, through various committee processes, have developed considerable experience in allowing the telephone system to evolve in an interoperable and largely transparent fashion. However, these vendors have traditionally played very little role in the deliberations of the Internet Engineering Task Force. That will either change or a new center of standards activity will emerge. Either way, the telephony industry will emerge as an important new voice.

The U.S. Internet backbone infrastructure provides an excellent example. In 1995, the key system interconnection points were handed over from the government's National Science Foundation to seven companies: the ANS unit of America On-line, Apex Global Information Services, BBN, MCI, PSI, Sprint, and UUNet Technologies now owned by MFS Communications. It has been the cooperative agreements between these companies that have kept the Internet running. It is only a small step to this function's eventually being taken over by the major communications carriers as it is with voice services today.

Among the areas most likely to be affected are billing, pricing, encryption, security, site registration, domain naming, addressing, directory services, routing and switching systems, broadcasting, audio, video, real-time services, and even the TCP/IP protocol itself. All of these are currently considered the domains of the computer industry. In sum, a major shift in IT industry power is just now beginning but will accelerate greatly over the next few years.

The End of the Internet?

This scenario is one that could well lead to the end of the Internet as we know it. This does not imply that the ubiquitous interoperability of the Net and the Web will vanish. Rather, the operation of this system will go from today's impromptu supplier structure to a more formal one that closely resembles that of the telephone industry. In such a system, the owners of the underlying infrastructure will also be the primary transmission service providers. These major players will have a strong incentive to work together to assure interoperability as they do with telephones today. In so doing, they will impose new structure and discipline on computer hardware and software providers alike.

Although some might find the arrival of this new, more structured phase psychically disappointing, it should be viewed as an important step toward stability, longevity, and improved service. As the Internet moves from a grass-roots to a more corporate culture, some of its mystique will clearly be lost. However, in exchange the market should get improved service, security, and reliability as well as a much clearer path to the future.

Over time, as this transition is completed, the very word *Internet* may come to seem increasingly passé and will likely disappear. Computers calling each other will become a routine service. One will not need to say, "I can reach you via the Internet," any more than today one would say, "I can reach you via the telephone network." From a linguistic perspective, the words *Internet* and *Worldwide Web* are proper nouns; a more appropriate future form of speech will likely be a verb or regular noun, analogous to the way *call* is used today for voice services. As the Net becomes increasingly intermingled with existing telephone services, it would not be surprising if the words *Internet* and *Worldwide Web* were largely out of general use by the end of the century. Consider that they have already been shortened to "Net" and "Web."

Toward a Converged National Network Infrastructure

The movement toward a converged communications industry value chain will take place in stages. As discussed in the previous section, much of the activity over the next few years will be focused on the integration of the Internet with today's telephone industry. Toward the end of the decade, a second major wave will evolve, this one involving the wireless and high bandwidth cable industries.

This stage is both more complex and more fundamental; whereas today's battle for control of the Internet can be viewed as one where the telephone companies are trying to reassert their natural role in data transmission services, the move toward a high bandwidth industry expands to include the entertainment-driven cable TV industry, opening up a whole new set of video services and greatly expanding the IT industry's scope and power. This will eventually lead to a major restructuring of the industry itself.

However, like the merger of the computer and communications industries, the convergence of the telephone and cable businesses has also been discussed for years. Almost since the beginnings of the cable industry, futurists have speculated about the possibilities of high bandwidth, interactive services. Indeed, pilot tests go back more than a decade to the Qube system experiments in Columbus, Ohio, in the early 1980s.

Obviously, meaningful convergence has taken time and still has a long way to go. In the past, major advances have been held back by three main issues:

1. Most cable systems are in fact analog in nature, requiring expensive upgrades to support digital services. Those investments are now being made but at a much slower pace than many expected. With the successful launch of low-cost satellite TV and so-called wireless cable, the cable companies are under considerable financial pressure.

2. Whether the connection was to a more functional cable set top box or to a personal computer, the price for each end user has historically been far too expensive. Falling cable modem prices and rising numbers of home PCs will soon create a viable new market. Additionally, a new generation of lower cost set top boxes should be out in a couple of years with new services following thereafter; these devices are critical to reaching the broader consumer market.

3. Regulatory restrictions and uncertainties have limited supplier cooperation and dampened investment enthusiasm. The February 1996 Telecommunications Reform Act goes a long way toward eliminating these constraints. Although the pace of regulatory reform was often criticized for being too slow, the extra time proved worthwhile. Over the last few years, a much deeper and broader consensus has emerged than would have been possible earlier in the 1990s. The mass appeal of the Internet has played an important educational role in what was once considered a highly esoteric subject. By taking longer, Congress has produced a better bill, and as will be made clear in the next chapter the pace of U.S. regulatory reform is considerably ahead of that in other major nations.

Taken together, an upgraded cable network, affordable PC connections, and a much more supportive regulatory climate provide a clear path toward the long-term evolution of the U.S. telecommunications industry. In trying to forecast how this evolution will play out, it is useful to first review some of the key aspects of the recent industry deregulation.

1. The regional RBOCs can enter the long-distance telephone market once they can prove to the FCC that their local market is open to competition.

2. Long-distance, cable, and wireless firms can enter local phone service markets. The FCC will oversee the critical issue of local company interconnections support and prices.
3. All cable rates will be deregulated within three years. On systems serving less than one percent of the nation's subscribers, they are lifted immediately.
4. Local and long-distance phone companies can provide video services via telephone or satellite transmission.
5. Telephone and cable companies can own each other in small markets and can have up to a 10 percent cross-ownership stake in major markets.
6. TV broadcasters are expected to get valuable new digital spectrum at no cost, although it was also agreed that this controversial issue would be revisited separately. So far, this reconsideration does not appear likely.
7. It is a crime to transmit "indecent" material over the Internet without "good faith" efforts to restrict access by minors.
8. The FCC continues to play an important role in making critical implementation decisions.

With the exception of the controversial Internet content provisions, currently being reviewed by the courts, the legislation sends a clear message that the U.S. Government supports broad industry deregulation and eventual restructuring as long as a competitive environment is maintained. As it currently stands, the bill has something for all of the major vested interests: local and long-distance telephone carriers, broadcast and cable television providers, and even the FCC. Current opposition tends to be focused on three main areas: the ambiguity of the Internet content rules, the proposed digital spectrum giveaway, and possible local phone and cable TV rate increases. All three issues are considered to be manageable. Few bills of this significance have been so universally applauded by businesspeople and politicians on both ends of the spectrum.

What Happens Now?

As the government steps back, in many ways the U.S. telecommunications industry is being asked what sort of competitive environment it really wants to build and is willing to pay for. The strategic challenges and investment stakes are daunting, and this will clearly not be a business for the faint of heart.

As so much will depend upon the strategies and decisions of particular executives, predicting specific future events is difficult. However, it is possible to identify the range of potential mergers, acquisitions, or partnerships, and discuss the soundness and likelihood of each. Seven major supplier options are described.

Long-distance companies and cable TV companies. This appears to be a natural means of delivering end-to-end high bandwidth services for video as well as advanced Internet services. It would allow a long-distance company to bypass much of the local telephone industry. There are few competitive overlaps.

Long-distance, cable TV, and wireless companies. The addition of wireless capabilities to the above would allow high bandwidth video and end-to-end voice without the complexities of forcing regular telephone service through the cable infrastructure. The addition of wireless capabilities also offers the possibility of both low local telephone rates and national telephone service mobility. This is probably the most likely strategy for AT&T.

Local telephone companies, or RBOCs, with each other. This would allow local telephone companies to enter the long-distance business without requiring support of the long-distance carriers. By joining their various cellular efforts, it would also allow the support of national wireless services. Internet cooperation would also be natural, as would any high bandwidth over twisted pair copper efforts, such as ADSL. Overall, it is highly likely that at least some of the RBOCs will work together closely in these areas. The pending merger of Bell Atlantic and Nynex is the most visible example thus far.

RBOCs with digital satellite service and wireless cable providers. This would allow the RBOCs to quickly enter their local video markets, providing real competition to today's relatively high cable TV rates. In addition, a high bandwidth satellite delivery system coupled with a standard telephone back channel is an inexpensive way to deliver various interactive services. Long-distance companies might also want to work with these players. An appealing side effect is that the success of satellite or wireless cable TV could put considerable financial pressure on today's cable players, many of which are already highly leveraged.

RBOCs and cable providers. Within the same region, such cooperation is not allowed except in small communities. Despite all of the excitement caused by the proposed but never consummated merger of Bell Atlantic and cable giant Tele-Communications, Inc. (TCI), it is difficult to imagine significant benefits resulting from cooperation between an RBOC in one region and a cable provider in another unless the RBOCs decide to go after one another, an increasingly unlikely scenario.

Long-distance companies and RBOCs. As the RBOCs assess the long-distance opportunity, close cooperation with a long-distance company such as MCI or Sprint will be one way to keep pressure on an increasingly aggressive AT&T. History suggest that it is often the number three player, in this case Sprint, that takes the most chances.

Keep things the way they are. Now that the laws have changed, this is no longer a realistic option. In theory, in a massive act of essentially illegal collusion, the long-distance carriers, the RBOCs, and the cable vendors could all stay out of each other's areas. But even in the extremely unlikely event that such an agreement could be reached, market forces would not let it last for long. Technologies such as cable modems and ADSL are inherently competitive, as is wireless and local telephone service. In addition, ambitious executives and demanding investors will ensure that each company tries to maximize its own potential and shareholder value.

In sum, the upcoming changes in the telecommunications industry are likely to be some of the most complex and dramatic in the history of American business. Since increasingly the telecommunications infrastructure is the technological underpinning of much of society, everyone has a major stake in a positive outcome. The transition of such a critical resource from a mostly public to a mostly private domain represents a dramatic show of faith in both the power of technology and the market system itself. A successful completion will mark the single biggest accomplishment of the network-centric era; despite all of the current excitement, it will likely take a decade or more.

From a historical perspective, the process is coming full circle. In 1982 government pressure led to the breakup of the vertically integrated Bell system into separate long-distance services, regional services, and equipment businesses. Over time, as a structural analysis would predict, the equipment business has stayed and in fact has become increasingly separate.

However, although it was certainly necessary at the time, the divide between local and long-distance services was always inherently arbitrary and inefficient. Neither networking technology nor consumer requirements would suggest, let alone dictate, such a structure. In this sense, the changes now underway should be seen as way of allowing the development of a more rational U.S. service structure.

What Exactly Are the Carriers Selling?

Assuming that the restructuring proceeds along the general lines described, perhaps the single biggest conceptual question is whether a uniform and rational pricing scheme will also emerge. Today, all of the major constituencies are coming from sharply different service pricing backgrounds.

   Voice telephone services are basically sold by the minute, with significant differences for time, distance, and geography.
   Internet services are sold by the hour, with no real differences for time, distance, or geography.
   One-way cable TV services are sold by the month, with additional charges for special events. There are no limitations on use.
   One-way broadcast TV is free to the users and is supported by advertisers. There are no usage limits.

In short, in the past the carriers were selling a specific function, a telephone call, a TV show, or an Internet connection. Interestingly, today cable, telephone, wireless, and Internet pricing all tend to gravitate into the $20 to $50 per month range for most consumers.

However, in an increasingly digital age, all of these services are essentially matters of moving bits through a network. In theory, a bit is a bit, and the cost to move a bit from one place to another should not vary by whether that bit represents voice, data, text, or video. However, there are order-of-magnitude differences in the number of bits required for video, voice, and text applications. Clearly, strictly proportional bit-based pricing would result in radically different prices and thus is highly problematic.

This dilemma has led to much speculation regarding how future service pricing will work. However, rather than any overarching scheme or philosophy, pricing will ultimately be determined by one thing—competition. If a truly competitive national infrastructure emerges with serious rivalry at each level of the industry value chain, market prices for various services will, over time, tend to reflect supplier costs. These costs will likely vary significantly by type of transmission activity.

Imagine a U.S. market led by several competing national telecommunications companies, each offering a broad range of voice, text, data, and video services. Unlike today's Internet, these organizations will in many cases have to absorb the full costs of end-to-end delivery. In other cases, they will need to connect to another vendor's infrastructure. Either way, the telecom supplier will have precise knowledge of the actual costs of various transmission services and, in a competitive market, will have little incentive to use one type of traffic to subsidize another. It can then relate investments in additional network infrastructure to the development of particular capabilities and services; costs can then be accounted for accordingly.

Voice services will require investments in synchronous real-time switching and related software; video requires powerful servers and high bandwidth channels; text transmission can be handled through asynchronous, store-and-forward capabilities. Each of these applications has its associated costs at the end user, network node, and network backbone level. They can be priced based on what it costs to provide them, not on the actual number of bits involved or the perceived value of those bits. Value-based pricing is viable only when monopoly supplier structures are in place.

If the differences in delivery costs turn out to be significant, services will be priced separately. If not, they will be bundled. If the patterns of heavy users start to significantly affect supplier costs, tiered prices will be implemented. If bandwidth turns out to be so plentiful that the amount of usage doesn't really affect cost, a flat rate system can be used. Traditional tiering schemes will likely be employed to simplify both billing and customer decision making. Competition will fine-tune these models over time.

In short, once a competitive and rational industry value chain emerges, the market becomes capable of solving problems that appear unsolvable in the loosely structured world of the Internet. Mundane as it may sound, the development of coherent pricing mechanisms will be essential to fund the investments needed to drive the market forward.

Implications for Supplier Market Power

One of the key characteristics of the PC era has been that the key technology driver—microprocessor performance—is also the source of supplier market power for both Intel and Microsoft.

The obvious question is whether the scarce resource of the network-centric era—communications bandwidth—will become the source of monopoly power in this period. In the United States, the answer seems clear. Although the primacy of bandwidth and the increasing role of communications carriers in setting networking standards will cause power to shift toward the telecom suppliers, given the deregulated nature of the market no one supplier is likely to get anywhere near the influence of Microsoft and Intel.

Outside the United States, where competitive telecom markets are less certain, local country monopolies may well develop. This subject is addressed in more detail in the next chapter.

CHAPTER 12
COMPETITION BETWEEN NATIONS

*Clearly, an advanced network infrastruc-
ture has become a cornerstone of a modern economy. Whereas chapters 9, 10,
and 11 discussed global competition from
a vendor and technology perspective, in
this section, we analyze the overall
strength of nations. Once again, Michael
Porter's global competitiveness model will
be used, this time to evaluate the infrastructures of the United States, Japan,
and the major countries of Western
Europe.*

Chapter 3 described how the great changes of the PC era led to a new global supplier system. Chapters 6 through 11 explained how the paradigm shift to the network-centric era will change key technology, business model, and structural dimensions as much or more than the PC era did. Taken together, all of this analysis strongly suggests that the global competitive situation is also likely to change significantly as the network wave moves forward. This chapter forecasts how this is likely to occur.

Two key factors will drive the competitive shifts to come. First, the network-centric era will tend to make both hardware and software products subordinate to higher value network services. Therefore, U.S. dominance of key product markets, even if it continues, will not equate to the same global IT industry dominance that it did during the PC era.

Second, as national structures rise to preeminence, individual country dynamics will be the driving force in shaping the overall network services environment. Although many products will still tend to be global in nature, many services will not. It is the interplay between these local and global forces that will define much of the network era.

Chapter 11 provided an overall picture of the U.S. telecommunications industry. Before attempting any comparisons between the United States, Europe, and Japan, some background on the latter two is required.

Japan

For a country that is generally eager to adopt electronic technologies, Japan has a telecommunications industry that has been remarkably sluggish. Cable TV, Internet usage, home PC usage, and email all lag substantially behind the United States. In addition, voice and computer networking service prices tend to be among the world's highest.

From a structural point of view, Japan's Nippon Telephone and Telegraph (NTT) was clearly modeled, down to the name itself, after the old AT&T. However, the AT&T divestiture went into effect in 1984. Japanese officials are still debating a comparable break-up of NTT more than a decade later. The additional U.S. telecom reforms of 1996 put another layer of distance between the two systems.

Part of the issue has clearly been political. The combination of a deep and prolonged recession and frequent scandals have forced numerous changes at the highest levels of government. Japan's powerful ministries, which in the past have often been able to overcome a lack of political leadership, have themselves been squabbling over both turf and policy. The two main groups are the Ministry of Posts and Telecommunications (MPT) and the Ministry of International Trade and Industry (MITI). The Ministry of Finance (MOF) is a third player since it is by far the largest stockholder of NTT.

MPT's traditional domain has been the communications and broadcast industries. It thus reflects a domestic perspective with a high tolerance for monopoly and a generally conservative attitude toward technology. It is considered to be a stodgy organization that tends not to attract Japan's best and brightest.

In contrast, MITI is responsible for Japan's "hard" industries—automobiles, computers, semiconductors, and so on. Consequently, it tends to be much more export oriented and much more enamored of the latest technology. It also is known for being Japan's most prestigious ministry and thus easily attracts graduates from Japan's leading universities.

As the boundaries between computers and communications blur, the two ministries have found themselves at odds over authority, influence, and policy. In the United States no such conflict emerged. Although the FCC plays a role similar to that of the MPT, there was no group comparable to the MITI to argue U.S. computer industry concerns. (In theory, this could have been the Department of Commerce, but this agency has nowhere near the influence that the MITI has in Japan.) Thus, the FCC became the primary locus of U.S. policymaking, with occasional but crucial Justice Department and congressional intervention.

In Japan, despite the general paralysis, some progress has clearly been made. Cellular telephone usage has taken off since the government lifted restrictions on individual ownership of portable phones. In addition, the cable TV industry has begun to grow from today's very small base. A 1994 MPT report predicted that cable TV would reach 60 percent of Japanese homes by the year 2010, up from about 10 percent today.

However, as of mid-1996, the overall policy gridlock remained in place. In fact, the more time that passes, the more unlikely a breakup becomes. Many in Japan would still prefer an NTT go-it-alone strategy, more along the lines of French or Singapore Telecom than the U.S. model. NTT clearly has the financial resources to sustain heavy investments in telecommunications infrastructure. The question is whether such investments could be justified if a largely monopolistic environment persists. The next year or two will likely be critical, although this has been said before.

A Pan-European Perspective

Since the beginnings of the computer industry, it has generally been a good idea to forget about the notion of "Europe" and, instead, focus on the needs and opportunities within particular European countries.

However, in the early 1990s, a real push for a United States of Europe began, capturing the attention and imagination of the global business community. Promises of Pan-European economic, social, and foreign policies were advanced by major heads of state such as Jacques Delors and Helmut Kohl. The Maastricht Treaty's commitment to a common European currency provided a tangible symbol to demonstrate a changed world. From an IT industry perspective, in 1994 the European Union announced its commitment to an open, deregulated market for telecommunications services and infrastructure by January 1, 1998, an enormous change from today's mostly monopolistic, state-owned structures.

However, over the last several years, most of the pillars of this European integration strategy have been weakened. High country deficit spending and various exchange rate crises seem likely to postpone or reverse the commitment to a single currency. The prolonged and embarrassing failure of European initiatives within Bosnia has destroyed confidence in a common foreign policy, and at a more mundane but perhaps more telling level, many Pan-European economic laws either have not been implemented or are simply not enforced within many European countries. Given this history, confidence in rapid and meaningful European telecommunications reforms has fallen greatly. Many businesses have gone back to the view of Europe as a collection of unique country markets.

From an IT vendor perspective, given the great diversities in infrastructure and policy, such a view is certainly warranted. Some countries are open, others closed, and still others mixed. Some have a thriving cable industry; others have none. Some nations have made information infrastructures a priority; others have not. Given these extremes, European averages must be used carefully.

Nevertheless, in terms of IT development, the major economies of Europe do have many things in common, including strong local telecom vendors, globally weak computer vendors, strong local sources of information and entertainment, strong labor unions, and generally large public sectors with a commitment to advancing social concerns. In addition, the great national diversity within Europe tends to follow a relatively consistent pattern. The level of technological sophistication steadily rises the farther north one travels. The Nordic countries of Sweden, Denmark, Finland, and Norway are among the world's most developed. Germany, France, the Netherlands, and the United Kingdom are generally a notch below but still well developed. Italy, Spain, Portugal, and Greece fall substantially below virtually all industrial world averages.

Comparing the United States, "Europe," and Japan

In trying to rank the major world players, once again, Michael Porter's models will be instructive. Porter's "diamond" as described in detail in chapter 3 will this time be used to assess the key dimensions of the current period. Porter's model stresses four main variables—factor conditions, related industries, demand sophistication, and domestic rivalry. Each is discussed in turn, with the emphasis on the relative positions of the United States, Western Europe, and Japan. In each case, a general one through five star rating is provided, with five stars being very strong and one star being very weak.

While the comparison of the United States and Japan is straightforward, for the reasons cited earlier, comparisons with "Europe" are inevitably difficult. This section will take an approach of compromise. Rather than discuss each European country in detail, the analysis will provide general comments regarding the distinctive characteristics of northern and southern Europe, while pointing out any major anomalies found within particular countries. In terms of the specific ratings provided, the extreme cases of Greece and Portugal are largely left out of the European evaluations.

Factor Conditions

In terms of human capital, all three economies have significant resources. A slight edge might go to the United States and Europe with their significantly longer experience in building and managing complex information networks and on-line systems. On the other hand, the often poor precollege education standards in the United States are a significant long-term negative as a mass market IT industry emerges. In terms of financial capital, the United States and Japan have a meaningful edge over Europe. Unlike the United States, neither Japan nor Europe has a strong venture capital culture, but Japan has a long list of cash-rich vendors willing to invest in long-term technology projects. European firms have found such investments difficult, hence the long history of reliance on grants from the European Commission.

However, at least in the near term, the single most important factor condition is the state of the current network infrastructure. Here, the clear leader is the United States. On the telephony side, the United States is roughly equivalent to—perhaps even a little behind—parts of northern Europe, but any deficit is more than offset by the relatively poor infrastructure of most of southern Europe, particularly Italy and Spain. The U.S. telephone infrastructure is also generally superior to much of Japan's, particular in rural areas.

But this small edge in telephone systems pales in comparison to the huge advantage in cable TV infrastructure. With the exception of Germany and the smaller Nordic and Dutch markets, most of Europe, including France, Italy, and the United Kingdom, has little or no cable infrastructure. Japan also has only a small cable industry today. In contrast, roughly 80 percent of U.S. homes are now passed by cable. As noted in previous sections, cable or fiber-optic lines are likely to prove critical to high bandwidth interactive services.

Several Asian countries without a cable infrastructure are pondering a concerted effort to lay coaxial cable or fiber-optic lines directly to most homes. This could potentially leapfrog the U.S. infrastructure, but it would take time and be very costly. As mentioned earlier, Japan is the most likely major nation to undertake such an effort on a massive scale, although a smaller, more decisive nation such as Singapore is likely to get there first.

Overall ratings for all factor conditions: United States, 5 stars; Europe, 4 stars; and Japan, 3 stars.

Related Industries

There are four main industries to be evaluated: computers, telecommunications, consumer electronics, and the content industries of publishing and media. These, not coincidentally, are also the four converging industries discussed in chapter 6. A possible fifth set of related industries might be those service sectors such as banking and other financial services that are most likely to be transformed by the network-centric era. This last group will be discussed at length in the customer implications sections. Each of the four main related industries are discussed and rated as follows:

Computer industry suppliers. This topic has already been sufficiently covered. From a global perspective, U.S. firms have a big lead, with Japan a distant second, and Europe clearly third. However, within any particular country market, local computer services and application software vendors are prominent and often dominant.
Overall computer supplier ratings: United States, 5 stars; Japan, 3 stars; and Europe, 1 star.

Telecommunications industry suppliers. On the equipment side, there is rough parity. All three rivals have vendors with strong PBX and other voice switching capabilities. All three also have solid positions in end user and other customer premises equipment markets. From a service perspective, the United States has by far the most competitive overall market, although some European countries such as the United Kingdom are also highly competitive.

On the other hand, much of Europe is equal or ahead in ISDN experience as well as digital cellular telephony through its Europe-wide GSM standard. Japan, although competitive in most areas, is not a clear leader in any major sector. Again, the main U.S. advantage is its robust cable and datacom equipment industry, and much more competitive long-distance and Internet access businesses. Relative worldwide cable usage is shown in figure 12-1.
Overall telecommunications industry ratings: United States, 4½ stars; Europe, 4 stars; and Japan, 3 stars.

Consumer electronics. Current markets for TVs, stereos, CD players, VCRs, and so on are all led by the Japanese, with European vendors second, and U.S. vendors barely active. In fact, Korea is by far Japan's

Figure 12-1. Relative worldwide cable usage, 1994.

Country	% of Homes Cable Access
Netherlands	84%
U.S.	83%
Germany	56%
Denmark	52%
Sweden	46%
France	23%
U.K.	16%
Italy	0%

Note: Cable access refers to the number of households passed by cable, not the number of actual subscribers.
Source: International Data Corporation.

most serious rival in these core consumer electronics markets. However, the United States has the lead in cable set top box technology as well as the use of personal computers for traditional consumer technology functions such as answering machines, CD players, fax machines, and other such equipment. European companies such as Philips have often been innovators in consumer electronics but have usually been unable to translate new concepts into significant business. This shows few signs of changing.

Overall consumer electronics ratings: Japan, 5 stars; Europe, 3 stars; and the United States, 2 stars.

Publishing/media. Due to cultural and local language issues, local content will always be a strong—and perhaps the strongest—component of network service offerings. Consequently, each region is to some extent immune from competition from the others. However, there is also a market for global content. Today, this market is almost exclusively in English and is thus led by English-speaking nations, principally the United States, but also with key contributions from the United Kingdom, Australia, and Canada. However, over time, large transnational, non-English content markets are likely to emerge in Chinese, Spanish, and French. In addition, contrary to many concerns regarding so-called cultural imperialism, network technologies' ability to create geographically independent virtual communities will likely prove a boon to many of the world's less used languages.

Overall, because of its strong English language global content and early experience with all forms of electronic content, the United States has an important lead, with Europe a reasonable second, and Japan clearly third. However, because of the local content issues, vendors from all three markets will continue to prosper.

Overall publishing/media ratings: United States, 5 stars; Europe, $3\frac{1}{2}$ stars; and Japan, 2 stars.

Overall ratings for all four related industries: United States, $4\frac{1}{2}$; Japan, $3\frac{1}{2}$ stars; and Europe, 3 stars.

Demand Sophistication

According to Porter (and certainly borne out through the history of the IT industry), the sophistication of local demand is critical in driving the creation of world-class vendors. Within the IT industry, there are four main sources of demand—business, consumer, government, and education. Of these, the first two have clearly become the most important, but government and education will continue to play a significant role, especially in Europe. The relative positions of the three regions are:

Business market. By almost any measure—IT spending per employee, percentage of workers with PCs, percentage using email, and so on—the United States and northern Europe are comparable in sophistication. However, southern Europe, especially Italy, often lags considerably, as does Japan. Although computing in Japan is increasingly following world market patterns, the usage gap is still quite significant. Differences in PC and electronic mail usage are shown in figures 12-2 and 12-3.

Additionally, there is now even some evidence that as the returns

Figure 12-2. Personal computer use per 1,000 inhabitants, 1995.

- United States -- 233
- Germany -- 152
- United Kingdom -- 147
- France -- 109
- Japan -- 88

Source: International Data Corporation.

Figure 12-3. Electronic mail use by country, 1995.

- United States --   64%
- United Kingdom --   59%
- Germany --   38%
- France --   34%
- Italy --   31%
- Japan --   21%

Source: International Data Corporation.

Figure 12-4. Percentage of homes with personal computers, 1995.

U.S.	**39%**
Germany	**30%**
U.K.	**25%**
France	**22%**
Japan	**21%**

Source: International Data Corporation.

on technology investments improve, usage gaps might actually widen until less developed markets reach a certain critical mass. This important developmental issue is explored more deeply in the customer implications chapter.

Overall business market ratings: United States, 4 stars; Europe, 3 stars; and Japan, 2 stars.

Consumer market. With the exception of the very small Nordic markets—Denmark, Sweden, Norway, and Finland—the United States has a large lead over Western Europe and an even larger lead over Japan. Figure 12-4 provides a view of the percentage of homes with personal computers as of the end of 1995. The U.S. lead is compounded by the much larger U.S. population. Looked at in terms of absolute numbers, as of the end of 1995, there were some 40 million homes in the United States with a PC as opposed to about 10 million in Japan. Given the powerful computer network scale economies described in chapter 6, these differences are dramatic and will not be eliminated quickly.

Overall consumer market ratings: United States, 5 stars; Europe, 3 stars; and Japan, 2 stars.

Government. Once a driver of computer technology, national government usage has in recent years tended to lag behind the commercial sector in most developed countries. In the United States, there is still a positive technology push coming from the defense R&D sector, but U.S. administrative systems have generally stagnated in recent years. Given the current anti-Washington mentality, aggressive technology deployment and service reengineering will likely prove difficult.

In theory, government computer systems should be most important in Europe where the public sector often consumes 50 percent or more of the national GDP. If Europe is to shake off its competitive problems without radical economic reforms, an active, efficient, technology-driven public service system will likely be essential. The Nordic, Dutch, German, and French markets are likely to be most active.

France's government-driven Minitel system is a good example of both the pros and cons of public sector initiatives. On the bright side, it made possible an unprecedented large-scale experiment in the use of public networks. On the other hand, by giving away dumb terminals, the government unintentionally set back the market for home PCs by a number of years. Nevertheless, France is likely to remain a leader in using technology for public sector projects and services.

The Japanese government, never an IT leader, has been so paralyzed by the current political environment that it is unlikely to have much of an impact on overall Japanese computer usage. However, in certain critical areas such as rail transportation, air traffic control, and seismic analysis, government investments will likely remain substantial.

Overall national government ratings: Europe, 4 stars; United States, 3 stars; and Japan, 2 stars.

Education. At university and postgraduate levels, the U.S. educational system is the world's most sophisticated computer environment, with a considerable portion of academic debate now occurring online, often making obsolete traditional forms of journal publishing. European universities are often connected to these networks, although individual use and access is not nearly as widespread. The situation in Japan is another step down both in terms of network usage and the overall dynamism of university education.

At the grade and secondary school level, all three markets are lagging. The scarcity of funds, the need to maintain and upgrade equipment, teachers' unfamiliarity with IT, and myriad other challenges make computers in the classroom more hype than reality. Indeed, many serious educators rightly question the importance of computers to the overall grade-school learning experience. On a more positive note, today's short computer life cycles are creating large quantities of surplus PCs that will be increasingly donated to schools. However, until school usage happens on a much wider and more intensive scale, none of the three regions is likely to gain any major advantage.

Overall education ratings: United States, 3½ stars; Europe, 3 stars; and Japan, 2 stars.

Overall demand sophistication ratings: United States, 4 stars; Europe, 3½ stars; and Japan, 2 stars.

Domestic Rivalry

Given the industry convergence scenarios previously described, the nature of future domestic rivalry will likely be driven by the movement toward the converged information industry value chain as discussed in chapter 7. The key question is how intense the domestic competition will be for vendors competing in an increasingly integrated device, transmission, software, and network content environment. Keep in mind that, according to Porter, intense domestic rivalry is the single most important competitive factor.

A converging device market. As discussed in chapter 9, the critical high volume devices of the network centric era will be PCs, CATV set top boxes, Internet terminals, PDAs, ADSL adapters, and cable modems. From Porter's analysis, the key question is not just which nations are ahead in these particular areas but which countries have the most open, direct, and active competition.

From this perspective, although the United States is the clear current leader, competition from Japan will likely pick up. As pointed out in chapter 9's discussion of hardware competition, current U.S. PC players, with their low margins and modest R&D capability, will likely have trouble investing in emerging product areas. In contrast, the diversified Japanese model may well prove to be better suited for pursuing a diverse but interrelated IT device market.

As noted earlier, the European position is generally weak. However, in areas such as ISDN, cellular telephony, and perhaps eventually Internet terminals the European market has the potential to emerge as the world's leader. If these opportunities could be married to a more competitive domestic market, some hardware market recovery might be possible. However, the overall position is still highly likely to be a distant third.

Overall converged device market ratings: United States, 4 stars; Japan, 4 stars; and Europe, 2 stars.

A converging transmission market. Because of recent history, this area should no longer be seen as a "natural monopoly." Countries that have enabled a competitive environment have seen clear evidence of lower prices, improved services, and heightened innovation. Unlike a decade ago, there are few major countries that would argue otherwise.

Here, an enormous advantage accrues to the United States, which with its recent telecom reforms now seems assured of fierce cable, copper, fiber, and wireless transmission service competition for the rest of the decade and beyond.

In contrast, despite government promises to end monopolies on basic voice services and telecommunications infrastructure by 1998, progress in this area has been slow. Only the United Kingdom, Sweden, and Finland would be described as having truly open competition, while most other European countries are dominated by either de jure or de facto monopolies. European carriers have traditionally taken advantage of these monopoly positions to slow service adoption and charge artificially high rates. This has certainly proved true with the Internet where European Internet access is still significantly more expensive than in the United States in most European countries.

Many European ministers, conscious of this history, are trying to spur reforms, but it remains a slow and uncertain process, subject to unpredictable political whims. Should lack of innovation, marketing, or competitive rivalry slow European ISDN adoption, an important opportunity will have been missed. As progress toward an integrated economic union slows, it seems likely that meaningful telecom reform will stall in at least a few countries and perhaps more.

What about Japan? Like most of Europe, Japan currently does not have a widely deployed cable industry. However, unlike Europe, it is unlikely to be content with a low bandwidth, ISDN-type infrastructure. Given Japan's strong face-to-face business culture, its powerful vendor groups eager to pursue fiber-optic and video processing technology, and the inherent difficulties in using text-based systems with a character-based language such as Japanese, a high-performance video infrastructure is seen by many as an important societal goal.

Building such a network would require massive up-front investments in fiber-optic cable installation. Fortunately, although its relative wealth has declined in recent years, as a society Japan clearly has the financial resources. The question is whether it has the political will and political capability to initiate and manage a major national investment project. Given the long-term economic importance of developing an advanced information infrastructure, Japan's decisions in this area are likely to be crucial to its future and may well determine whether its global economic power has peaked or only temporarily leveled off. The choice seems clear, Japan must either try to leapfrog the United States or accept that it will fall further behind. Either way a fiercely competitive domestic telecommunications services sector appears unlikely anytime soon.

Thus, in the critical carrier competition segment, the United States should race ahead of both Japan and much of Europe over the next few years. If Europe can instill a competitive climate, it could, however, become a world leader in ISDN products and services. In the case of Japan, a large centrally driven NTT effort seems to be the fastest way to catch up. But a sustained commitment to this sort of massive push is by no means assured. With a few key exceptions such as the United Kingdom and Sweden, neither Europe or Japan has generally accepted the type of wide open competition that the United States has embraced.

Overall converged transmission rivalry ratings: United States, $4^{1}/_{2}$ stars; Europe, $2^{1}/_{2}$ stars; and Japan, 2 stars.

Software and content. Over time, both end user devices and transmission services tend to take on commodity attributes. Indeed, turning bandwidth into a commodity is one of the principle missions of the network-centric era. In contrast, the software required to coordinate and manage these systems as well as the content that runs on top of them offer almost unlimited potential for increasing value-add.

Clearly, from a software perspective, the U.S. lead is enormous. Although there are pockets of expertise all across Europe, the ability to keep up with, let alone drive, the market is questionable. With Japan, it seems as if the nation has, at least temporarily, given up any hope of being a major world software player. U.S. software companies are becoming increasingly dominant even in Japan. The sort of competition that drives Japanese hardware companies just isn't there with software.

Issues regarding the overall strength of the content companies in each region have been discussed in the related industries sector. However, from the perspective of domestic rivalry, the United States, because of its large and increasingly deregulated industry, would again have a distinct advantage. However, unlike the situation in both computers and telecom, the publishing/media industry in Europe and Japan is also highly competitive. This avoidance of the national champion syndrome bodes well for future country content competitiveness.

Overall software ratings: United States, 5 stars; Europe, 2½ stars; and Japan, 1 star.

Overall content ratings: United States, 5 stars; Europe, 5 stars; and Japan, 3 stars.

Overall domestic rivalry ratings: United States, 4½ stars; Europe, 3 stars; and Japan, 2 stars.

Overall country ratings for factor conditions, related industries, domestic demand, and domestic rivalry: United States, 4½ stars; Europe, 3½ stars; and Japan, 2½ stars.

Summary and Conclusions

While this chapter has focused on the major markets of the United States, Western Europe, and Japan, other nations will also take advantage of global telecommunications technology. The potential for even a small nation to have impact through a unique business model, more open laws, or lower telecom costs can be considerable. Islands as remote as Sardinia hope to become the information-age equivalent of Hong Kong. Singapore, on the other hand, may become the first nation to have a truly all fiber telecom infrastructure. Israel hopes to drive a number of key networking technologies.

Nevertheless, the United States, Europe, and Japan today account for some 70 percent of the world's gross national product (GNP), and although this share will fall, it will remain over 50 percent for at least the next decade. Even emerging powers such as China, Korea, and India are unlikely to be leaders in terms of network products, infrastructure, and services for a very long time.

For nations large and small alike, global competition in the network-centric age has two different but interrelated meanings. First is the traditional definition of competitiveness, which seeks to identify those countries that will produce world leaders in hardware, software, or services. A second view seeks to evaluate the sophistication of each country's overall network infrastructure with the implicit assumption that an advanced information infrastructure will be to the benefit of both business and society. It is with both of these definitions in mind that the overall U.S. position is best understood.

In terms of designing and building the hardware and software products that will drive the network-centric era, U.S. vendors remain extremely well positioned. Japanese and other Asian players will likely become much tougher competitors in many existing hardware sectors, but the overall dynamism of the United States should continue to drive success in new and existing areas alike. On the software front, although the Net makes it easier for non-U.S. vendors to reach the global market, this minor increase in competition is more than offset by the dramatic overall expansion of the global software market opportunity. From a traditional professional services perspective, much of the market will stay local, particularly as small business IT services activity picks up. However, where global service support is required, U.S. firms remain extremely well positioned.

However, despite this generally positive picture, in terms of using those products and services as part of a larger set of network services offerings, each country will generally determine its own pace of development and direction. Differing infrastructures, public sector goals, and levels of supplier competition will result in a wide spectrum of national network characteristics. This increased importance of national infrastructures is perhaps an ironic result of telecommunications technology that in and of itself does not recognize or respect national borders. Indeed, the arrival of global communications will clearly result in all manner of global virtual communities and related transborder challenges.

However, the geographic strength of the network-centric era stems from the fundamental fact that most businesses, services, forms of entertainment, education, and government are national or local in nature. Thus, the increasing influence and leadership of network content will bring about this more heterogeneous world. As network technology improves, this trend will only accelerate. The ramifications of a truly content-driven world will be explored in the final chapter of this book.

Additionally, given the overall national importance of telecommunications, local country ownership, management, and oversight seem highly likely. Most countries will be no more willing to give up control of their information infrastructures than they would their railroads, highways, airports, and postal, electrical, and water services. Thus, despite numerous global alliances, national players will dominate much of the critical network infrastructures. It is in this important sense that the U.S. global industry dominance gained through the PC era is likely to be significantly diminished.

However, when one looks beyond the IT business toward the overall global economy, these same national infrastructures and related services must be seen as global competitors in and of themselves, with some country's networks being fundamentally more capable than others.

When the current and likely infrastructures of the United States, the major nations of Europe, and Japan are compared, the edge also goes to the United States. With the exception of the northern European countries, European aims are generally less ambitious. In contrast, Japanese goals may eventually be very aggressive, but the serious pursuit of these goals has hardly even begun.

What could go wrong to cause the United States to lose its leadership position? Of course, there is always the possibility that an unforeseen technology, event, or leader could arise to change the competitive landscape. Multimedia microprocessors, global antitrust action against Microsoft, or a charismatic figure who could truly unite Europe are possible examples. There is also the converse—that the United States through ineptitude, misfortune, or conflicting special interests could fritter away its edge.

Perhaps a more philosophical answer would be that almost the entire analysis is dependent on the assumption that largely free market forces can effectively bring about an advanced telecommunications environment. Certainly, this has been the case thus far in both the telephone services and and data communications businesses.

However, although unlikely, it is certainly not outside the range of possibilities that at some point simple competitive forces could wind up either unable to justify the capital expenditures needed to drive the industry forward or, perhaps more likely, unable to agree upon the standards and procedures needed to assure the desired interoperability. In either case, such a market breakdown might allow another country, using another approach, to assume world leadership. Fortunately, should the U.S. private sector box itself into such a position, the U.S. Federal Government has repeatedly shown an ability to effectively intervene. The past and future roles of government are discussed in chapter 15.

In summary, the U.S. IT industry seems highly likely to make an important contribution to overall U.S. competitiveness during the next decade. As Michael Porter's models make clear, the two forces do tend to feed off one another. The critical relationship between advanced information utilization and global economic power is intrinsic to the very idea of an information society.

One of the paradoxes of our time is that it is often said that the twenty-first century will be dominated by Asia. But the twenty-first century is also called the "Information Age." Given the wide gap between U.S. and Asian information usage, it is difficult to see how both of these statements can be true.

CHAPTER 13

IMPLICATIONS FOR ENTERPRISE COMPUTING

The network-centric era will reshape business computing even more than the PC era did. Whereas information systems in the past mostly automated internal functions, in the network age IS priorities will shift toward building external links to customers, suppliers, and other key third parties. Additionally, industry usage patterns will begin to diverge, as information-intensive industries become transformed and the emergence of the "wired consumer" begins to fuse notions of business and consumer computing.

As recently as 1991, the outlook for large U.S. corporations was openly pessimistic. In sector after sector, global (often Japanese) competition seemed to be getting the upper hand, and despite years of heavy investments in information technology, measurements of worker productivity remained stagnant. Corporate emphasis on layoffs, outsourcing, and offshore manufacturing suggested an uncertain economic future.

By the end of 1995, the situation had turned around completely. Not only had the U.S. economy enjoyed four years of recovery and expansion but U.S. companies regained competitive leadership in many key global industries. Perhaps even more heartening, U.S. worker productivity, always difficult to measure, began showing strong signs of improvement. The soaring 1995–1996 U.S. stock market was perhaps the most visible sign of this heightened sense of corporate optimism.

Understandably, these striking changes have attracted global scrutiny. Among a long list of possible explanations, two are most commonly cited: (1) the flexibility and adaptability of the U.S. economy and (2) U.S. corporations' aggressive use of information technology. There is no doubt that U.S. companies are now far more computer intensive than most of their major multinational rivals (see figure 13-1). There is also good reason to believe that computers have been indispensable to the ongoing competitive restructuring of the last

Figure 13-1. Major country IT spending as percentage of GDP.

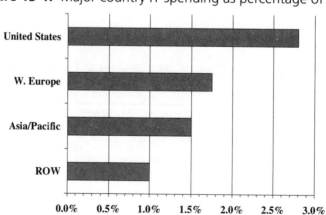

Source: International Data Corporation.

decade. Although this sort of statistical evidence is always difficult to amass, the investments of the last decade finally seem to be paying off. The growing belief that information technology has become a critical component of national competitiveness is making these heady times for the information industry and information systems professionals. This is particularly so since the great majority of chief executive officers have made it clear that their IS organization has in fact been entrusted with most key technology responsibilities. Indeed, the IS community hasn't been in such a favorable position since the glory days of the 1970s, the "decade of the DP shop."

All evidence suggests that these trends will strengthen over the rest of the 1990s. The arrival of the Internet and the Worldwide Web opened up a whole new technological frontier, and once again through investment, infrastructure, and inclination, U.S. firms are best poised to exploit the new opportunities presented. This is especially so in the consumer sector. The combination of high home PC penetration levels and a strong Internet infrastructure will allow large U.S. businesses to directly reach their consumer customers well before many major Asian and European rivals.

These mutually self-reinforcing economic and IT-related factors may actually accelerate future IT investments. As stated in Metcalfe's law, the value of information networks grows exponentially with the number of nodes. As the number of people connected to the Internet reaches critical mass thresholds, the incentive for others to join increases greatly. Idealists have even suggested a powerful virtual circle where IT investments spur productivity, which drives growth, which enables more IT investment, and so on.

Although it is highly unlikely that the business cycle has suddenly become obsolete, it is true that in recent years U.S. IT spending has grown substantially faster than that of Europe or Japan. Certainly, much of this can be explained by the stronger overall U.S. economy. However, the critical mass effects described here also have likely played an important role.

Quantitatively, separating the short-term influences of economic and specific industry factors is largely impossible. However, over time, patterns of economic growth can be correlated with various factor effects. One possible upcoming test will be to measure how global IT spending behaves if the European and Japanese economies fully recover or if the U.S. economy dips into recession.

Defining the End User Paradigm Shift

Although much of this book focuses on how changes in IT industry structure have affected global supplier competition, each wave of industry change has also shifted customer computing paradigms. End user spending on in-house staff and related infrastructure accounts for roughly 50 percent of the total IT spending for most medium-size and large businesses. In this sense, end user activities are the single largest segment of the overall industry value chain. For the IT industry to move ahead smoothly, these internal resources must be successfully aligned with the changing technology and supplier realities.

Indeed, for many information systems organizations the transition from a mainframe, data center oriented framework to an end user driven IT environment has proved to be unnecessarily difficult and painful. Like their mainframe and minicomputer vendors, many IS departments saw PCs as either a threat or as an immature and therefore unreliable form of computing. Consequently, they tended to continue to align themselves with existing mainframe and minicomputer products and suppliers who encouraged and supported their views.

The consequences of those attitudes were often severe. IS became perceived as stodgy, unresponsive, and in some extreme cases irrelevant. Individuals and departments, sometimes by desire, sometimes by necessity, saw fit to make their own technology decisions, introducing unnecessary friction and complexity into many large organizations. In short, end users and IS professionals often found themselves at odds.

Over the 1993–1996 period, much of this damage was repaired, with top management showing renewed confidence in IS management and most end users recognizing the need for professional information systems support. IS seems to have learned the lessons of the past. Even though today's Internet is every bit as immature and unreliable as some of the early PCs, IS has learned to see the glass as being half full and is working hard on overcoming the current problems. This is a wave they don't want to miss.

This more open attitude is an important factor, since the changes of the network-centric wave are likely to greatly exceed those of the PC period. The nature of these changes is depicted in figure 13-2.

The diagram is intended to portray a relatively simple but fundamental shift. Throughout the IT industry's history, virtually all major

Figure 13-2. Changing IS customer priorities, 1985–2010.

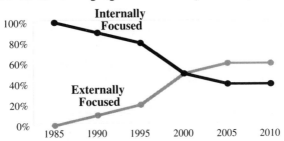

customer computing initiatives have been focused on various forms of internal automation. For both the mainframe and PC eras, emphasis has been on key applications such as accounting, financial analysis, human resources, inventory, transaction processing, document management and production, internal messaging, and so on. Most of this work has been intended to improve internal efficiencies.

In contrast, despite the current focus on "intranets," much of the coming wave will be focused on external forms of automation, using computers to reach customers, suppliers, investors, and other key third parties. In this sense, the network-centric wave will reach much deeper into the core activities of the overall organization, directly affecting sales, marketing, customer services, and support. "Electronic commerce" is the phrase most often associated with this increasingly external focus.

In retrospect, perhaps it is not surprising that during the 1960s, 1970s, and 1980s, there was so much debate regarding the overall return on IT investments. In addition to the lack of critical mass defined by Metcalfe's law, it seems probable that there are inherent limits to how much productivity can be gained by merely automating oneself. In contrast, as business moves out into the emerging cyberspace, the potential exists for much higher IT investment returns. Entire processes can move away from people and buildings and onto the network.

As figure 13-2 shows, the early years of the network-centric era correspond to the early experiments with electronic commerce. As of 1995, research by IDC suggests that there was a core group of roughly 15–20 percent of large and medium-size U.S. corporations and other institutions that already have a strong focus on these new external systems. Unless companies become bogged down in intranet initiatives, this number can be expected to increase rapidly over the next five years, particularly as critical security and other transaction processing concerns are overcome. (See chapter 7.)

By the early twenty-first century, external systems should become just as important to the typical IS department as internal systems. Internal systems clearly will not go away; companies will continue to develop new applications and enhance existing ones. However, priorities will steadily shift outward. Perhaps more important, the boundaries between internal and external systems will, in many case become indistinguishable. A good example is the current Federal Express package tracking system, whereby customers can access a FedEx Web site to obtain package tracking and other information. Allowing electronic customer access to critical corporate and customer records will no doubt be a driving consumer and business-to-business application.

Today's heavy emphasis on intranets (using the Internet as a supplement or replacement for traditional internal networks) both supports and delays this long-term evolution. On the bright side, as the internal and external worlds fuse, the power of the network-centric era will emerge. As large amounts of information begin to flow freely and automatically between individuals and organizations, the meaning of previously vague phrases, such as the virtual and boundless corporations, start to become much more tangible and intuitive.

On the other hand, the heavy supplier emphasis on intranets runs the risk of distracting the industry from the network-centric era's real external mission. Too much of the intranet emphasis so far has been placed upon internal efficiencies, productivity, and cost savings. On-line employee benefits books, internal calendars, price and client lists, and executive communications all may be great information to put on-line, but what do they really do for the customer?

Too much of the intranet emphasis sounds like a replay of the client/server promises of the early 1990s or even the paperless office claims of the mid-1980s. To the extent that incremental investment and critical IS staff time is focused internally, some of the Internet's external promise will be delayed. The task for today's IT suppliers and the IS user community is to make intranets a step toward true electronic commerce and not a sidestep away from it.

But Not All Industries Will Evolve in the Same Way

A second major difference between the network-centric wave and that of the mainframe and PC era is that technology use by industry will vary greatly. Certainly, there have always been significant differences in computing between, for example, manufacturing, banking, and government organizations. However, differentiation tended to be primarily at the application level. The underlying technologies and the effects of IT on the overall enterprise were often surprisingly similar.

While some industries spent more on IT than others, expenditure differences remained within a relatively narrow range. For some two decades, systems vendors such as IBM, Digital, Unisys, and their global competitors have experimented with various industry-specific sales, marketing, and support groups. Although there have certainly been some successes, in general these groups have had little industry impact and in virtually all cases have remained subservient to these same vendors' product activities.

As the network-centric era moves information technology closer to core business functions, industry variances are likely to increase. They will do so along lines defined by the nature of each individual sector.

Professor Nicholas Negroponte, founder and head of the Media Lab at the Massachusetts Institute of Technology and perhaps best known for his monthly columns in *Wired* magazine, wisely suggests that to understand the oncoming digital world, one should adopt the habit of viewing various events and activities as being either matters of atoms or matters of bits.

Issues of atoms, such as building a house, growing food, and producing clothes, have a fundamental physical essence that cannot be changed by computers. In contrast, matters of bits are fundamentally information based and thus fully susceptible to digital manipulations. Professor Negroponte suggests that, as the power of digital technology increases, the behavior of the world of atoms and that of the world of bits are beginning to rapidly diverge.

This general framework can be applied to the major industry sectors that together comprise the bulk of the world economy. Figure 13-3 provides a simple view of a selection of major industries along an atom/bit continuum. Clearly, the industries on the left—manufac-

Figure 13-3. Potential for transformation, major industry sectors.

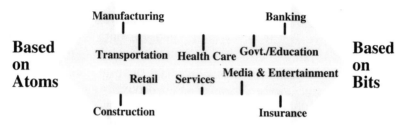

turing, construction, agriculture, and others—are least likely to be transformed by computer networks. Those on the right—banking, insurance, media, publishing—will change the most.

This is hardly surprising. Companies whose main product is information are the ones whose business is most likely to be affected by the technologies of cyberspace. For example, virtually everything that a bank does is a form of information processing and therefore could, at least in theory, be conducted over a network and managed by software without any theoretical need for buildings or even people. Compare this to, for instance, automobile manufacturing, which although it relies on computers in countless ways could never use them to actually replace its current end product.

This underlying potential for transformation explains how a seemingly minor event such as Microsoft's proposed acquisition of Intuit could have stirred such a loud reaction within both the software and banking industries. However, market resistance to the merger probably reflected too much of a product orientation, generally missing the main message of the network-centric era. It will be banking services that drive the market, not any particular piece of software.

Banks intuitively understand their vulnerability; they are scrambling to restructure themselves to compete in a network-driven industry. That this is happening most visibly in the United States is perhaps another example of the importance of overall U.S. economic flexibility. Similar restructuring within the publishing and content industries will be the focus of chapter 16.

Given that bit-based industries have a potential for transformation that atom-based industries do not have, it seems likely that the former will show markedly higher rates of overall IT investment. Certainly, the early evidence suggests that this is becoming the case. The overall importance of computer networks by industry is shown in figure 13-4.

In theory, the atom/bit spectrum of industries shown in figure 13-3 should mirror the network importance data shown in figure 13-4. In general, they do. However, in the key public sector industries of government, health care, and education, the rankings differ.

Certainly, these industries are a mix of physical and information services. Government functions such as defense, law enforcement, and policy development can be provided only by people; doctors and nurses provide direct physical services that information technology can only supplement; and all evidence shows that the teacher-to-student ratio is one of the strongest predictors of overall educational success.

However, it is also true that all three have a very large information processing component; yet, for various financial and cultural reasons, each has generally lagged in using IT technologies. Although separating cause and effect is difficult, it does not seem unreasonable to suggest that the current low productivity of all three sectors is related to insufficient technology utilization, particularly given the significant bit-based aspects of all three industries.

One doesn't have to be a technology promoter to see the potential for computers to improve government and health service delivery and to significantly lower education costs, especially at the university level. However, given the current low, often inefficient, investment climate

Figure 13-4. Importance of computer networks by industry, 1995: percentage of IS managers viewing networks as critical.

- Business Service --   74%
- Banking --   71%
- Insurance --   71%
- Retail --   59%
- Transportation/utilities -- 55%
- Process manufacturing --   53%
- Discrete manufacturing --   51%
- Education --   49%
- Government --   48%
- Health care --   35%

Source: International Data Corporation.

in each sector, we may never know whether lack of technology utilization is a core problem or not. Perhaps another country will show the way.

From a longer term perspective, across all industries there is a widespread IS consensus that the Internet is a significant industry development and that electronic commerce will rapidly gain in importance. IDC research shows that as early as January 1995, some 25 percent of all large and medium-size organizations were actively hiring people with Internet-specific skills, up from virtually zero as recently as 1993. No doubt the figure is significantly higher today. The resulting skill shortages are creating lucrative Internet-related opportunities for new and existing professional service firms, a business that should remain strong for years to come.

A Widening Array of Corporate Challenges

Although the future holds tremendous potential, the typical IS department needs to live in the present. From a current perspective, perhaps the main downside of living in such technologically exciting times is that the list of IT opportunities, challenges, and issues often seems endless and only gets longer over time. As each new wave of technology innovation—mainframes, minis, PCs, LANs, Internet—arrives, the old waves don't disappear; they become yet another thing to manage. Although the phrase has now become passé, internally focused "client/server computing" will still be the core activity for most IS departments for at least the next three years. It won't be until roughly around the end of this century that network-centric activity becomes the top IS priority.

Overall, the migration toward a network-centric, electronic commerce environment should be seen within the overall spectrum of current IS priorities. Consider the following ten IT issues faced by virtually all large enterprises today:

1. *End user training and support.* As computer products and internal systems become both more complex and more pervasively deployed, end user training and support require extensive and sustained commitment. How much of this should be provided by the corporation, the supplying vendor, or employees themselves? As technology

becomes increasingly embedded in almost all industries, the ability of employees to absorb new ways of working will emerge as a major national competitiveness issue. Given relatively weak U.S. elementary and secondary school education, it is a clear cause for long-term concern.

2. *End user device and software management.* Windows 95 provides an obvious example of the challenges involved in keeping thousands of desktops running compatible software with sufficient memory, storage, and processing speed. How does IS justify the considerable costs of such a major end user upgrade? When is the best time to migrate? Can some generations be skipped altogether? In a true network-centric era such problems will be minimized, with migrations often handled by the network itself. However, until then, just keeping up with PC technology is an enormous financial and human resource drain.

3. *LAN/server architecture.* The arrival of Windows NT provides a real challenge to Netware's long LAN dominance. Should IS go with one or the other, or should they expect both products to coexist? How does network server software from Netscape, Open Market, and others fit into this decision? Throughout all the waves of technology change, basic IS decision making continues to be heavily driven by colleagues, word-of-mouth, and the momentum of the marketplace. Many customers prefer to pursue safety by following the herd.

4. *Wide area network management.* The arrival of the Internet is causing many companies to rethink their current internal network architectures. So-called intranets offer potentially great savings, but how should the transition from numerous existing systems be managed? Expect the rate of change here to be rapid, particularly for geographically dispersed organizations.

5. *Application development.* Software development is one of the most commonly outsourced IT functions. Which applications should be developed in-house and which should be outsourced? Should IS go with a mostly Microsoft environment, or should they mix and match? Since Microsoft has traditionally provided good products at low prices, customers are not nearly as concerned about Microsoft's market power as many suppliers are. Additionally, the actual share of a typical IS budget that is spent with Microsoft is less than 5 percent. This is a major difference from the IBM-dominated era, where IBM

often took 50 percent or more of a company's total spending with outside suppliers.

6. *Data center evolution.* The stronger economy has led to re-newed investment in mainframe systems and software that remain a large share of many IS budgets. Can the new server and parallel processing machines help reduce costs? Or should the entire data center be outsourced? In general, outsourcing seems to be highly correlated with the economy. It increases during recessions and falls back during strong economic times. As new technologies allow mainframe processing costs to decline, in-house processing will likely retain a strong position. As distributed servers become a critical part of most enterprise information systems, full-scale hardware outsourcing becomes more difficult.

7. *Security.* The Internet is leading to greatly increased information flows both within and between organizations. Given the known security issues, how can the risk/benefit trade-offs best be managed? For many IS professionals, major mistakes in this area can become a career-breaking issue. However, as discussed in chapter 8, the industry is making rapid progress with security technology.

8. *People skills.* What skills are truly needed in-house—Internet, Lotus Notes, Netware, security, database, or others? How does IS keep its people current as technology rapidly changes? The lessons of the PC era suggest that IS would be best served by having new Internet capabilities in-house. It is easier to manage the outsourcing or subcontracting of older, better understood PC and mainframe skills. However, this is often precisely the opposite of what many companies do. There is a natural human reaction to keep in-house that which is established and familiar and outsource the new and strange. As the network-centric applications become the most important IS priority, the precariousness of this strategy will become increasingly obvious.

9. *Internal partnering.* As information systems become increasingly operational and line-of-business driven, how does IS work with its key internal constituencies? Who is really in charge? How are costs and responsibilities actually allocated? This is perhaps the single biggest IS management issue. In the end, there is an inherent conflict in viewing IS as both strategic weapon and as a stand-alone cost center. On the other hand, the existence of such a major business challenge creates the potential for achieving an overall enterprise competitive edge through more effective IS management.

10. *Budgets.* The list of potentially worthwhile technology spending seems limitless, but the reality is that most IS budgets increase 4 to 8 percent per year. Where should the money go? Who should decide? This sort of budget growth will likely prove to be insufficient to make the network-centric era a rapid reality. To fulfill a broader electronic commerce mission, companies will have to supplement IS budgets with increased business unit spending to lift overall annual computer and communications investments into the 10 percent or more range. This is occurring now in the United States but in general has yet to catch on elsewhere.

The list of challenges could go on, but the point is clear. In order to avoid being pulled in too many directions, the modern IS organization has to have a clear set of priorities. These priorities should be driven by the needs of the overall enterprise, not those of the IS organization itself. Top management and key line-of-business operations must give the IS team a clear sense of mission along with the resources and authority to carry it out.

Many have taken this a step farther to say that, in order to really have an effective technology strategy, everything must be driven by a company's major lines of business that can then evaluate IT investments and their related returns. Some have gone so far as to say that the goal should be to eliminate as much of the central IS function as possible. However, given the cross-boundary nature of information and the need to leverage skills and infrastructure, this seems unlikely for the foreseeable future. Although individual business units will increasingly have and require their own technology professionals, the need for a strong IS management function is still increasing.

Indeed, from a long-term perspective, it is easy to see the IS professional becoming the equivalent of the landlord of cyberspace. As an increasing share of the business is moved on-line, IS becomes a key part of the business, not just the technology infrastructure. In this sense, IS necessarily becomes highly strategic. A successful cyber strategy clearly requires successful technology decision making.

IS Meets the Consumer

Given this situation, it seems likely that IS will steadily evolve over the remainder of the decade, embracing new technology opportunities while being responsible for managing a complex transition to a network-centric future. Large businesses' new faith both in technology itself and in the technology professional community could not come at a better time. From a business point of view, the changes over the next ten years will be far more dramatic than those of the past. Since their inception in the 1960s, corporate computers have generally been used to improve business productivity, efficiency, and effectiveness. Over the next decade, they will in many new and existing industries come to approximate the business itself.

From a broader industry perspective, the network-centric era should ameliorate a long-standing industry rift. Throughout the PC era, there was frequent discussion as to whether the industry was becoming consumer driven, with the role of the enterprise customer declining.

As we look forward to an era of increasingly wired consumers, it becomes clear that, rather than creating divisions, the network-centric era will in fact unify business and consumer computing missions. After all, a large share of consumer Web access today is aimed at reaching the corporate systems of Federal Express, Citicorp, Fidelity Investments, Sony, and other companies. As the number and importance of these connections increase, the business and consumer worlds will merge in an unprecedented manner. In this sense, the technologies in the home will become one of the drivers of what businesses can and can't do to reach their customers. This evolution of the wired consumer marketplace is the focus of chapter 14.

EVOLUTION OF THE CONSUMER MARKET

In many ways, the expansion of the consumer market is likely to be the single biggest test of the network-centric era. Unless telephone-like ubiquity can eventually be reached, large-scale societal transformation will prove impossible. Fortunately, the combination of lower prices, expanded applications, improved ease of use, and steadily more favorable demographics all argue strongly for information technology to be in use in 80 percent or more of U.S. households within a decade. Other major nations will not be far behind. This eventual ubiquity provides the structure needed to advance the industry toward a truly content-centric phase.

The mid-1990s have been milestone years for the home computing industry with U.S. unit sales passing those of both televisions and automobiles. From a consumer electronics perspective, PCs continue to gain in popularity. Although nowhere near the 95 percent household penetration level of televisions or the more than 80 percent for VCRs, PCs are now in use in more than one-third of U.S. households and exist in numbers roughly equivalent to video game machines.

During 1994 and 1995, the explosion of the Internet opened up yet another great consumer frontier. After years of largely unsuccessful videotext-style projects, the world of the wired consumer has started to become a reality. The combination of rising PC penetration rates, aggressive marketing by America On-line, CompuServe, and others, and, most important, the explosion of the Worldwide Web has created vast new possibilities that have captivated the minds of American businesspeople.

These market movements have been matched by equally important conceptual shifts. Since its earliest days, the computer industry had followed what could be called a trickle-down technology deployment pattern. New technologies—be they multitasking, disk drives, or 3-D graphics—tended to be introduced first for expensive, high-performance systems, and then, as they rode down the cost curve, they would make their way into more mass market devices.

During the first half of the 1990s, at least some of this process became inverted, with the home market becoming the driver of many of the industry's most important new technologies such as video and audio processing, CD-ROMs, color printers, and even the Intel Pentium itself. As businesses struggled to understand and implement multimedia technologies, these same technologies were readily adopted by consumers who naturally expect integrated audio, text, and video capabilities.

In the second half of the 1990s, the very image of the home PC itself will shift dramatically from that of a primarily work-at-home, desktop processing device toward one that is increasingly communications oriented. Today, only 15 percent of all U.S. home desktops are linked to some sort of on-line service. By the year 2000, this figure will approach 80 percent. As home PCs become linked to both businesses and other consumers, business and consumer technology will become increasingly inseparable.

Sizing the Home Market Today

Statistically, there are a number of useful ways of viewing today's home computing industry.

From an overall information industry perspective, the U.S. consumer computing market, including all home systems, peripherals, software, and on-line services as well as all upgrades, add-ons, and replacements, reached $18 billion in 1995, accounting for roughly 8 percent of the total U.S. information processing market. The global home market in 1995 was $37 billion, or just under 7 percent of the $530 billion 1995 global IT market (see figure 14-1).

Forecasts by IDC show this worldwide consumer share rising to roughly 15 percent by the year 2000, making the home market a significant but still far from dominant IT sector. As this chapter shows, a number of important application, demographic, and pricing obstacles will need to be overcome before the home market can become comparable to any of the major business sectors; this process will take a decade or more.

However, from a strictly personal computer industry basis, as early as 1994 U.S. home PC sales already accounted for more than 40

Figure 14-1. Home market share of global IT industry, 1995.

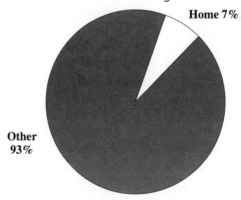

$530 Billion

Source: International Data Corporation.

percent of the U.S. personal computer market. Given this still rising share, it's no wonder that most major PC vendors, with the notable exception of Digital Equipment Corporation, have recommitted themselves to the highly competitive, and still largely unprofitable, consumer marketplace. By the end of the century, it is quite likely that, in developed markets such as the United States, the home market will account for 50 percent or more of total PC unit sales. With 100 million U.S. households and a labor force of 130 million and with multiple device possibilities in both segments, rough long-term unit parity between the consumer and business PC markets seems probable.

Measuring the U.S. Lead

Among developed markets, the United States has been the clear early market leader. Only smaller nations such as Australia and the northern European countries of Denmark, Sweden, Norway, Finland, and the Netherlands approach the United States in terms of percentage of households with personal computers. However, because the populations of all of these countries are quite low, their overall impact on the global PC market is not significant.

In the major markets of Europe, IDC data indicates that Germany, France, and the United Kingdom tend to be a couple of years behind the U.S. pace of adoption. In the case of Italy, the lag is much greater. Only about 5 percent of Italian homes have a PC installed today.

As for Japan, as of the end of 1995, roughly 20 percent of Japanese homes had a PC, although the number has been rising quickly.

Given the critical mass aspect of on-line services, the higher U.S. penetration rates and the larger overall U.S. population should virtually ensure that the United States will continue to have the most advanced consumer marketplace for at least the next few years. This should allow U.S. Internet service providers to stay at the forefront of service delivery technology. However, unlike in the PC product sectors, the competitive skills honed in the U.S. market will not be so easily extended into non-U.S. markets. Each country will tend to create its own array of service leaders, especially for non-English language offerings.

What Are Consumers Doing With All of These Machines?

As discussed in chapter 8, much has been said about the search for "killer" consumer applications, the 1990s equivalent to word processing and spreadsheets, which so clearly drove the early years of the PC market. However, a broader look at this issue suggests that the driver of the PC market in the 1980s was individual productivity. In the network-centric 1990s, the driver of the industry will be communications applications of all types and in audio, text, and eventually video form. From this larger perspective, consumer computing is already well on the path to success. Indeed, the rate of acceptance of consumer email should prove to be a benchmark measure of broader consumer on-line acceptance.

However, given today's roughly $1,500 PC price points, it is not surprising that today's PC user has a strong practical orientation. Job-related applications, be they work-at-home or running a home-based business, remain the leading consumer activity, with education, entertainment, and on-line services all popular but still lagging significantly. According to IDC, at the end of 1994, adults still accounted for 80 percent of all home computer usage, although the purchase of a home PC primarily to aid with children's education is becoming increasingly common.

As more people work independently and as improving technologies and evolving corporate cultures become more supportive of tele-commuting, this work-centered consumer usage will continue to expand and be aggressively upgraded. Telecommuting often requires an advanced home technology environment. In addition, this customer segment will tend to follow software and communications standards established by the workplace.

However, work-at-home patterns show strong national variations. Obviously, both telecommuting and home-based businesses in the United States are acceptable, and even trendy. In contrast, in countries such as Japan or Italy, they are not so popular. With their small houses and strong business emphasis on face-to-face discussion, most Japanese would not seriously consider doing most of their work in the home, this despite often grueling office commutes.

In Italy or France (to risk cultural stereotyping), home is usually seen as where one goes to be away from work, and the always-on-call work ethic increasingly found in the United States is neither desired nor widely adhered to. In addition, two-worker families are also often ideal customers for a home PC. Such families are more common in the United States than Japan, Italy, or France. In short, different attitudes toward working at home can explain a considerable portion of today's global differences in home PC usage.

Over the long term, entertainment, education, lifestyle, and transaction applications might at least in theory be more broadly appealing across national boundaries. However, even in the United States the viability of many of these ideas has yet to be decisively demonstrated in the marketplace, and there are certainly a number of naysayers who continue to dismiss consumer computing as being substantially and even dangerously overhyped.

Perhaps the most articulate of these voices is renowned computer hacker Clifford Stoll. In his 1995 book *Silicon Snake Oil,* * Stoll provides a series of simple but valuable reminders that the real world is indeed generally superior to a virtual one and that the role of face-to-face work, communication, entertainment, and shopping may not be greatly diminished by on-line alternatives.

Clearly, the early years of consumer computing have witnessed numerous failed projects and services, and overall profits have been scarce. Although work-at-home, children's education, specialty hobbies, and general curiosity are enough to continue to move the market forward, more compelling financial or entertainment services will be necessary to make computers a universal household item. Even today, one can't generally do even mundane things with a computer like booking theater seats, paying bills, reserving restaurant tables, or renewing parking permits, let alone take a university class or get advice from a lawyer or doctor. For most consumers, today's Web experience is still much less compelling than industry boosters would like to admit.

Additional Challenges and Pitfalls

Consumer computing faces a number of other important challenges. Narrow user demographics, high system prices, inadequate ease of

*Clifford Stoll, *Silicon Snake Oil* (New York: Doubleday, 1995).

use, insufficient communications bandwidth, and rapid technological obsolescence form a set of interrelated inhibiting factors largely unique to the information technology industry. Each of these is discussed in turn.

Demographics. Today's PC buyer comes from a narrow slice of the overall demographic base. The typical customer is highly educated (college or above), young (less than forty-five years old), affluent (over $50,000 per year annual income), and male.

Obviously, this current base will be quickly saturated, at least in the United States. To sustain growth, new sectors must be reached. Some will prove easier than others. Certainly, educated, affluent females are now an established growth area. In addition, there is evidence of increasing success in reaching relatively wealthy, older, and, in particular, retired workers. However, lower income groups, particularly when older and less educated, are likely to prove to be difficult to reach, especially at current PC prices. These groups comprise roughly half of the potential market. (See figure 14-2.)

Price. At configured system prices often running well over $2,000, the PC is the most expensive consumer electronics product ever, and for a typical consumer its cost is often exceeded only by that of the automobile. There is no doubt that many potential new customers would be far more comfortable with traditional consumer electronics

Figure 14-2. Changing PC user demographics.

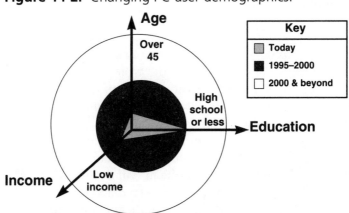

prices of $200 to $500. This is the price point being targeted by both Web TV and network computer manufacturers, as well as used equipment resellers. Useful systems in this price range would greatly increase overall household penetration levels.

Ease of use. Unless they have gained experience and training through school or the workplace, many consumers continue to find personal computers too difficult to use. Experimental interfaces such as Microsoft's Bob or voice recognition technologies are not likely to solve this problem in the next few years. The incremental improvements of Windows 95 over Windows 3.1 show that the rate of innovation in this area has slowed. Apple's industry-leading Macintosh interface really hasn't changed much in over a decade.

End user bandwidth. Even with 28K modems, current transmission speeds to the home greatly limit the quality, scope, and variety of home computer offerings. Clearly, ISDN and cable modems will eventually bring the higher speeds required, but this will take several years to be widely and cheaply available and another few years to become extensively deployed. Many consumers understandably will not have the patience to put up with today's transmission technologies. In many ways, if IT vendors could know one thing to help them forecast consumer market evolution it would be when various increases in bandwidth would be broadly available. Almost every other advance will flow from there.

Technological obsolescence. IDC research shows that the single most unsatisfying aspect of computers to the typical consumer owner is the constant need to upgrade. Televisions, telephones, and stereos can all be used for a decade or more with minimal maintenance. In contrast, the computer industry demands a steady stream of significant upgrades in systems, software, communications, and perhaps most bothersome of all, memory. As technology improvements migrate onto the network, at least some of this problem will eventually diminish, but consumers who bought 4MB or even 8MB machines in the 1993–1995 period are no doubt already facing significant constraints.

A Range of Solutions

Given the long list of hurdles described above, it should be kept in mind that the entire history of the information technology industry is one of overcoming barriers to expanded use, and vendors all around the world are busy trying to translate today's problems into tomorrow's opportunities.

Part of the solution is time. With each year, the generational barriers to usage are reduced. Within ten years, the age problem will be largely overcome in the workplace; within fifteen to twenty years, it will be minor in the home. Time is also a factor in overcoming some of the ease-of-use problem (consider plug and play) and today's current bandwidth limitations. In ten years time, communications bandwidth will likely be as cheap and plentiful as microprocessor MIPS are today.

The network-centric era will also help overcome issues of price and technological obsolescence. In the future world of an increasingly converged industry value chain, network-enabled access devices will span a range from $200 (and eventually less) up to $3,000 and more. The four most important developments are:

1. PC vendors are making a renewed effort to drive entry-level PC prices below the $1,000 range.

2. Video game manufacturers now use powerful 32-bit microprocessors in their new offerings. They are also beginning to add incremental word processing, Internet, and related services while staying in the $300 or less range.

3. Network computers when coupled with a high-speed ISDN, cable, or ADSL link can offer high-performance Internet and other application services without the need for local disk drives, large memories, or high-performance PC processors. By using remote network as opposed to local resources, these products, at least conceptually, can solve many ease-of-use and technology obsolescence problems as well. Internet appliance vendors are also targeting the $300 to $500 price range, but there is also talk of bundling them as part of a monthly Internet service from, for instance, a local telephone company.

4. Cable TV or Web TV set top boxes will most likely offer substantial point and click capabilities but, at least initially, not full key-

board driven applications, making them well suited for entertainment and transaction systems, with much less emphasis on text and messaging.

These new devices and price points will be critical to reaching a more universal audience. There is little doubt that the network-centric era will soon provide enough utility for most households to make an initial investment of, say, $400 with additional payments based on monthly usage. As the market expands, some of these users will want to buy service packages of as few as five hours per month. As Internet access competition increases, expect the basic charge for minimal connection to fall sharply.

The Long March to Universal Service

Given improving demographics and technology along with falling hardware and network services prices, the most likely home market scenario is one of a long and generally steady march toward ubiquity. The current rate of progress should be sufficient to attract 75 to 80 percent of U.S. homes by 2005, with other major countries likely following close behind. The connection of literally hundreds of millions of homes around the world will be one of this period's greatest accomplishments. The movement to a content-centric era really can't begin until this type of ubiquitous network infrastructure is in place.

Nevertheless, during this buildup period, it is virtually certain that many more affluent citizens will have access to on-line technologies, while many of the less well off will not. It is outside the scope of this book to make in-depth social judgments about the implications, if any, of this division. However, from a historical perspective, none of this should be surprising. For a very long time, both automobiles and telephones were also used mostly by the wealthy. On the other hand, televisions were in 90 percent of U.S. households just fifteen years after the first sets were commercially available. VCRs also sold quickly, going from 1 percent to 75 percent of households over the 1980–1994 period.

Given that the first PCs became commercially available more than fifteen years ago, it is clear that the consumer uptake of PCs is dramatically slower than for TVs and VCRs, although considerably faster than for telephones or cars. Consider that it took roughly fifty years for telephones to be in use in 50 percent of U.S. homes and another twenty-five years to reach the 90 percent level, which first occurred in 1970. The long-term U.S. pattern of phone, automobile, TV, and PC acceptance was shown in figure 5-1.

Much of the more rapid TV and VCR acceptance is, of course, due to price points. However, when one considers that a TV and VCR together might sell for close to $1,000, not counting the additional monthly cable subscription charges that might run $300 per year and per use VCR rental fees of perhaps $100 per year, it is clear that consumer preferences today are still far more oriented toward the major video appliances than they are toward PCs.

Yet, despite these clear consumer decisions, there are still a number of influential political figures who will raise the specter of a world divided into the computer haves and have-nots in a way that no one would dare do for cable TV, cellular telephones, or even automobiles. The roots of this anxiety are somewhat mysterious, perhaps even irrational. It generally stems from a belief that those without computers are missing out on something of great importance. Given the way home computers are used today this is by and large not true. Nevertheless, it is almost certain to become a frequent topic of debate. The next chapter, which concerns the role of government, will examine issues of equity from a long-term policy perspective.

Vendor Positions

One of the current anomalies of the consumer market is that although work-at-home remains one of the key consumer applications, PC vendor market shares in the corporate and consumer worlds vary greatly. Whereas Compaq, IBM, HP, Digital, Dell, and others have a strong presence in the corporate desktop market, the U.S. consumer market has in the first half of the 1990s been led overwhelmingly by two vendors—Apple and Packard Bell—neither of which has established a comparable presence in corporate America. Additionally, outside of the United States, vendors such as NEC in Japan, Vobis in Germany, and Olivetti in Italy are strong enough that, with the exception of Apple, no single hardware vendor has anything close to a strong worldwide consumer market position.

The situation on the software side is, of course, entirely different. Microsoft's dominance in operating systems is global, and its strength in core applications is nearly as pervasive. No other software vendor has anything even remotely comparable. Only the graphical browser and related network-centric developments have the potential to challenge Microsoft's consumer software position.

On the services side, the U.S. market is intensely competitive. In addition to the long-term battle between America On-line, Compu-Serve, Prodigy, and, most recently, the Microsoft Network there are literally hundreds of large and small Internet access suppliers, thousands of private bulletin board operators, and tens of thousands of Web sites. European and Japanese markets, although generally less competitive, still have a number of primarily local service providers. Only CompuServe has been successful in exporting its services to a number of countries around the world. This has put it on the frontier of managing the differences between local country customs and laws.

Where Does It All Lead?

Consumer computing is a large and expanding space. Usage will span the spectrum from the technology professional to grandparents wanting to use email to reach their grandchildren. Consequently, consumer price points will run from $300 to $3,000 and higher. Expanded price points imply expanded vendor offerings. Some of these offerings will come from today's computer leaders, but consumer electronics, CATV, and telecommunications vendors will be active as well. As PCs take on some of the tasks once dedicated to the television, the telephone, the stereo, the VCR, and the answering machine, the boundaries between devices will blur.

In the end, the drive toward ubiquitous consumer computing will be at the heart of the network-centric era. Unless computers are as pervasive as telephones, it will be impossible for many aspects of life to move primarily, let alone exclusively, into cyberspace. If computers remain mostly a business and affluent consumer phenomenon, there is only so much social transformation that can occur. If 80 percent or more of U.S. households are linked to the Net within a decade, the network-centric era will have fulfilled its mission.

CHAPTER 15

THE ROLE OF GOVERNMENT

As the deregulated world of computers merges with the heavily regulated world of telecommunications, government policy will inevitably become an important part of overall IT industry development. Research and development, the fostering of a competitive environment, and various forms of consumer protection can benefit from, and will sometimes require, national government intervention. This chapter outlines the major relevant activities of government and describes how each of these roles should change as the network-centric era evolves.

National governments around the world have always played such a significant role in the development of the IT industry that it should be unnecessary to say so. Nevertheless, given the strong antigovernment views that have taken hold in much of the United States and a number of other countries around the world, the contribution of government to the overall growth of the IT industry often seems to have been forgotten or at least deemed somehow irrelevant to the current period. This is remarkable given that even recent industry driving phenomena such as packet switching, the Internet, Mosaic, and the Worldwide Web all have their roots in public sector initiatives.

Given both the importance of information infrastructure issues and the long history of government involvement in the telecommunications sector, it is inevitable that public policies will play a key role in shaping the overall IT environment. The major elements of the U.S. Telecommunications Reform Act signed into law by President Clinton in February 1996 are a major reaffirmation of this long-standing role. However, deregulation is only part of the story. This chapter begins by describing ten major roles of government, summarized in figure 15-1. It then provides a framework for viewing the specific roles of government at various stages of the IT industry's evolution.

1. Sponsor of Research and Development

The U.S. Government, particularly the Defense Department, has always played an important R&D role and continues to do so. Looking

Figure 15-1. Summary of key government roles.

1. Sponsor of research and development
2. Investor in pilot projects
3. Regulation of competition and tariffs
4. Protector of privacy and copyrights
5. Maintenance of public "decency"
6. Assurance of fairness, equity, and access
7. As a leading-edge user demonstrating what can be done
8. Industry promotion
9. Setter and/or arbiter of standards
10. Guarantor of competitive and "fair trade" between nations

forward, because of the structural changes brought on by the PC era, the role of the public sector, broadly defined to include government and universities, is likely to remain important and perhaps even to increase.

During the era of vertical integration, companies such as IBM and AT&T drove much of the IT industry's basic R&D, using their superior profits, diverse interests, and secure market position to pursue a wide variety of long-term, pure science research efforts. As the industry changed to a horizontal and more commodity-based structure, such long-term projects became harder to fund and justify.

Today, although IBM and AT&T are both still important, their ambitions have been necessarily scaled back. Among the newer U.S. companies, only Microsoft and Intel have the size and profit margins to pursue truly long-term R&D projects. Both companies have already shown a willingness to invest heavily in research; they have also shown that they realize that in order to move the industry forward they need to help develop areas outside of their individual and relatively narrow slices of the industry. Witness Microsoft's efforts in designing 3-D chips and Intel's work in both multimedia and communications software.

Nevertheless, in today's highly competitive horizontal structure, private sector research is likely to continue to become more short term and practical in nature. Given that basic scientific research is still a requirement for long-term industry advancement, there is an opportunity for both government and universities to fill the void.

However, over the last decade, U.S. Federal Government IT research often focused on what have proved to be largely unproductive areas such as supercomputers, massively parallel systems, and artificial intelligence. Closer business cooperation is clearly needed to help select more appropriate topics. Although the Sematech semiconductor manufacturing initiative has had its share of both fans and detractors, it was clearly a good example of allowing industry to drive research and development decisions.

As things stand today, federal government R&D efforts will likely continue in areas such as high-performance systems, defense, aerospace, and health care. Universities, many of them state owned, seem likely to continue to drive most IT-specific work in software, networking, and human interface engineering as well as the relevant basic work in chemistry, biology, and physics. As more universities develop particular IT competencies, this increasingly decentralized national R&D structure will likely prove to be better suited to accurately reflecting overall industry needs. Nevertheless, there is still the risk that today's horizontally structured, commodity-driven industry may not generate sufficient R&D. It is at least an area for regular government/industry/university discussion.

2. Investor in Pilot Projects

This role is often viewed as being more important in Europe and much of Asia. However, even in the United States, many such partnerships and programs have contributed to overall industry development, especially in telecommunications.

Certainly, government seed money played a useful role in launching the Internet. In the mid-1980s, the National Science Foundation (NSF), through its NSFNET, took the lead in changing the ARPANET from being a relatively closed military network to an increasingly open system that eventually became the Internet. In the late 1980s and early 1990s, the NSF essentially ensured the operation of the overall Internet backbone. In fact, it wasn't until 1995 that NSFNET was officially shut down, with the U.S. portions of the Internet being completely privately run for the first time.

In the United States today, the telecommunications industry has sufficient revenues to fund advanced pilot projects; therefore, government activity in this area is currently quite modest. Given the active work with cable modems, ADSL, fiber optics, and all forms of wireless, it is not clear where additional government support might be needed. The technology behind high bandwidth communications is not the main problem; the real issues today are those of implementation and cost justification.

3. Regulation of Competition and Tariffs

Prior to the telecom reforms of 1996, government regulation was often viewed as a major barrier to industry advancement. However, now that a generally well-received bill has been enacted, a more accurate and positive perspective has emerged. The fact is that, historically, the U.S. government's major regulatory decisions have made important industry contributions. Indeed, at least arguably, they have made a significant contribution to global U.S. IT leadership.

On the computer side, the U.S. Government's 1956 Consent Decree forced IBM to fully exit the computer processing services business until 1979, accelerating the development of an independent processing services industry. Additionally, government jawboning and overall antitrust oversight also encouraged IBM's 1969 decision to unbundle its software and hardware product pricing, again greatly accelerating the viability of an independent software industry.

From a less interventionist perspective, the Reagan administration's 1982 decision to drop its thirteen-year-old suit against IBM, showed an important ability to not intervene in the marketplace unless clearly necessary. In retrospect, this decision may seem to have been an obvious one. However, in 1982, IBM's market power was enormous and seemed to be increasing. There were many who thought that action should have been taken.

More recently, the Justice Department's decision to modify some of Microsoft's operating system practices but to at least for now give the company a free hand in networking reflects a similar wisdom. We will never know whether the government would have formally blocked the Microsoft/Intuit merger or not. It would have been a close call and rightly so. Similarly, there is now heated industry debate as to whether Microsoft's freeware and bundling efforts constitute "predatory" behavior.

On the telecommunications side, the history is also generally positive. Going back to the so-called Carterphone decision of 1968, which allowed non-AT&T equipment to be connected to the U.S. telephone network, through the 1978 decision to allow long-distance service competition, to the monumental 1982 agreement that broke up AT&T itself, the federal government has played a critical, even essential, role in increasing telecom competition. Although this progress has not always been as rapid or as extensive as many suppliers have wished, when compared to that of any other major nation, the U.S. record is outstanding. Japan, for instance, is still considering making changes to Nippon Telephone and Telegraph comparable to the AT&T breakup of almost fifteen years ago.

Although telecom reform appeared to be slow, each year greatly improved policymakers' understanding of the overall issues. The result was a generally sound bill that is likely to move the market smoothly toward increased competition, with multiple long-distance and local providers using a mix of twisted pair, cable, and wireless technologies. As real competition emerges, rate regulation will be phased out, eventually even for local services where wireless technologies will clearly challenge today's relatively high local service rates. Overall, the explosion of the Internet has helped to foster broad support for moving telecommunications services toward an open, unregulated, competitive market. It took time for this consensus to emerge.

From a global perspective, the United States continues to have a much more open market than most of its major national competitors, although the United Kingdom has moved very quickly in this area. Given the recent legislation and the other powerful advantages enjoyed by the United States, a clear and supportive policy framework should assure a competitive U.S. position through at least the first half of the network-centric era.

4. Protector of Privacy and Copyrights

Government efforts here have also tended to be supportive. As early as 1972, the U.S. Supreme Court accelerated the development of the independent software industry by making it clear that it did not endorse software patents, preferring the more nebulous copyright law. Government agencies such as the CIA, Defense Department, and the FBI have always been leaders in security and encryption technology. On the privacy front, laws regarding the use of computer-based information have become an important form of consumer protection in many countries, especially in Europe.

As the network era emerges, all of these issues are arising once again. So-called public key encryption schemes provide very good mass encryption protection, certainly far superior to the general lack of security readily accepted for traditional postal mail systems. In fact, these new private/public key systems are actually too good for many in the law enforcement area who would like to retain the right to tap into electronic communications when necessary. It appears that the technologies to prevent easy surveillance can no longer be prevented from becoming available to the marketplace.

As with Xerox machines, VCRs, digital tape players, and even the floppy disk the Internet has raised serious copyright concerns. However, just like all of the earlier examples, through a combination of sound legal precedents, acceptable social behavior, and adaptation to changing market conditions these concerns will ultimately prove to be exaggerated. Although there will clearly be significant violations, copyright infringement is unlikely to become a major growth inhibitor. The history of the major replication technologies suggests that, although there will be some illegal copying and content prices will fall, overall unit volumes will increase more than enough to grow the total revenue base.

Over time, network-based content will likely follow the same pattern. There are a number of reasons for this. The first is that most people are basically honest, especially if there is enough social stigma associated with a particular form of dishonesty. In the end, if a business or consumer wants to receive a particular form of content, few consumers and virtually no businesses are going to want to steal it on a regular basis. Second, as usage patterns and customs develop, government will enforce laws on "unacceptable" usage.

In this area, government clearly plays a dual role of protector of both consumers and copyright holders. Consider the case of the VCR; it was the U.S. courts that decided over the loud objections of the motion picture industry that consumer taping for personal use was not a violation of content owner copyrights. However, the court also added that any unauthorized taping for commercial purposes would be clearly illegal. This balanced view benefited consumers, the motion picture industry, and VCR manufacturers while creating countless video stores and all manner of promotional, commercial, and how-to video products.

From a global perspective, the situation will likely be more problematic, especially in the short run. Less developed nations today have little incentive to police copyright violations, which affect only well-off, foreign-based content or software providers. Given rapidly rising PC use in countries such as China and India, should current software piracy patterns continue, copyright violations will soon occur on an unprecedented scale. It is hard for these countries to feel sorry for a Microsoft.

However, as these countries grow and develop, countervailing forces almost inevitably will emerge. The most important of these is local content. In the end, Chinese and Indian consumers will want local music, local films, and local software. Local producers of this software and content will seek and receive local support for copyright protection. Once acceptable usage patterns are established to protect local players, these same practices will eventually be extended to foreign offerings. Indeed, the recognition of software value and the stigma associated with illegal copying is already emerging as an important indicator of national development and as a crucial stage in moving toward an information society.

This generally appealing climate should prevail with one possible and noteworthy exception. As PC use in Asia and India swells into the hundreds of millions, these countries might balk at paying high machine royalties to Microsoft. Should Microsoft hold its PC operating system monopoly for another five to ten years, don't be surprised if a country such as China tries to force more favorable licensing terms.

5. Maintenance of Public "Decency" in Areas Such as Gambling and Sexually Explicit Materials

That sexually explicit material has emerged as a high-profile Internet issue should not be surprising. As the examples of cable TV, VCRs, 900 telephone numbers, CD-ROMs, the Internet, and, more recently, virtual reality suggest, pornography has often been closely associated with the early development of new technologies. In fact, many of the earliest written and printed books featured suggestive, often explicit drawings.

In the past, society has always found a way to manage controversial technology applications. Adult cable TV offerings are available only through special, paid subscriptions; X-rated VCR rentals require age identification; and sexually explicit magazines are kept behind special counters. Nevertheless, none of these generally accepted practices are anywhere close to being 100 percent effective in shielding children from offensive materials.

The Internet controversy stems from the valid concern that no such protective mechanisms have yet emerged. Yes, there are now some software programs that can screen for offensive materials, but these often require the provider to identify materials as such and are not today either widely available or in use.

Furthermore, the nature of packet-switching technology can make it difficult to know exactly what information is being transmitting until it is fully available on the recipient end. Here, initially, different countries will have very different standards, which will clearly be problematic. Current Internet technologies are not well suited for recognizing national variations, although vendors such as AOL and CompuServe are scrambling to develop this capability.

Progress on all of these issues will be made over time. Most content providers will not refuse to label their products as sexually explicit. Laws will emerge to punish those who falsely label or fail to label such materials. Each country will be allowed to influence how these content descriptors relate to their own local laws. The system will not be perfect, but it should be manageable enough not to impede overall network expansion. All that is necessary is that most believers see the new preventive practices as being generally effective and heading in the right direction.

Nevertheless, as the Internet provisions in the recent telecommunications reform bill demonstrate, this issue is not likely to be fully resolved any time soon, at least not to many key groups' satisfaction. In the interim, it will be up to politicians, content providers, and the Internet industry itself to convince the general public that progress is being made and that the extent of the overall problem is not sufficient to risk the many benefits of today's rapidly evolving Internet. However, aggressively defending a system that cannot currently prevent the free flow of pornography is a lot to ask of today's U.S. politicians. Since consumer Internet usage in most of Europe and Asia is still quite low, the issue has yet to fully emerge in many countries. It will be interesting to see what happens when it does.

The gambling issue may actually prove to have more staying power. Some would go further to suggest that, without government efforts to control it, gambling might become a driving network-centric application. Certainly, the potential appeal of national or possibly even worldwide interactive gambling is enormous.

Given current U.S. state governments' infatuation with gambling revenues, the public sector might even become the driver. More likely, in the United States at least, vested interests such as the states themselves, existing gambling centers, and a wide array of antigambling organizations and even antinetwork types will do their best to prevent organized gambling from gaining a presence on the Internet. In these efforts, concerns regarding the Internet's security and privacy should prove to be a handy, even if self-serving, rationale.

From a global perspective, gambling, much more so than pornography, has the potential to become one of the biggest transborder data flow tests. In theory, Internet-based gambling could become a way around widely diverse national laws. However, even if untraceable digital cash were available, the placing of essentially nonenforceable and probably illegal bets across geographic regions would no doubt scare off many consumers. As with pornography, national laws should generally but certainly not uniformly prevail.

6. Assurance of Fairness, Equity, and Access

This is also a politically sensitive issue. In a country increasingly concerned about widening income gaps, the arrival of the Internet and the move toward an information-based economy is viewed by some with alarm. To these observers, the Internet looks like just another example of a world increasingly divided into the haves and have-nots.

Governments around the world should resist encouraging this view for two main reasons. From a practical perspective, unless governments are willing to embark on a massive technology giveaway program, it is clear that wealthier and more educated citizens will have access to information technologies sooner and more often than the less well off and less educated. This has been the case with virtually all major new technologies.

It is simply incorrect to imply that not having a computer in the home today is any sort of major economic, educational, or lifestyle disadvantage. The majority of home computer usage is for work-related activities. However, for many service and other forms of employment, working at home is really not possible. On the education side, although children with PCs at home will gain some advantage in having early access to this important new technology, there is little to no evidence that a home computer is a crucial component of a successful grade school education. However, to some extent in high school, but most definitely at the university level, easy access to the Internet is now a near requirement in many fields.

Finally, given that only one-third of U.S. homes currently have a PC and fewer than half of these are actually connected to an on-line service, there are currently no essential or even near essential services provided exclusively over this medium. There won't be for at least another five years.

In sum, government should be sending the message that society is on a long march toward an information economy where PCs will be nearly as universal as phones. However, this process might take ten years or more; in the early years those with machines will be like those with automobiles in the 1920s, 1930s, and 1940s, adopting a new form of transportation while others still rode trains, buses, and trolleys. This difference in mode of transportation did not lead to vast economic or social inequalities and neither will today's gaps in PC usage. Providing sufficient Internet access through schools and libraries can also help diminish any anxieties. Unfortunately, politics being what it is, there will always be those who will resort to demagoguery to gain attention and votes.

7. As a Leading Edge User Demonstrating What Can Be Done

Of all the government areas, this is perhaps the one where the U.S. Government has been least successful. In the 1960s, in addition to the Department of Defense, government social services agencies such as the Social Security Administration and the Internal Revenue Service were considered to be among the leaders in terms of large-scale, database, and transaction processing applications. However, over the course of the last twenty years, government information processing activities have clearly fallen steadily behind those of the private sector.

Upon their election in 1992, the Clinton/Gore administration talked of restoring government technological excellence. In particular, Vice President Gore's "reinventing government" initiatives placed great emphasis on the role of technology in delivering faster and more efficient government services. However, four years into this administration, it is clear that only modest improvements have been made, and prospects for reaching private sector parity anytime soon are poor.

Given the strong public sector role in their overall economies, this issue should be of particular importance to the nations of Western Europe. As in the United States, both national governments and the European Union itself have talked extensively about the role of technology in delivering public sector services. At the height of the United States of Europe enthusiasm, European leaders talked openly about on-line Pan-European job listings, educational offerings, anticrime

efforts, telecommuting support, medical advice, government information, and similar social applications. However, with the exception of
some of the reform-oriented economies of northern Europe, meaningful change has not really occurred, with organizational and labor rigidities remaining a formidable barrier to real innovation and change.

8. Promoter of Technology Through Visible Advocacy Efforts

The importance of this role has been often overstated, but clearly in
the 1992–1994 period, political leaders, such as U.S. Vice President
Gore and U.S. House Speaker Gingrich as well as then European
Union President Jacques Dolors and Commissioner for Industry and
Telecommunications Martin Bangemann greatly helped publicize in-
formation technology.

However, given the extraordinary publicity of the Internet over
the 1994–1996 period, such advocacy is no longer really needed except
for specific IT initiatives. Perhaps not surprisingly, neither President
Clinton or any of the major Republican leaders are strongly associated
with this issue. More tellingly, the U.S. Government has taken a very
low profile approach to the one area where aggressive leadership
might make a real difference—installing computers and Internet access in the nation's schools. In 1992, Vice President Gore pushed hard
for a National Research and Education Network (then known as
NREN), originally proposing to spend some $2 billion connecting
U.S. schools and libraries. These plans have been largely dropped. In
their place, private sector led efforts such as TechCorps and Net Day
have emerged.

9. A Setter and Arbiter of Standards

In addition to the ARPANET/Internet/TCP/IP work previously discussed, the U.S. Government has played an important role in a number of other standards areas. In the early 1960s, in cooperation with
the CODASYL (Conference on Data Systems Languages) task force,
the Department of Defense (DOD) played a critical role in the establishment of COBOL as the primary business processing language. The
1976 approval of the IBM-designed Data Encryption Standard by the

National Bureau of Standards (NBS) was instrumental in the establishment of this still widely used security technology.

Overall, the NBS, which in 1988 was renamed the National Institute for Standards and Technology (NIST) has set a number of Federal Information Processing Standards (FIPS), many of which also became important to the private sector. However, in recent years, these efforts have become less frequent and less successful. Perhaps the last major effort was in the early 1980s, when the Department of Defense, swamped by incompatible systems and applications, attempted to standardize around the ADA programming language. Although ADA usage became considerable, overall DOD standardization was not achieved. More important, ADA usage outside of DOD has been minimal.

As the industry's largest buyer of IT equipment and services, the U.S. Federal Government could be an important standards setting influence. However, this can only occur if the government is a coordinated and state-of-the-art user. Since the latter is unlikely to prove true, the U.S. Government will likely continue the recent pattern of being more a standards follower than a leader. Additionally, since no other national government is large enough to drive the market, this lack of leadership should occur on a worldwide basis as well. A unified European Community might someday change this, but a uniform, leading edge European technology strategy is unlikely anytime soon.

10. Guarantor of Global Competitiveness and "Fair Trade" Between Nations

Many nations view a competitive local IT industry as a high strategic priority. Given this, it is hardly surprising that information technology has been the subject of many trade disputes between the United States, Europe, Japan, and other nations. It has also been a key aspect of the industrial development strategies of countries such as Japan, Taiwan, Korea, Israel, and India. Virtually all developed and developing markets put at least some emphasis on an overall technology trade policy.

The goals and effectiveness of these efforts comprise a complex and controversial topic well outside the scope of this book. However, during the network-centric era, it is clear that such issues will remain and likely intensify. As national information infrastructures emerge as cornerstones of the modern economy, the temptation for government intervention aimed at producing "fair trade," "level playing fields," and "strategic self-sufficiency" will almost certainly prove to be irresistible for some.

Historically, most nations have grudgingly accepted relatively open computer industry competition and trade but insisted on relatively protected telecommunications development. As these two industries merge, regulatory and policymaking attitudes will have to evolve accordingly. This is unlikely to go smoothly. The potential for major international trade disputes regarding network equipment, services, and content is very high. Nations that have allowed U.S. firms to dominate their computer markets are likely to draw the line at telecommunications. Despite tolerating or paying lip service to global markets and joint ventures, national governments, with few exceptions, will be no more likely to allow foreign firms to control their telecom infrastructure than they would their roads, airports, water, or electricity. For computer firms, used to a free-wheeling laissez-faire style, this will likely come as a considerable shock.

Changing Roles Over Time

The ten roles described in the previous section, and no doubt others as well, have all been important at various times and in various countries, particularly within the telecom sector. Governments around the world continue to debate whether and how these activities should relate to the IT development challenges ahead. No one answer is likely to emerge. More likely, a wide array of national responses will essentially become a laboratory for experimentation and policy refinement. Policymaking will be heterogeneous, implying that national competitive differentiation and advantage is achievable. From an IT policy perspective, the next ten years will be far more interesting than the previous twenty.

Although it is too early to say with certainty which specific policy strategies are likely to be most effective globally, some general patterns can already be discerned. This section will suggest that the role of government must evolve over time, with different priorities at different phases of industry development. This policy-organizing principle is illustrated in figure 15-2. By using a standard S-curve for market development analysis, government roles can be broadly mapped into four main stages.

1. *The prelaunch phase.* This is primarily an R&D period, largely restricted to those nations capable of conducting leading edge research. It is by definition a period of unpredictable duration and direction that often only clearly emerges in retrospect. In terms of the network-centric era, this period ran from the late 1960s up until the late 1980s when the Internet began to be privatized. The government role during this phase is largely one of ensuring that its own needs in areas such as defense are being met and that, overall, a competitive national R&D structure is in place through some combination of private, university, and government research initiatives. Relevant proof of concept pilot programs are also generally associated with this phase.

2. *The launch phase.* During this period, government policy is focused on catalyzing the desired developments. Appropriate actions include overall technology advocacy, sponsoring projects with seed money, creating sufficient market incentives, understanding progress within other countries, and, most important, getting the proper regulatory framework in place. The leading edge user role is also highly relevant in this stage for those government bodies capable of such activity. In terms of the network-centric era, the launch phase can be viewed as beginning with the emergence of NSFNET in the mid-1980s, and ending with the development of Mosaic at the University of Illinois in 1993.

Figure 15-2. Changing role of government over time.

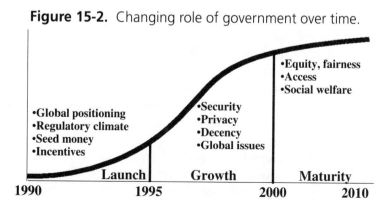

3. *The growth phase.* This period began in early 1994 with the explosion of Internet and Worldwide Web usage and will continue until at least the end of the century. The growth phase will be characterized by regulatory challenges typical of any new frontier without clear laws or enforcement procedures. The development of the American West is a frequently cited and still surprisingly relevant analogy.

In particular, issues of security, privacy, and decency will need to be understood and socially integrated once the mass deployment of new applications and services begin. However, history suggests that these frontier civilization issues will not be resolved until accumulated experience begins to shape accepted usage and behavioral attitudes. Some issues such as copyright infringement will need to be coordinated on a global basis while others such as privacy and decency will show considerable country variation.

4. *The mature phase.* Once pervasive networking begins to become a reality, it then becomes important to fully consider issues of equity, fairness, and universal access as well as the inevitable trade-offs between free market development and overall social welfare. The mature phase in the United States will begin early in the next century. Once three quarters or more of consumers have easy access to the new technologies, then increasingly essential citizen services will begin to emerge, perhaps requiring government-led efforts to extend network service offerings to the remaining population in the same way that rural telephone service received important subsidies to enable virtually universal telephone service.

Timing the Emphasis

Although virtually all of these government roles will need to be discussed throughout the life cycle of information infrastructure development, their emphasis should vary considerably over time. Perhaps the most obvious example is universal service. Consider the historical example of the telephone industry. If universal service had been required in the early years of that industry, the business might never have developed.

Similarly, since personal computers are currently the main means of access to the information infrastructure and since personal computers are still only in use by a relatively small percent of the citizenry, it would be highly counterproductive to insist on universal access at this stage of the industry's development. This message needs to be fully understood by both the political and regulatory regimes and effectively communicated to the public in order to manage potential fears concerning the gap between those connected and those not.

Perhaps a more subtle, but equally important, set of distinctions exists between the launch and the growth phases. Should society wait until the rules of copyrights, privacy, and decency are fully written and implemented, pervasive network service development would be considerably slowed. The Internet pornography issue is a clear example of a growth phase problem that should not be allowed to become a long-term market inhibitor. In the end, the most effective usage laws and customs have been those that evolve out of experience.

Thus, the role of government is necessarily far more complex than simple discussions of market and regulatory philosophies. The complex challenges ahead represent a real opportunity for governments to demonstrate their ability to assist the private sector through a major economic and social transition. The regulatory issues alone provide a great test of public/private cooperation. Government policymaking is also an area that allows for a wide range of national experimentation and diversity, while providing an environment that although competitive can also be cooperative, with governments learning much from each other over time. Ten years from now, it is likely that certain governments will be able to look back and say that they helped their countries develop an important competitive edge. However, given the vagaries of politics and policy, it is all but impossible to say which nations these will be.

CHAPTER 16

THE FOURTH WAVE: TOWARD A CONTENT-CENTRIC IT INDUSTRY

The establishment of a network infrastructure is a means of moving the IT industry forward, not an end in itself. This chapter looks beyond the current period to speculate what sort of IT industry will emerge once a high-performance network infrastructure is finally in place. How will business models and supplier structures evolve? What type of economic transformation can we really expect?

If one were asked to briefly describe the history of the computer industry in terms of its changing overall mission, one might come up with something like the following:

1. *Pre-1964, research and development.* Let's see how computers work and what they are capable of doing. Maybe there is a real business here; maybe not. Let's put some of our best scientists to work and see what happens.
2. *1964–1980, the rise of the computer professional.* Computers are potentially a powerful business management tool that can be very effective in certain controlled environments. However, they are too expensive and difficult for wider market use; they should be used by large organizations and run by specialists.
3. *1981–1994, computers for the office worker.* Computers can improve almost anyone's productivity and are now widely affordable. From an employee perspective, those who learn to use a PC will probably be more successful than those who don't.
4. *1994–2005, wiring the planet.* Now that so many people have computers, it would be nice if they could communicate with each other as easily as humans do over the telephone. It would be even nicer if they could do this at computer as opposed to human speeds. Let's build the infrastructure necessary to do this and find a way to pay for it.
5. *2005–2015, what do we really want to do?* Assuming that there are virtually no constraints on computer power, information storage, and communications bandwidth, and that just about everyone has access to computers that are fully connected to one another, what would happen then? As Microsoft says: "Where do you want to go today?"

Once a high bandwidth infrastructure is ubiquitous, inexpensive, and easy to use, the industry, for the first time, will face the question of what can and cannot be done with computers, or perhaps more accurately, what makes sense and what doesn't. How much of life can and will actually become virtual—working, shopping, communicating, recreating? To what extent will sources of information content—print, audio, video—actually merge? In short, what will the market *really* want?

Predicting the specific new applications of the twenty-first century is generally recognized as an impossible task and is not the focus of this book. The author makes no claims to being a long-term, societal futurist. However, it is possible to use the analytical approach applied to the previous waves to at least identify the general patterns and issues that are likely to emerge during the content-centric era. This chapter provides a framework for thinking about the future based on what we know about both technology, technology economics, and the underlying realities of the world economy.

First of all, what do we mean by "content-centric"? In this book, the word *content* is used broadly to include not just news, information, and entertainment but all manner of computer-based services and applications. In this sense, content is meant to include just about everything that information technology will be used to do.

Skeptics might ask whether, by this definition, we have always been in a content-centric world in that applications have always been the reason businesses or consumers spend money on IT. Although this is clearly true, what defines the content-centric era is that for the first time the range of technology usage will be defined far more by the demand for an application as opposed to the historical pattern of having to always factor in what is technologically possible. Although some technical restraints will certainly continue to exist, their movement from being a primary to a secondary or even tertiary factor represents a major industry shift.

To begin to define what this content-centric era might look like, first recognize that this fourth wave will likely prove to be yet another

Figure 16-1. Summary of content-centric era dynamics.

1995–2005	2005–2015
Network-centric	Content-centric
Electronic commerce	Virtual businesses
Metcalfe's Law	Law of transformation
Wired consumer	Individualized services
Communications bandwidth	Software, information, services
Online demand	Narrowcasting
Converged structure	Embedded technology

major paradigm shift whose principal dimensions can be identified, debated, and separately analyzed. The general pattern of fourth-wave change is summarized in figure 16-1 and explained as follows:

From a network-centric to content-centric industry. The fundamental shift characterizing a content-centric era is that the industry will not revolve around any particular technological capability. Instead, it will center around particular audiences and the content they choose to value. *Audience* here is defined broadly to include various consumers, a business, even an industry. The content that serves this audience will be delivered in a wide variety of increasingly interchangeable forms and media. More important, content will be increasingly intermingled with context as content is increasingly screened for and targeted at particular audiences.

From electronic commerce to virtual businesses. Whereas network technology can be used by every major business sector, in the content-centric world some industries will be much more affected than others. To return to the terminology of Professor Negroponte of MIT (see chapter 13), inherently bit-based industries such as finance, publishing, and entertainment will be much more affected than atom-based industries such as agriculture or construction. More than anything else, the content-centric industry is about transformation and moving much of the world economy and society into cyberspace.

From Metcalfe's law to the law of transformation. Each preceding wave has had its own governing law articulated by an industry pioneer such as Herb Grosch, Gordon Moore, and Robert Metcalfe. This history suggests that the fourth wave might also have a conceptual and exponential driving dynamic. However, this time it probably won't be a technical issue such as system size, semiconductor density, or number of connections. Rather, it is likely to be grounded in the relationship between content and transformation.

Consider the following conceptual formula. The extent of an industry's transformation will be equal to the square of the percentage of that industry's value-add which is accounted for by pure information (bit) as opposed to atom processing activity. In other words, the Transformation Potential of Industry I, TP_I equals %bitsI squared, where %bitsI represents an estimate of the share of an industry's value-add accounted for by bit-based, information processing activities. The use of the squared relationship has the effect of widening industry differentials. If the banking industry is 90 percent information processing and the manufacturing industry is 30 percent, the law of transformation would suggest that the banking industry will be roughly nine times more transformed by IT than is manufacturing: .9 × .9 = .81, .3 × .3 = .09, .81 ÷ .09 = 9.

Obviously, measuring %bitsI precisely is difficult, but it does provide a starting point for the process of trying to forecast the extent of the impact of IT on any particular industry.

From the wired consumer to individualized services. Today, most Internet and Web activity consists of broadcasting information to selected audiences, with some individual feedback returning to the broadcaster. In a content-centric world, the delivery itself will be far more customized around individual needs and preferences. Software agents derived from today's customization programs are likely to be the key enabling technology. In addition to providing unprecedented customization, tireless, constantly active agents will dramatically increase network traffic, perhaps eventually becoming the majority of communications activity. Should individuals end up dealing mostly with their chosen agent, it will be a large step in making the network itself truly invisible.

From communications bandwidth to software, information, and services. The scarce resource in the industry has always been one of hardware resources—MIPS, bandwidth, and so on. Once the overall hardware infrastructure is in place, industry focus will shift to software, content, and services, all of which are much less likely to be subject to diminishing investment returns. Information economics, which combines the nearly infinite scale economies of software with the nearly infinite variety of content, will become the main industry driver.

The patterns of previous waves suggest that in a content-centric era, content would start as a scarce commodity and wind up as a surplus one. Given the vast array of content on the net already, this might seem like an overstatement. However, when one takes the broader view of content to include applications such as shopping, banking, and related services, one realizes that there is still a very long way to go. Today's Web offers no truly essential services. By the end of the content era, network access will be a necessity.

Even for the vast store of information already on the Net, given the serious problems in finding content, paying for it, and establishing real multimedia capabilities, it is clear that a true content-centric industry cannot emerge until a ubiquitous, high bandwidth network infrastructure is in place.

From on-line channels to customer pull. Each of the first three waves has been characterized by its own dominant channel—direct, followed by indirect, then on-line. It is clear that the content-centric era will take this one step farther. Today, most of the marketing on the Net is still one of pushing various information at potential customers. As information access and related services become increasingly customized, the majority of information will be pulled by individuals and their agents. This sounds obvious, but the impact of a shift to predominantly customized information and service streams will have a profound effect on overall technology usage, supplier structure, and brand. In effect, the nature of individual needs as reflected in software will begin to define the information channels of the future.

From a converged computer/communications/consumer electronics industry value chain to one of embedded systems. To truly move toward an information society, technology must extend beyond today's world of encoded bits and abstract information to include ubiquitous links to the physical world. Smart cameras, sensors, and other analog inputs will become embedded in a wide range of products and systems. As information processing capability becomes increasingly bundled into a virtually infinite array of products and applications, the size of the overall IT industry will become essentially unmeasurable. Describing and quantifying the full IT value chain will become as difficult as defining and measuring the full electricity value chain would be today.

Envisioning a Content-Centric Information Industry

Figure 16-2 shows the changed model of a content-centric industry. At the center of the industry will be a community or audience that has a particular set of needs and interests. These communities can range from the highly specialized such as Chicago-area chiropractors

Figure 16-2. Understanding content-centered communities.

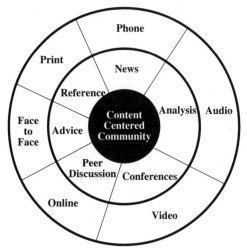

to a mass market such as World Cup soccer fans. As with today, various types of content will continue to emerge to meet the needs of each community. So far, nothing new.

The second layer portrays some typical forms of this content. Although the terminology will differ across various business and consumer markets, the key idea is that increasingly content providers will serve their audiences through multiple types of offerings, all driven by and revolving around the overall community and the content brand that serves them. This brand-driven strategy will be necessary to compete for mind share in increasingly competitive content and services industries. Examples of this strategy have already started to emerge in both the business and consumer sectors, but they cannot come to full fruition until after the work of the network-centric era has been completed and a multimedia world is truly enabled.

This idea of a broad range of services revolving around a particular content brand is fundamentally different than the situation today, where content providers are often closely associated with a particularly technology—TV, print, film, audio, and events. In other words, in today's world, services and media are usually tightly integrated, often by law. In the future, they will become increasingly independent. The regulatory reform to allow this to happen is now well underway.

This uncoupling of services and media is shown most clearly in the outer ring. Not only are the needs of a particular audience met by a spectrum of content-branded services but each of these services is free to employ a variety of technologies and media. Taken together, the broadening of service forms and the interchangability of media constitute a working definition of a multimedia, content-centric era.

Differentiating Content from Software Economics

For more than a decade it has become fashionable for many industry participants to use the words *content* and *software* interchangeably. In this book, the two terms have generally been used separately. Software is used to describe instruction sets such as computer operating systems, utilities, and application programs. Content is reserved for various forms of information, be they text, data, audio, or video. Although the two are sometimes bundled together, as in an interactive product (in this book referred to as "rich content"), in most cases the two can be clearly discerned.

Software and content do, of course, share some important traits. Each tends to have high initial development expenses but then effectively zero marginal unit cost. Therefore, both benefit heavily from volume markets. Additionally, since both software and content are composed purely of bits, both share similar concerns regarding copyrights and other intellectual property protection issues.

It is debatable which industry faces the more serious intellectual property problem. Since content often requires no support or upgrades, illegal copies are often virtually the equivalent of the original. For software, the need for support is perhaps the main pragmatic (as opposed to moral) reason to buy a given product.

On the other hand, content product pricing is generally much closer to actual marginal unit cost than is most software. In contrast, today's comparatively high software prices provide a much stronger financial incentive for illegal copying.

However, these premium software prices are almost entirely due to either near monopoly vendor shares in certain markets or strong customer lock-in, which effectively gives a vendor monopoly-like control over its own customers. As discussed in chapter 10, at least some of this privileged position is likely to diminish over time, resulting in much more competitive, "contentlike" pricing for many mass market software products. Corel's willingness to provide an entire suite of office software for as little as $10 per machine is a sign of the changes that truly competitive software markets would bring. Should a competitive, unbundled, browser market emerge, prices might fall to just a few dollars or even less.

However, there is one large difference that tends to make these two markets behave and be structured differently. Whereas many consumers might wish to own or have on-line access to hundreds or even thousands of CDs and movies, most individuals need and want only one word processor, one spreadsheet, one database. In addition, many software applications programs can be used by everyone, but most content is designed for some audiences but not others. This is why software markets have historically been highly concentrated, while content markets have usually been highly fragmented.

Furthermore, content products are produced and then sold with little customer lock-in or follow-on activity. Software, on the other hand, generally requires user training and often needs to be continually upgraded. In this sense, it has important service attributes. For these and other more cultural reasons, software and content companies are likely to stay separate over time.

A company such as Microsoft by sheer strength of effort might have major content successes, but such successes will not come easy and will tend to be more the exception than the rule. On the other hand, the content-centric era presents such tremendous opportunities for both the software and content-centric industries that there is often far more reason to cooperate than to compete. Moreover, close cooperation between software and content providers will be required to bring about a truly interactive and multimedia content industry. Accordingly, the cooperation between Microsoft and NBC is appropriate in a way that a stand-alone Microsoft on-line news magazine probably is not.

Structural Implications

If this holds true, it would appear that overall the software and content industries will remain more separate than converged. Rich content will be developed through joint ventures, contract programming, and increased in-house software resources at many content companies. In the end, however, the software business is about building tools; these tools should be used as broadly as possible and therefore should not be restricted to inherently more narrowly focused content companies. The software efforts of content companies will be aimed primarily at providing customized applications and services. The tools used for this customization will come from the software industry.

Perhaps a less predictable issue is whether today's mostly media-specific content companies will successfully evolve into the multimedia companies of the future. There is no more clear-cut example of this question than the competition between on-line and print publications.

Print vs. On-line: The Search for a "Natural Transformation"

Computing power will soon be sufficient to virtualize into bits many products currently consisting of atoms. The question is whether this is something the market will want to do. The author has labeled the process by which the market decides which areas will be virtualized and which will not as one of "natural transformation," borrowing the connotations of the term "natural sizing" used by many economists to describe the long-term shape of various national economies.

There is perhaps no better example of this issue than the long-standing debate about the future of printed paper publishing. Clearly, some industry observers have been predicting since the 1970s that on-line information would soon make printed paper obsolete. Word processors, integrated office automation systems, personal computers, email, and now the Worldwide Web have all been expected by some to make paper go the way of the horse-drawn carriage.

Some forms of print publishing have in fact become largely outdated. Perhaps the most prominent example is scientific publishing. When new scientific research is announced, the reaction and debate over the Internet has largely bypassed the need for specialized journals, which cannot possibly provide the same level of low-cost speed, distribution, and interaction. However, this case is still clearly the exception. Despite the explosion in electronic media, print volumes continue to steadily rise. Will this change?

One way to address this question is to draw up a list of the strengths and, by implication the weaknesses, of electronic and printed material. This will help define a rational basis for coexistence or replacement at various points in time. These functional distinctions can then be combined with critical cultural and inertial issues. Some of the defining attributes to both print and electronic media follow.

Strengths of newspapers and magazines

Low risk	Insignificant financial penalty if lost or stolen
Disposable	Can be thrown away when no longer needed
Portable	Easy to use and carry when moving
Lightweight	At least for shorter documents
Detachable	Individual can carry only what's needed
Flexible	Can be bent, folded, or packed without real concern
Off-line	Never needs batteries or power. Never experiences network delays
High resolution	Capable of very high print and image quality
Inexpensive	Requires no up-front technology investment
Sharable	Can be easily and legally given to friend or colleague
Easy to store	In small quantities can be easily put aside for future use
Multiuser	Household or office members can read different material simultaneously

Strengths of electronic

Current	In theory can be updated twenty-four hours a day
Searchable	Reader can search for specific things
Customized	Individual can receive only specifically requested information
Interactive	Individual can respond immediately to received information
Multimedia	Text, audio, and video can be intermingled
Depth	Potential for additional depth virtually unlimited
Hyperlinks	Direct links to other related information easily available

Network stored   No need to keep old paper copies for ref-
                        erence
Communal   Contacts with others with similar interests
                        are easy
Ubiquitous   Delivery instantaneous everywhere in the
                        world

Although electronic technologies offer tremendous new capabilities, paper's advantages in mass availability, image quality, flexibility,
weight, powerless operation, and the ability to be lost, stolen,
dropped, spilled on, taken to the beach, or simply thrown away are
still compelling. Put more simply, the advantages of paper tend to be
ones of convenience, whereas those of electronic publishing tend to be
ones of substance. There is plenty of room for both in the marketplace.

Major technological progress is required if electronic products
are to neutralize the current print advantages. In addition to much
higher levels of device ubiquity, very light weight, very high resolution,
low power consumption, and inexpensive devices would be required.
In addition, power sources in airplanes, airports, train stations, cars,
and perhaps even coffee shops would help, as would detachable flat
panel screens that could be "docked" with a notebook computer
when necessary.

However, progress in all of these areas will take considerable time.
The need for high screen quality conflicts with the requirements of
low price and power. Ubiquitous plug-in capabilities will await overall
infrastructure improvements that will take years, if not decades. Detachable screens with their own memory and power exist largely at a
theoretical level.

When combined with cultural and inertial effects, it seems clear
that paper will be around for a long time to come. Not only do many
readers still prefer paper but business practices surrounding paper
pricing, advertising, copying, and distribution are well understood,
further increasing user and provider comfort levels.

In sum, print and electronic media will coexist for the foreseeable
future. Given that the strengths and weaknesses are so different, a
rational positioning of both media should be a fairly straightforward
process. Computers will be used mainly when searchability, depth,

specialization, currency, interaction, mass storage, group interaction, and multimedia capabilities are desired. Paper will still be ideal for mass market reading convenience, particular for those on the move. The two media should evolve in a complementary manner. Most print publications will also offer electronic services. The two offerings will be positioned as part of an overall strategy with much complementary interaction.

Over time, reading habits will change, especially for professional and business reading. Electronic technology's ability to store and retrieve virtually everything means that information can be accessed when necessary. This will tend to diminish the need to browse weekly or monthly journals to keep up. In addition, the Internet provides a powerful tool for product and services companies to provide content directly to an audience without the support of publishing intermediaries.

Many have argued that eventually the significantly lower costs of on-line delivery will tilt the competitive balance decisively. A typical newspaper or magazine spends far more on paper, printing, distribution, and postage than on editorial content. If these costs were borne by the readers, incentives to read lower cost on-line products might well drive the market. Indeed, this is likely to be the case in many specialty areas such as academic journals. It was the core founding idea behind the creation of Microsoft's *Slate,* edited by Michael Kinsley.

However, in the mass market, print costs are not borne by the reader, they are principally paid for by advertisers. Therefore, unless advertisers shift their money to on-line media, the underlying cost differentials are not likely to seriously affect the consumer. With on-line media's inherent ability to be customized and linked to other services, and perhaps more important, its ability to be accurately measured, many advertisers are eager to go on-line as soon as possible. However, in the end, advertisers will follow the readers; if they prefer paper, then advertising will continue to support paper.

It must also be realized that the print-to-electronic transition will vary greatly by type of publication. Audience size, computer device and bandwidth availability, and cultural affinity are among the driving forces that will differ sharply for different types of publications. As a general rule, the transition should occur in roughly the following order:

1. *Academic journals.* In fast moving areas such as science, has already changed
2. *Other highly specialized areas.* Already many exist only on the Net
3. *Computer trade press.* Should move in next few years
4. *Other business trade press.* Will take three to five years at best
5. *Mass market business press.* Five years or more
6. *Mass market newspapers and magazines.* Ten years or more

Academic and other specialized publications have shifted because of speed, cost, and lack of advertising. The computer trade press will then likely be next because of its wealth of available devices and bandwidth and because of its strong cultural identity with on-line services. If this segment does not shift, then many of the others probably won't either.

The trade press in other industries will then follow because of device and bandwidth availability and limited advertising revenues in certain mature industries. After that, the next major challenge should be the mass business press such as the *Wall Street Journal.* If anything is going to drive this transition, it will probably be depth, searchability, and customization. Finally, it will likely take a decade or more for an electronic experience to match that of the daily newspaper for most consumers.

Competitive Implications

The competitive implications of this slow transition are significant. Unlike the computer industry, the media industry has historically shown high levels of stability. Although there has always been room for new entrants (*USA Today,* Fox TV), many of the world's major TV networks, newspapers, and publishing houses have existed for decades or longer. On the other hand, each industry has tended to remain separate. Newspaper companies did not succeed in the television business; television networks missed the film business, and so on.

As vendors see the content-centric era approach, they are either analytically or instinctively recognizing that these traditional separations are starting to break down. This has led to the current period of cross-media mergers and acquisitions—Disney and ABC, Westinghouse and CBS. These deals should be seen as an essential part of the process of creating the multimedia content companies of the future.

Clearly, the Web was the first major step in this direction. On the Internet, given the current emphasis on text and graphics, most media companies' sites—be they print, TV, radio, or film companies—tend to look alike. As the Internet begins to offer integrated audio and video support, it is likely that this resemblance will continue. In other words, as the network becomes capable of supporting multimedia applications, most content companies will want to take advantage of this. This will tend to transform these content companies into true multimedia companies in sharp contrast to today's technology-specific content providers.

It is easy to imagine some obvious examples. A *New York Times* Web site will support audio or video clips of related newspaper stories. In the same way, a television station site might have the entire text of a presidential speech available for those who want it. A film industry company will want to have various reviews and textual information available for the films it is promoting. As each tries to better serve its audience, the temptation to use all available media will prove irresistible. This will have the effect of making these companies increasingly alike and competitive.

In addition, the slow pace of change and the high investments required will likely make it difficult for new companies to supplant today's leaders by focusing solely on the electronic marketplace. If the market was going to shift in just a few years, such dedication might well create an important competitive edge. However, given the more evolutionary process forecasted, the established players will likely continue to lead. The real question is how these companies will fare in competition with each other. There will be clear winners and losers, but since they will largely be determined by the decisions of the companies themselves, they cannot be predicted.

Getting Back to Bits and Atoms

Content is not just the news and media; it embodies just about everything that computers will be used for. Although the former has attracted most of the attention, the biggest question for the content-centric era is to what extent the overall economy is transformed.

Over time, an industry's potential for transformation will be directly proportional to its underlying bit/atom ratio. Publishing, entertainment, banking, insurance, and other financial services will likely be the most radically transformed.

Mixed environments such as health care, education, and government services should comprise the next tier, especially if the public sector can reduce or even reverse the currently widening gap between its technology utilization and that of the private sector. This will become a critical issue in controlling the overall costs and improving the quality of public sector services. Perhaps more than any other area, it will be the use of technology in these public or quasi-public areas that will determine national competitiveness in the content-centric age. This is, at least arguably, the biggest area of U.S. strategic vulnerability. However, given the current wide-open competition, it also remains a tremendous opportunity.

Figure 16-3 puts these three groups in perspective in terms of their overall share of the U.S. economy. Clearly, deeper analysis would be required to measure the precise extent of potential transformation, but the data are sufficient to suggest that roughly a third of the U.S. economy is already bit-based in nature.

Integrating the Physical World

What will happen to the other two-thirds, those industries that are fundamentally of a physical nature? Manufacturing, wholesale and

Figure 16-3. U.S. Gross Domestic Product by industry sector, 1992.

Agriculture, mining, construction --	7%
Manufacturing --	18%
Transportation and utilities --	9%
Wholesale trade --	7%
Retail trade --	9%
Finance/insurance/real estate --	18%
Private health care --	6%
Other services --	13%
Government --	13%

Source: Latest data available from U.S. Department of Commerce, 1996.

retail distribution, construction, agriculture, and many services such as cleaners, florists, and restaurants will likely undergo the least change, at least initially. In these sectors, information technology may well be a critical tool in terms of overall business efficiency and effectiveness, but in the end, cyberspace-based offerings have little opportunity to replace the tangible products and services provided. All of these sectors will no doubt continue to invest heavily in information technology, but the issue in the content-centric era will not be the ability to spend but rather the ability to be transformed.

Some have taken this argument a step further to predict that as information businesses are increasingly automated, these physical services will assume even greater social and economic value. This, however, would run against hundreds of years of history that consistently demonstrates that new and changing industries tend to produce the greatest opportunities and provide the highest wages.

Although the world of atoms will never be transformed as much as the world of bits, the content-centric era will likely start to dramatically affect atom-based industries sometime in the early twenty-first century. Technologies such as smart cameras, microphones, and other sensors and the increasingly intelligent software that will manage them will move the industry far beyond today's mostly general purpose computers and related software and services.

Smart automobiles, houses, roads, buildings, and factories, along with intelligent machines, robots, appliances, and other devices, will bring a much larger slice of everyday life into the digital world. Although some of this technology exists today, its potential cannot be realized until the network-centric era's information infrastructure is in place. This is especially so in the consumer sector. Once sufficient bandwidth to the home is available, these new types of applications and services can be quickly integrated, leading to the intelligent homes and offices of the future.

As technology becomes a basic component of nearly all other industries, the size of the IT industry becomes essentially unmeasurable. Additionally, as atom-based industries such as automobiles, consumer appliances, construction, and even agriculture take on a strong technology dimension, further IT supplier restructuring is highly likely. More broadly, this marriage of the virtual and physical worlds will complete a major phase of this industry's century-long efforts to create a true information society.

Implications for Leadership

Almost by definition, a content-centric industry cannot have companies with overwhelming market control. Be it information content or content-driven services, the market will tend to support a nearly infinite variety of often conflicting content types. More than in any other area, it is here that the distinctions between software and content economics are critical.

Additionally, as an increasing share of IT hardware and software is embedded in other types of products and services, the product subordination patterns that began in the network-centric era will be even further amplified. The close link between a microprocessor and an operating system with a PC will generally not occur in the case of a home security or electric power management system. Hardware and software in these emerging applications will clearly be enabling components and not ends in themselves.

CHAPTER 17

WAVES OF POWER

This book closes with a few final remarks regarding the past, present, and future of supplier market power, this time through the eyes of an observer in the year 2010.

Given today's world where information processing is so pervasive as to be largely invisible, it is difficult to believe that, for most of the computer industry's history, computer vendor competition was dominated by just a few suppliers who wielded extraordinary influence over the worldwide information technology community.

Today, of course, there is a nearly infinite array of different computer-based hardware devices coming from large and small electronics firms alike. The idea of any one manufacturer dominating the market for what is now such an embedded capability has become hard to imagine. Similarly, software today exists in such countless quantity and variety and is so intrinsic to nearly every activity that the fact that any one vendor could dominate both the production and sale of software also seems a remote possibility.

Nevertheless, for most of the computer industry's history this was precisely the case. Indeed, the story of how this great supplier power was initially created and why it was steadily eroded reveals much about the course of the IT industry's evolution.

Looking back, both supplier market power and the overall IT industry were largely shaped by the interplay between three main forces: new waves of technology, shifts in overall information industry structure, and the actions of individual market competitors. All three factors proved to be critical determinants in each of the first three great waves of IT industry expansion—mainframes, personal computers, and network-centric computing.

In the 1920s, 1930s, and 1940s, before the electronic computer industry began, IBM aggressively grabbed nearly total control of the market for electromechanical punch-card equipment, using tactics that simply would not be tolerated today. At a time when the concept of antitrust enforcement was only beginning to emerge, IBM founder Thomas Watson, Sr., drove hard not just for industry leadership but for total market control. As IBM went on to take some 90 percent of the punch-card business, it was also setting the future course of the next fifty years of computer industry competition.

In the 1950s and 1960s, IBM, to its great credit, succeeded in transferring this dominance of electromechanical corporate information processing into the electronic era, with its S/360 family representing its most symbolic and long-lasting triumph. Although competitors built many equivalent or even superior machines, they never managed to even approach IBM's share in the major general purpose computer sector. IBM's vast base of electromechanical customers and its control of the still-critical punch-card equipment business gave it enormous advantages over any would-be rivals.

IBM's near monopoly systems market power was coupled with a vertically integrated hardware, software, and services business model, giving it leverage over the entire IT industry and making it one of the world's largest, most powerful, and most admired corporations of its time. By the mid-1960s, the competitive ruthlessness that lay at the heart of IBM's great initial success had largely been forgotten, replaced by what was often called the "IBM mystique," a rare combination of fear, admiration, and mystery.

IBM's apparent ability to dominate any information technology sector it chose became a significant cause of industry and government concern. Throughout the 1970s, there was persistent talk of either breaking up IBM or finding some other means to check its power. However, the threat of government intervention officially ended with the arrival of the laissez-faire Reagan administration, which dropped the Department of Justice's thirteen-year investigation of IBM in 1982.

Ironically, the 1982–1984 period marked the peak of IBM's perceived global power. A booming mainframe market, the widespread success of its S/36 small business systems, and its stunning takeover of the emerging PC market seemed to demonstrate an awesome across-the-board prowess. IBM executives talked openly of becoming a $100 billion company by 1990; few observers disagreed.

Amid all of the great market success, hardly anyone realized that the eventual humbling of IBM had actually begun three years earlier in 1981. In that year, IBM made its fateful decisions to outsource its key PC components to Microsoft and Intel. What IBM and most others at the time saw as a simple time-to-market decision turned out to be a total loss of control over the most important IT market of the next decade. IBM's great divestiture also triggered a thirty-year process of IT industry power diffusion.

Just as the history of the computer industry would have been radically different had not Tom Watson, Sr., had the ambition and drive to so totally dominate the accounting machine market, so did IBM's PC decisions mark a critical industry turning point. Even today, historians continue to debate what would have happened had IBM approached the PC market with its traditional proprietary technology strategy.

As fate would have it, both Microsoft and Intel were also run by extremely able and aggressive executives. Once power was given to them, they were nearly always successful in not letting IBM or anyone else take it back. Intel invested massively to exploit its opportunity and become the overwhelming world leader in microprocessors. Microsoft leveraged its operating system and user interface position into additional leadership in tools, languages, and, most important, applications. The interests of the two companies were highly synergistic as suggested by the then popular term "Wintel."

From an overall industry perspective, IBM's loss of PC market control quickly led to the collapse of the long-standing vertically integrated supplier model in favor of a highly horizontal structure. Whereas in the past, computer companies had produced their own hardware and software and handled their own sales and customer services, new PC-oriented entrants focused on particular layers of an emerging IT industry value chain. With this narrow focus they tended to move with a speed, openness, and deftness that the older systems companies could not match. IBM's initial PC design leadership provided the critical interface specifications, allowing standard products to be produced from an increasingly specialized and multivendor environment. Indeed, the shift from a vertical to a horizontal supplier structure dominated the IT industry competition of the 1980s.

Over time, each layer of this new horizontal value chain began to be defined by either de facto or de jure standards. De facto layers supported monopoly supplier positions for vendors such as Microsoft, Intel, and Novell; de jure segments tended to produce the sort of brutal commodity competition common to many industries but unlike anything the IT business had previously experienced. However, whether competition was de facto or de jure in nature, individual vendor power was consistently restricted to a single layer of the value chain, a significant overall diminishment compared to the vertically integrated era.

It soon became clear that long-lasting de facto monopoly positions would exist in just two main areas—microprocessors and operating systems. There were a number of interrelated reasons why this proved to be the case. Both microprocessors and operating systems were complex technologies with intricate inner workings that proved very difficult for other vendors to duplicate. Additionally, not only did both products occupy neighboring layers in the overall industry value chain but, because operating systems and microprocessors defined the point where hardware and software technologies are joined, the boundary between these two layers was considerably less clear than with other industry segments. Finally, thanks to IBM's initial influence, the Microsoft DOS operating system was tailored specifically for Intel's microprocessor designs.

During the 1980s and into the early 1990s, the PC market grew beyond anyone's expectations, and the power of Microsoft and Intel expanded accordingly. By 1993, it was clear that this power would no longer be restricted to the PC marketplace but would begin to move into the larger systems and server arena. To many observers at the time, this put the two industry leaders on a path to try to duplicate the industry-wide power that IBM had once enjoyed. Microsoft's publicly stated aims soon reached a point where even the U.S. Justice Department began applying close scrutiny, actually intervening in several then important areas.

However, as successful as these two firms were, even their combined power was nowhere near what IBM's had once been. Because both companies sold indirectly with little or no customer service activity, they could not begin to match the combination of both product and customer control that IBM enjoyed in its day. In reality, the two companies had monopoly shares in what were now relatively small slices of the overall industry value chain. By 1993, Intel and Microsoft combined accounted for just 4 percent of overall IT industry revenues. However, because of their monopoly positions, their share of gross industry profits was consistently over 10 percent. In contrast, in 1982 IBM had roughly one-third of industry revenues and more than 50 percent of its profits.

Additionally, and in hindsight remarkably, in all of the excitement over the extraordinary success of "Wintel," it often seems to have been forgotten that Microsoft and Intel were in fact *two* companies, not one. IBM had not just handed over its systems market power to the new leaders, it had forever divided it. For the next decade and beyond, advances in microprocessors and operating systems would proceed increasingly independently, making cooperation between the two leaders difficult.

It was therefore only a matter of time before the link between hardware and operating systems (which had existed since the industry's origins) was finally broken. This meant that any one vendor's market power would henceforth be largely limited to a single layer of the value chain, making it much harder to defend and leverage. As obvious as this seems in retrospect, it went largely unnoticed at the time due the tremendous staying power of the "Wintel" platform and the PC industry itself.

From a mass market perspective, the perceived power of Microsoft peaked in 1995 with the extraordinary publicity over relatively minor new product offerings such as Windows 95 and the Microsoft Network, indicative of the exaggerated industry fears of the software market leader. As primarily a component provider, Intel consistently kept a much lower end user profile.

As was the case with IBM, however, the source of Intel's and Microsoft's diminished market power was apparent several years earlier but not widely recognized. By late 1993 and growing rapidly thereafter, the power of the Internet had begun to emerge, challenging the fundamental premises of the PC market leaders.

Although it had been slowly gathering momentum for over a decade, the development of the Worldwide Web in 1989 and the graphical Mosaic interface in 1993—combined with the underlying pent-up demand for linking existing but previously incompatible mainframe, minicomputer, LAN, and on-line services networks—resulted in an almost totally unforeseen explosion in public network usage, quickly making the Internet the industry's most powerful new force and shifting the industry toward a new network-centric paradigm.

From a supplier power perspective, the Internet ushered in its own combination of technology change, structural transformation, and individual executive and company actions, generally repeating the pattern of both the PC and systems eras but with some significant variations.

The core technology changes quickly became apparent. Improving communications bandwidth through technologies such as cable TV, fiber optics, ISDN, and others replaced faster microprocessors as the primary industry requirement. Additionally, user investments began to shift away from funding ever more powerful desktop hardware and software. Instead, incremental investments increasingly went into developing the network infrastructure and related network applications.

This change in technology was accompanied by a significant change in structure. With the arrival of the Internet, the true merger of the computer and telecommunications industries finally began. After all, the Internet was almost completely dependent on the underlying telephone infrastructure. It was only a matter of time before the carriers that owned these resources began to exploit them. Thus, as the industry emphasis shifted toward network services and their bandwidth requirements, the lines between the computer and telecommunications industries became indistinguishable, fulfilling a decades old industry prediction. Digital information transmission became an essential and increasingly integrated part of the overall IT industry value chain.

These changes in technology and structure had truly startling implications for new and existing vendors as well as the very nature and source of network-centric IT industry leadership.

Whereas IBM's leadership was created by aggressiveness and Intel's and Microsoft's, at least initially, by inheritance, the core elements of the Internet emerged nearly by accident. Technology initially developed for government and research use quietly seeped into the open market and then exploded in use as an appealing and inexpensive means of rapidly overcoming decades worth of proprietary vendor networking strategies.

This temporarily tilted the industry toward a more de jure structure. Whereas so much of the history of the IT business had been characterized by strong de facto vendor leadership, suddenly, the critical technologies of the Internet—TCP/IP, HTML, Mosaic, Hypertext Transfer Protocol (HTTP)—had no real vendor leadership or ownership at all.

What little overall management existed was done by formally powerless, relatively slow moving standards bodies such as the Internet Engineering Task Force. This collegial structure worked fine during the Internet's government and academic past, but was ill suited to the fast-paced, high-stakes network-centric IT industry that the Internet triggered.

As the Net grew quickly to become a powerful market force, vendors such as Netscape, Sun, Microsoft, and others attempted to move various aspects from the de jure to the de facto domain. Additionally, the Internet's grass-roots legacy brought with it unusually immature network usage and pricing structures that were not well suited to the order-of-magnitude increases in network utilization and the required bandwidth investments. In short, over the 1995–1998 period, fierce and often frenzied competition broke out in virtually every aspect of the now wide-open Internet-centric industry. Given the myriad uncertainties involved, many wondered if the Internet would even survive.

This competition took place layer by industry layer as a horizontal industry structure remained even through the convergence of the computer and communications industries. PC hardware vendors were challenged by a variety of new devices, including so-called network computers, personal digital assistants, video games, TV adapters, and eventually cable set top boxes. Microsoft and other software leaders faced new competition on virtually all fronts from Netscape, Sun, and many others. Finally, the specialized Internet Access Providers eventually came to face brutal price competition first from the telephone carriers and eventually from the cable TV service providers.

As the computer and telecommunications industries converged and as powerful individual vendors or alliances of vendors tried to set important new Internet standards, the old Internet de jure structure crumbled. Once again, vendor competition became the main driver of market evolution. During this transition, the Internet experienced its share of problems—product incompatibilities, bandwidth shortages, service disruptions, security breakdowns, and more. Nevertheless, the industry proved to be remarkably adept at making the transition from a public standards structure to a competitively driven structure. The much feared collapse of the Internet never really occurred.

The resulting vendor competition was some of the most fascinating and complex in the industry's history. Most of the leaders of the PC industry were determined not to let the Internet industry do to them what the PC era had done to the mainframe and minicomputer companies. In addition, all of the surviving systems companies, such as IBM, Hewlett-Packard, and Digital, saw the Internet as a second chance to regain their lost market leadership. Finally, a powerful wave of well-financed start-ups was launched in virtually every major Internet-related niche. In short, three generations of U.S. vendors, not to mention their global competitors, were doing everything they could to earn their place in a rapidly shifting industry. The ensuing and intense value chain competition produced different results in different sectors.

In hardware, the expanded range of new devices and a slowdown in traditional PC hardware product cycles posed fundamental challenges to that era's PC hardware industry business model. Increasingly, the market moved away from one led by fast-moving PC-focused suppliers toward a more diversified consumer electronics approach. With this change in structure, Japanese and other Asian competitors, after nearly twenty years of struggling, finally resurfaced.

Although Intel went on to build enormous volumes of microprocessors, new IT devices tended to use chips from other suppliers. In addition, as network-centric computing eventually made longer PC hardware cycles viable, the market for Intel-compatible chips became viable, especially after the major Asian investments in this business in the second half of the 1990s. Although Intel was led by an extremely able executive, little could be done to prevent the microprocessor from taking on increasingly commodity-like status.

In software, the story was much more dramatic. Start-up vendor Netscape grabbed an early lead that clearly threatened Microsoft's software industry leadership. However, in the first half of 1996, Microsoft, still led by founder Bill Gates, engineered one of the most remarkable company responses in business history. Showing drive that would have made Tom Watson, Sr., proud, Microsoft went all out to destroy its last main rival, using all manner of technical, financial, and even legal initiatives.

It soon became clear that, left to its own, Netscape, despite its best efforts, might not stand up to its brilliant and powerful rival. If Microsoft were to sweep away Netscape the way it did its PC software rivals, its control over the industry would become immense. The industry had come to a defining moment.

Fortunately, both the industry (through explicit pro-Netscape financial and marketing support) and the government (by forcing Microsoft to curb its most predatory tactics) managed to ensure that the Internet software market would remain open to competition. Netscape and Microsoft each remained strong competitors. The long history of de facto software market monopolies was finally broken. This proved to be a critical step in reshaping overall industry leadership and influence.

Although Microsoft held on to its PC market leadership for another decade and made major roads into enterprise, its inability to control the Internet put a ceiling on its growth in power. Thanks to Netscape and its supporters in key markets such as browsers and server software, Microsoft was a major but not monopoly player. The effect of this on software pricing was dramatic. With browser products sold in the hundreds of millions of units, even advanced versions of these and other software products began to be priced at just a few dollars, sometimes even less. Reducing monopoly power proved to be critical in finally bringing the natural economics of software to the market. Overall prices for word processing, spreadsheets, and other applications fell dramatically.

In telecommunications, after years of sluggishness, the telephone companies eventually awoke and drove many of the early Internet Access Providers out of the business. These large communications vendors then began to work out Internet interoperability issues in a manner similar to their long-standing telephone interconnection cooperation. As high bandwidth national and global networking services became ubiquitous, transparent, and commonplace, the words *Internet* and *Worldwide Web* steadily dropped out of general usage. Using the network had become as simple and as commonplace as making a telephone call. The impact of this on overall IT leadership was dramatic.

Long the domain of the computer industry, the evolution of the Internet became increasingly shaped by the major global telecom players who went on to define critical architectural and interconnection issues. The computer industry, not used to such outside intervention, overall reacted badly to this changing reality, refusing to recognize that a sharing of power was implicit in the very idea of combining the computer and communications industries.

More specifically, as the network infrastructure providers and major network users became increasingly organized and influential, the ability of computer software and hardware firms to independently determine key Internet-related standards began to diminish. Increasingly, major de facto hardware and software standards became more difficult to establish. Even when they were set, the required licensing policies made exploiting them to obtain high monopoly rents much less likely. Although software remained an extremely successful business, its overall ability to control the industry steadily decreased. Software products became increasingly subordinate to higher level network services and content, a fact that seems obvious today but took a number of years to be recognized.

However, computer/communications industry convergence was only a part of the competitive story. Equally important changes were brought about by global telecommunications deregulation, which eventually led to the integration of previously separate long-distance, local, and wireless phone service, as well as the cable TV industry. With a few minor exceptions, countries that could not bring about this competition fell behind.

It was from this global perspective that the full extent of power diffusion became most obvious. Since the major nations of the world were no more willing to give up control over their network infrastructure than they would give up control of their roads, electricity, or water systems, each country developed and managed its own network infrastructure, resulting in a heterogeneous global network market that stood in sharp contrast to the globally proliferated, mostly U.S.-controlled technologies of the PC era. Although some telecommunications monopolies remained, their power was nearly always restricted to a single country market.

In addition, the great majority of the traffic transmitted across these national infrastructures consisted of local messages, local transactions, and local language information and entertainment. As network services, network applications, and network content became the dominant IT industry activities, country-specific issues and idiosyncrasies became increasingly important.

In short, the network-centric era transformed the global information technology market into a multinational and multicultural one. Hardware and software products remained global but were fundamentally less important. Network services became the driving force of the industry, but from both a technical and content perspective, these were predominantly local in nature.

By the year 2005, the mission of creating a high bandwidth information infrastructure was largely complete in most developed nations. Bandwidth had been successfully moved from being a scarce to a surplus resource. Additionally, vigorous competition had been restored to most layers of the now greatly extended industry value chain, diffusing industry power among a long list of both global and nation-specific industry leaders. No one vendor was capable of having any-where near the power IBM, Microsoft, and Intel had during their re-spective eras. This was a sign of overall industry stability and maturity.

Once the process of building this ubiquitous infrastructure was completed, the IT industry's emphasis shifted once again, this time toward the content and services that ran on top of this powerful tech-nological base. As has since become obvious to all, it is this content that defines the true utility and importance of information technology and has set the developed world along the path toward a true informa-tion society.

Content and services, of course, have their own sources of power and market influence, but they are now spread across the entire range of human activities and interests. Computer hardware and software vendors have made and continue to make great contributions to the enabling of this process, but no one vendor has any more market con-trol than one would see in other mature sectors such as automobiles, airlines, or entertainment. In the end, perhaps part of the price of building a real information society was that the computer industry needed to conform to the established standards of global economic competition. The IT industry had simply become too big and too im-portant for any one vendor to control.

INDEX